CALCULATED RISK

THE EXTRAORDINARY LIFE OF JIMMY DOOLITTLE – AVIATION PIONEER AND WORLD WAR II HERO

A MEMOIR BY JONNA DOOLITTLE HOPPES

SANTA MONICA PRESS

CALCULATED RISK

THE EXTRAORDINARY LIFE
OF JIMMY DOOLITTLE —
AVIATION PIONEER AND
WORLD WAR II HERO

★ ★ ★ ★

A MEMOIR BY JONNA DOOLITTLE HOPPES

Published by:
Santa Monica Press LLC
P.O. Box 1076
Santa Monica, CA 90406-1076
1-800-784-9553
www.santamonicapress.com
books@santamonicapress.com

S A N T A
M O N I C A
P R E S S

Printed in the United States

Santa Monica Press books are available at special quantity discounts when purchased in bulk by corporations, organizations, or groups. Please call our Special Sales department at 1-800-784-9553.

Library of Congress Cataloging-in-Publication Data

Hoppes, Jonna Doolittle, 1950-
  Calculated risk : the extraordinary life of Jimmy Doolittle, aviation pioneer and World War II hero / by Jonna Doolittle Hoppes.
      p. cm.
  Includes bibliographical references and index.
  ISBN 1-891661-44-2
  1. Doolittle, James Harold, 1896- 2. Generals—United States—Biography. 3. Air Pilots, Military—United States—Biography. 4. United States. Army Air Forces—Biography. 5. Aeronautics—United States—History—20th century. 6. World War, 1939-1945—Aerial operations, American. I. Title.

UG626.2.D66H67 2004
629.13'092—dc22

                                                                    2004029814

All photographs courtesy of the Doolittle Collection with the exception of: photos 12, 16, 34–36, 44, and 50 courtesy of the Carroll V. Glines Collection; photo 56

★　★　★　★

CONTENTS

★ ★ ★ ★

ACKNOWLEDGMENTS

CALCULATED *Risk* is a work of love dedicated to two people who left the world a better place than they found it. It is also a collaborative effort—a collection of memories, historical facts and talents. I would like to thank all the people who contributed so much.

My parents, John and Priscilla Doolittle, shared numerous stories that found their way into this project. I know that many of these stories brought back wonderful memories, but others made us sad. I depended heavily on C.V. Glines. He was extremely generous with his knowledge, editing and friendship.

I owe much to Bonnie Hearn Hill for her faith and her rule of twelve. Bonnie, I keep that picture and your words as daily inspiration. Cindy Woods and Jeannie MacNeil spent hours proofing this manuscript. Kevin Eldridge answered endless questions about airplanes and flying. Kevin I would fly with you anytime!

I greatly appreciate Bob Lindsey for his encouragement and coaching—especially early on through all the frantic phone calls and email. Maryjo Reed, Bill and Judy Nelson and Deborah Barrow Zak stayed the course with their friendship. I think they were almost as excited as I was each step of the way. Thank you Susan Howard for the last minute edit and Jim (Pooh) Partington for the daily quotes. Frequently they inspired stories.

I am indebted to all the people at the Planes of Fame Museum—especially the crew of the Photo Fanny. I should have made Shawna drive the car home!

A special thank you to the Cascade War Birds: Ken and Linda Morley (Ken I really wasn't afraid.), Willie and Mary Paterson, Dave and Shirley Desmond and Betty Sherman for welcoming me into their group and sharing their wonderful airplanes, stories and knowledge. I had an unforgettable time.

I began writing this book in response to the film *Pearl Harbor*. I particularly appreciated the efforts of Jennifer Klein, Bruce

Hendricks and Jerry Bruckheimer for listening to the family's objections and making many of the changes we requested. I very much enjoyed meeting and working with Jennifer.

I am grateful to the members of the Literary Guild of Orange County—Cindy, June, Linda, Marguerite, Phyllis, Teresa, Doreen, Mary, Pam, Joan, and all the wonderful women who spend so much energy promoting emerging authors. I value your friendship and thank you for your support.

I would like to thank publisher Jeffrey Goldman for taking a chance on a first-time author.

And finally, I'd like to express my profound gratitude to Stacy and Shawna, my daughters, who contributed their own special talents and to Steve, my husband, who gave me the freedom to follow my dream.

★ ★ ★ ★

FOREWORD

N o history of American aviation could be written without mentioning James Harold "Jimmy" Doolittle. Born before the Wright brothers made their first flights in a heavier-than-air flying machine, his life paralleled the history of fixed-wing flight and our ventures into space. He was an aerobatic and racing pilot, military aviator, aeronautical engineer, leader of the famed 1942 attack on Japan, commander of the 8th Air Force during the Normandy invasion, leader of the struggle for a separate U.S. Air Force, member of scientific governmental committees, and advisor to presidents.

Jimmy Doolittle was known in aviation circles as the "master of the calculated risk" because he always carefully considered the risks involved in flying and transferred this attribute to his undertakings on the ground. He felt that luck had been with him all his life and that's why when asked if he would like to live any part of his life over again, he replied, "No, because I could never be so lucky again." And he said the luckiest moment in his life was when Josephine "Joe" Daniels, his high school sweetheart, said she would marry him.

In the following pages, the reader will learn that during their 71 years together Joe also had to take calculated risks being married to a man so active in so many aspects of aviation, industry and government. She shared some of his flying records as a passenger and watched him perform dangerous aerobatics that few other pilots dared to try. As a military leader and business executive's wife, she made a home out of each house or apartment they occupied and raised two lively sons who also became military pilots.

Joe Doolittle traveled hundreds of miles during World War II to bolster the morale of service wives and their families and give inspirational talks to employees in war industries. She authored a syndicated newspaper column for wives of servicemen, built a corps of daily listeners for a wartime radio program to give them hope and advice, and gave speeches to help sell war bonds and encourage participation in volunteer activities. She wrote hundreds of notes to "my shut-ins" when she learned of friends who were ill or had suffered family tragedies.

Her concern for others continued after Jimmy left the military service and their family circle grew. What follows is a granddaughter's tribute to her gracious, beloved grandmother who shared her love of life with everyone she met. It is also a review of her famous grandfather's exciting life as a world figure with a reputation for personal daring on one hand and exemplary leadership on the other. It traces his early days in Nome, Alaska and maverick teenage years without a father to his gradual maturation into an aviator who changed the course of world aviation with his technological breakthroughs in instrument flying and development of more powerful aircraft fuels.

Although Joe Doolittle always remained in the background, provided encouragement and was a model of patience, it was Delores Hope, wife of Bob Hope, who summed up her life succinctly when both Doolittles were presented with Mutual of Omaha's prestigious Criss Award for their service to the nation. She said the wives of those who traveled as much as their husbands did, learned much from Joe Doolittle as she shared her courage with women everywhere.

Those of us who were privileged to spend any time with Joe always came away with the realization that we had been in the company of an extraordinary person whose gentle smile and wise outlook had brightened our lives. And those who were fortunate to know or serve with Jimmy learned the effect she had on his thinking about their family and the love they shared. And they also realized that he was truly a man of great wit and wisdom.

At least a dozen books have been written featuring Jimmy Doolittle's remarkable contributions to aeronautics and this one reiterates them. It also describes how Joe Doolittle, the love of his life, contributed her energy and selfless work as his goodwill emissary and spokeswoman for those serving our country. It is a granddaughter's loving and respectful review of the lives of two important people in her life who happened to be celebrities.

Carroll V. Glines
Colonel, USAF (Ret)
Curator, Doolittle Library
University of Texas at Dallas

★ ★ ★ ★

For Granny and Gramps,
I love you dearly.

★ ★ ★ ★

★ ★ ★ ★

INTRODUCTION

A s a child growing up in the Doolittle household, I was relatively unaware of the public personas of my grandfather Jimmy Doolittle and my grandmother Joe. To me, they were simply Granny and Gramps, and their home was Doolittle Central, a place of unconditional love and laughter.

As I matured, I learned about the public image of the general and the woman he called Duchess. I heard stories of the daredevil pilot who achieved numerous aviation firsts, of the scientist driven to expand the horizons of aviation and the general who asked only of his men what he himself was willing to give. I saw firsthand his insatiable thirst for knowledge and self-discipline, his sense of humor and his charm, his keen observations and his honesty and fairness.

He claimed that the luckiest thing that ever happened to him was when my grandmother agreed to marry him. I think that's true. My grandmother had the patience of a saint. She stood by him throughout his life, usually beside him, but occasionally prodding from behind and sometimes in the lead. She was gentle, kind, intelligent, loving, and equally determined.

They lived through extraordinary times of great change. Early in his career, Jimmy Doolittle was branded a daredevil pilot who would try anything in an airplane—a reputation that was reinforced by his devil-may-care attitude when dealing with the press. But in truth, he was blessed with an analytical mind and most of his "stunts" were the result of careful study and planning. He was the master of the calculated risk.

There were those who claim that the Tokyo Raid was a suicide mission. This is not true. Although it was dangerous, the planning and execution of the Raid were based on calculation and study. Every man on that mission had reason to believe that he had a good chance of returning home safely. The Tokyo Raid was a calculated risk.

In her own way, my grandmother was also a master of the calculated risk. An "A" student with an equally analytical mind, she gambled early on a boy who boxed for spending money and fancied finding gold on the beaches of Alaska. She traipsed around the country, pulling up stakes and replanting them every time Jimmy's career led them in a new direction. Never once did she stand in his way.

I would never claim that my grandfather's success was because of my grandmother, but I believe she made success easier for him—that his achievements were also her achievements. She was the good woman behind the good man.

He was best known for leading the Tokyo Raid, but the raid was not what he felt was his most important achievement. He firmly believed that his experiments, especially in blind flight, were his greatest contributions.

Although many of the books written about my grandfather mention my grandmother, this is the first book that tells her story, too. This is their story, the story of their partnership. He was in the public eye. She was his rudder and the "wind beneath his wings."

Calculated Risk is a biography, journal of historical events, memoir and love story. When Josephine Daniels met "that Doolittle kid," he was a scrappy young fellow with little interest in high school. Together they created a future that would span more than seven decades. Decades that witnessed aviation records set, broken and reset. Decades that spanned two world wars. Decades that fostered the development of both military and commercial aviation. Decades that gave birth to the U. S. Air Force as an independent branch of the military services.

Calculated Risk is a window into the public and private lives of Jimmy and Joe Doolittle as world citizens, parents and grandparents.

I relied in part upon his autobiography, and books by Carroll V. Glines. I read my grandfather's wartime letters to my grandmother, plus hundreds of letters sent to them over the years. But most of all, I drew from the stories my grandparents told us, my father's recollections and my first-hand memory of the people I knew as Granny and Gramps.

As time moves on and takes with it those who lived history, our memory dims and their stories fade. *Calculated Risk* is my attempt to pass to a new generation the story of Jimmy and Joe Doolittle, and to keep our collective memory alive for at least a little longer.

Jonna Doolittle Hoppes

PART I

PREFLIGHT

"Luck has been with me all my life. Fortunately, I was always able to exploit that luck during my flying years and at each turn in my career.

The best thing I ever did was to convince Joe that she should marry me; the luckiest thing that ever happened to me was when she did."

—I Could Never Be So Lucky Again, James H. "Jimmy" Doolittle

CHAPTER 1

THAT DOOLITTLE KID

"Jimmy was the school hero—
strong, absolutely fearless, and as
obsessed with speed as today's teenage hot-rodders. He terrorized the
local roads with his souped-up
motorcycle and twice broke his leg
in precipitous crashes. But even at
full-speed, the motorcycle was too
slow for Jimmy's tastes. The airplane was his real love."

—Lawrence Tibbett, well-known
opera singer

JIMMY Doolittle stood in the center of the dirt road, his feet
firmly planted, his hands doubled into fists. A ring of boys circled
Jimmy and the newcomer who faced him. Like all the other boys,
the *chechako* towered over the diminutive pugilist. Cocky, the new
kid grinned at the crowd in a way that said, "You've got to be kidding. This pipsqueak doesn't stand a chance." If Jimmy noticed
the look, he didn't acknowledge it.

"Hit him, Jimmy!" the boys cried. "Knock him flat!"

A few miners, standing on the boardwalk in front of Nome's
general merchandise store, placed bets on the pair of boys. The
old-timers bet on Jimmy.

"Show him who's boss!" shouted one kid.

"Wipe that smile off his face, Doolittle!" yelled another.

Hearing that, the big kid widened his grin, turned it on Jimmy, and lazily raised his fists. Without warning Jimmy plowed into the *chechako*. Punching furiously with flailing fists, he aimed for his opponent's nose, knocking him to the ground.

The fight was over before the older boy knew what happened. Blood streamed down his face, and he fought back tears of pain mixed with humiliation.

The ring of boys tightened, congratulating Jimmy as he reached down to help the other boy to his feet. Someone offered a less-than-clean handkerchief to stop the flow of blood. All around, the boys laughed, slapped each other's backs, and, ritual complete, accepted the new kid into the group.

Jimmy looked around. He hadn't always held this position. When he moved to Nome, Alaska, he had been the smallest boy in town and the target of most of the town bullies. But they shoved, and he shoved back. They hit, and he hit back. He quickly learned that speed and a fierce attack could take down most opponents, so he honed those skills.

Emily Borgenson stood on the outside of the pack, hands on her seven-year-old hips, tapping her foot. "Better hope your mama doesn't hear about this fight, Jimmy Doolittle!" she said to her cousin as he broke away and joined her on the boardwalk.

Jimmy reached over and ruffled her hair. "Who's gonna tell her?"

Absently he rubbed his right thumb, still throbbing from being tucked inside his fist.

Emily grabbed his hand and inspected it. "Did you hurt yourself?"

"Nah, not really."

He picked up his hat, waved goodbye to his friends and started off down the boardwalk toward his home. Emily, the first white girl born in Nome, skipped along beside him, chatting endlessly.

They stopped at the edge of the boardwalk and looked out at the Bering Sea. Rotten wood and the dismembered wreckage of forgotten dreams dotted the beach. Large ships anchored in the unsheltered harbor. Barges, tied to the vessels, received the last shipments of supplies before ice sealed Nome away for the long winter.

Jimmy looked back at the dried mud lane that ran down the center of Front Street. He hadn't felt the same about Nome since his trip to the "outside" with his father, two years before. Seattle, San Francisco, and Los Angeles sported *painted* buildings, and quivered with activity. The saloons and stores of Nome looked shabby compared to the bustling life in "real cities."

Nome boasted a population of 25,000 in 1900, the year he arrived with his mother and Aunt Sarah. By 1906, that number dwindled to 5,000 hardy souls, and most of them would climb on those big steamers and sail away. Only about 1,000 rugged die-hards would brave the long nights of Alaska's winter.

"Come on, Jimmy!" Emily tugged at his arm. "It's getting late."

Jimmy looked at the dusky sky. Summer's twenty-four hours of sunlight had faded, preparing for the long dark days of winter.

Reaching out to tousle her hair one last time, Jimmy turned, and with his customary grin, took off, his little cousin trailing behind.

The house at 301 Third Street was comfortable by Nome standards. Built entirely by his father with wood shipped in from Canada and the United States, it boasted four tiny, sparsely furnished rooms stacked in two stories, with a ladder that reached through an opening in the upper floor.

Frank Doolittle had followed the gold to Alaska, but made his living as a carpenter. His earnings, a dollar an hour, surpassed the twenty-five cent rate offered in the States, and provided the family with a steady income. But life remained hard, and both Frank and Rosa insisted Jimmy get an education.

Summers are short on the Bering Sea, but the winters, when school was in session, seemed to last forever. High noon offered only twilight that faded quickly into black. Nome's only public school clustered students by grades and Jimmy's small classroom held first, second and third. Three rows of desks stretched from the back wall, past the old Franklin stove, to the front of the room.

Each desk serviced two children by providing a writing surface for one child, and a seat to another.

Jimmy's gaze drifted out the window. School held little interest for him, and sitting still even less. He glanced up at the teacher who stood at the board diagramming sentences. He shifted the papers on his desk. With one last quick peek at the front of the room, he resumed work on his caricature of the principal. He studied the drawing, added a touch of hair to the ears, then smiled, pleased with the likeness.

A ripple of giggles passed through the room. Not wanting to miss out on the joke, Jimmy looked up. Mrs. Staples stood in the aisle beside his desk.

"I'll take that," she said, snatching the drawing from under his hand.

Like a specimen butterfly waiting for the pin to skewer him, he returned her stare with a boldness he didn't feel. The expected sentence fell.

"I'll see you after school, young man."

The rest of the afternoon dragged by. Finally it ended, and the other kids rushed outside. Jimmy sat at his desk near the back of the room, Mrs. Staples behind hers in the front. Scowling, she picked up his drawing. Reluctantly, Jimmy left the relative safety of his seat and shuffled toward her.

"Jimmy Doolittle, you are incorrigible. I'm not sure what to do with you." She sat quietly for a moment, then, shaking her head, pointed to the board. "I want you to write 'Jimmy Doolittle is the smallest boy in school' twenty-five times on the board before you go home." She handed him the chalk, picked up his drawing, and left the room.

Tears pooled behind his eyes and threatened to spill down his cheeks. Jimmy shuffled up to the black board. She didn't need to remind him. He was the smallest boy in school, and he knew it. But, he had carved out a place for himself in this Alaskan wilderness, and more than held his own with the older boys. His size hadn't stopped him, and, as he held the chalk in blanched white fingers, forming the letters of each sentence, Jimmy silently vowed that it never would.

Two sports captured the passion and imagination of the local boys: dog-sled racing and running. Although Jimmy's family owned a sled and a few dogs, they didn't own a competitive dog team, so he joined the ranks of runners who sprinted across the tundra on long summer days, and filled the gymnasium during the winter.

Marathon races, of one-and two-hundred miles, took place inside the gymnasium. Men and older boys ran for two days straight, stopping only for nourishment, or to relieve their bladders. Jimmy emulated them, running hours on end and occasionally collapsing from over-exertion.

Jimmy's size gave him a distinct advantage in gymnastics; another sport he performed indoors. He excelled in acrobatics, spending hours practicing tumbling routines and working out on the parallel bars, workouts that filled the long winter days.

By the time school ended, the children of Nome were tired of being indoors and ran wild through the Alaskan wilderness, exulting in the freedom of summer.

★ ★ ★ ★

Jimmy sat with his knees pulled tight against his chest and his back hunched against the rough sides of the shed. His backside ached from the whipping his father had given him, but not nearly as much as his insides ached from his father's lack of faith.

Jimmy didn't lie. Only weaklings lied, and although he was small, he wasn't weak. He wiped away a tear that stole down his cheek. He couldn't understand how his father could take the old man's side over his.

Rex crept up and licked the salty tear from Jimmy's cheek. The boy ran his hands through the thick mane around the dog's head, then buried his face in Rex's neck. His angry words to his father, uttered with ice cold resolve, echoed in his memory.

"I don't lie, and I didn't lie to you this time. But mark my words. When I'm strong enough, I'm going to whip you for this."

By late summer 1908, Rosa had had enough of Alaska. Eleven-year-old Jimmy helped his mother pack their meager belongings for the return to Los Angeles. Memories of his trip four years before with his father tumbled excitedly in his mind.

Rosa Doolittle was a tower of strength, stronger than anyone he'd ever known. Strict but loving, she had always been his safe harbor. But, Jimmy couldn't imagine her in a big city.

He studied her chapped and callused hands as they worked. Those hands guided the dog team, they carried water, they stacked logs. He couldn't picture her wearing fancy dresses, or living in a proper town. She belonged here in Nome, courageous and tenacious in the face of adversity. His mind drifted back to a winter memory from several years before that defined her character perfectly:

Perpetual dusk made cold days seem colder, as Rosa bundled Jimmy into the sled. Dark clouds clung to the horizon. She hoped the storm would hold off long enough for her to replenish their water supply from the river.

The dogs, unusually skittish, pulled in their harness, spooked by impending weather. Rosa stepped onto the sled and called to the dogs, urging them across the snow to the river five miles away. Cold wind, weighed down with tiny crystals of ice, stung the small area of exposed skin surrounded by the fur ruff of her parka. The silence of the wilderness settled around them, broken only by the swoosh of sled runners on snow, and the jingling of the harness that pulled tightly between the dogs.

The sharp crack could have come from a hunter's gun, or a clap of thunder, Rosa wasn't sure, but whatever it was, the sound startled the dogs. The handle jerked loose, and before she could react, it crashed into her chest. Stunned, she fought for air and to keep the circle of darkness from closing in.

The sled slipped over the ice and Rosa regained a strangle hold on the handle, each shallow breath painful, each jarring bounce of the runners on the snow threatening to cause her to blackout. Unacceptable. What would happen to Jimmy if she lost consciousness? Besides, they needed the water.

Unbelievable pain made her gasp involuntarily with every move as she crossed the rough terrain to the river, loaded the water and began the journey in reverse.

The trip home took hours, and Rosa held tight as the dogs made their way back to the small house on Third Street. She unloaded the water and fed the dogs. Chores done, she made her way up the ladder to the small bedroom she shared with Frank. Alone, she took a few minutes to examine the angry purple bruise on her chest, and to bind the three broken ribs before starting dinner.

Never once could Jimmy remember her complaining.

There were no tears as he and Rosa climbed aboard the ship that would take them to Los Angeles. Jimmy simply assumed that his father would join them in the near future. He had no way of knowing that his father would visit them only once, and then return to Alaska, never to see his wife again.

Rosa set up housekeeping in a modest two-story house at 1235 Catalina Street in downtown Los Angeles. She enrolled Jimmy in Borendo Grammar School, where he quickly became known as a scrappy young fighter who could easily defend himself against much larger boys.

By the time he attended Manual Arts High School two years later, his reputation as a brawler was well established, and local bullies felt compelled to call him out.

Forrest Bailey, an English teacher and boxing coach, stood in the shadows and watched as young Doolittle, flailing wildly, finished off his older opponent. When the crowd dispersed, he walked over to Jimmy.

"Look, young man, I know a little about boxing, and you're going to get hurt badly, fighting the way you do. You get mad when you fight. If you lose your temper, you're eventually going to lose a fight because you let your emotions, instead of your head, rule your body. Think about that. If you really want to learn to box, I'll teach you."

Jimmy jumped at the chance to be coached by Bailey. On pre-selected afternoons, he raced to the gymnasium, leaving both friends and schoolwork behind.

"Think, Jimmy!" Bailey instructed his student. "Anticipate what your opponent will do next.

"That's good! Put power behind your punch! Hit all the way from your heels with your fists!

"Bob and weave! Now set yourself. Strike the minute the other fellow's guard is down!

"That's right, Jimmy! Good job!"

Jimmy learned quickly, and by the time he turned fifteen, he captured the West Coast Amateur Championship as a Flyweight. Within two years, Jimmy boxed in an exhibition match with the Bantamweight World Champion, Kid Williams, and held his own, without getting hurt.

Split lips, bruises, and black eyes were impossible to hide from his mother, who repeatedly requested that he stop fighting.

"Boxing is nothing more than legalized brawling," she argued, encouraging him to focus on other sports.

And Jimmy did participate in other sports. He still worked out regularly with the tumbling team, practicing acrobatics and working out on the parallel bars. He joined the Pyramid Team with his close friend, Frank Capra, and represented Manual Arts High School in competitions. But boxing, with its seedy glamour and easy money, intrigued him, luring him into the professional world of prize fighting.

In addition to his prowess in the ring, Jimmy had an engaging personality. Quick-witted and outgoing, he easily made friends with adults, and was often invited to join them for parties and outings.

Jimmy moved easily between the dissimilar worlds of high school and professional boxing, gathering friends from both.

★ ★ ★ ★

Jimmy shivered under the worn thread-bare blanket. Sitting on the narrow cot, he rested his back against the cold cement block wall. A bare light bulb in the center of the cell chased the black night into the corners. The stench of stale urine permeated the bedding and appeared to draw the walls closer. Twenty-four hours stretched behind him, more that twenty-four more stretched ahead. Jimmy closed his eyes against the sound of metal doors slamming shut and keys grating in locks.

The stormy events of the previous night fought for assembly into chronological order. The party at a local dairy. The shoving match. Blinding anger. The circle of faces.

"Take it outside!" someone yelled. The crowd swept the two fighters out the door, forming a tight circle around them.

Jimmy swung wildly, fists flying, pummeling his larger opponent.

Angered, the trucker advanced, driving Jimmy toward the edge of the circle. Searing pain took Jimmy's breath away when a friend of his opponent gave him a kidney punch from behind, forcing him to drop his guard. Ducking to the right, Jimmy barely avoided an uppercut aimed at his jaw.

Jimmy knew he needed to stay in the center of the ring. Furiously, he thrashed out at the larger man. Step-by-step he was forced toward the edge of the circle. Another kidney punch from the crowd. Another near miss to the jaw from his competitor!

Jimmy danced around, using his speed and smaller size to avoid both the long arms and helpful friends of his rival. Abusive taunts, punctuated by feminine screams, infused the air. Eventually, the circle widened, the onlookers held back by two policemen who watched, but did nothing to stop the fight. Without the kidney punches, Jimmy began to hold his own, blow for blow.

Suddenly, whistles blew. The sergeant arrived, and the two officers snapped into action. A policeman grabbed each of the fighters, loaded them into police cars, and hauled them off to jail.

Charged with disturbing the peace, they were both fined a few dollars.

Jimmy, a minor, huddled in the corner of his cell.

"Is my mother here yet?" he asked.

The sergeant, not without a little sympathy, shrugged. "She wants you to stay here until Monday morning. She'll drop by then and get you out in time for school."

The sound of retching from an adjacent cell pulled Jimmy back to the present. The sergeant looked in from the hall, but said nothing. Jimmy turned to look out the small window. An enormous full moon hung in the sky, and the lively hum of the city drifted in as the weekend stretched into eternity.

Boxing was not the only thing that caught the young man's fancy. In January 1910, Jimmy found a passion that captivated him for life. At Dominguez Field, just outside Los Angeles, aviators gathered from around the world for the first U.S. Aviation Meet west of the Mississippi River.

Jimmy stood on the sidelines, his head thrown back, face framed by an unruly mop of dark curls, and watched as the Frenchman, Louis Paulhan, pushed his Farman higher and higher to a record altitude of 4165 feet. He held his breath as Glenn Curtiss stormed by with a passenger on board, at a record speed of 55 miles per hour. He cheered as local airmen, Roy Knabenshue and Lincoln Beachey, raced dirigibles, pushing each other until Beachey finally won.

Jimmy walked through the static displays, breathing in the fumes from gasoline engines, and inspecting the construction of each flying machine. He circled the Wright B Flyer flown by Arch Hoxsey, and the ship designed by Glenn Curtiss. He checked out the wing structure and landing gear of Paulhan's Farman. He scrutinized every single plane on display. They were beautiful, magical and radically different from each other in design. And, they all flew. He knew, because he stood there in the light ocean breeze until the field emptied and the sky reverted to an uninterrupted canvas of ebony.

Two years passed before Jimmy attempted his first flight. He studied shop at Manual Arts High School, learning about gasoline engines and wood working tools. He collected magazine articles on airplanes and the men who flew them. In the shed behind his house, Jimmy gathered the materials needed to make a glider based on an article by Carl Bates, in a 1910 issue of *Popular Mechanics*.

Rosa, anxious for Jimmy to find an interest outside of boxing, encouraged him. She sewed unbleached muslin for the wings of his glider. She gave him as much change as she could spare. The rest of the money he earned by selling newspapers and performing odd jobs in the neighborhood. He spent hours in the shed, studying the drawings, fashioning the spruce strips into a flexible skeleton, stretching the fabric skin over delicate wings—breathing life into a dream.

A few weeks later Jimmy carefully loaded the glider into his wagon and waved to his friend Lawrence Tibbett. He could already imagine himself soaring through the air.

"Where's the motor?" Lawrence asked, eyeing the glider.

"There isn't any," Jimmy said. "Where would I get money to buy a motor?"

"Then how does this—this thing get off the ground?"

"You just watch."

Jimmy pulled the wagon carrying his plane up the steep hill on the road to San Pedro. Leaving it there, he walked over to the edge. Sparse white clouds meandered lazily across a crystal blue sky. He wet his index finger and extended it, calculating the eastwardly direction of the light breeze. He looked over the edge of the bluff to the dirt field, fifteen feet below. Plenty of room to maneuver.

Jimmy walked back to the wagon, wiped his sweaty palms on his pants, and unloaded the glider. Careful of the fragile wings, he stepped into the contraption and strapped himself in. Confident that all he needed was enough speed, Jimmy held tightly to the frame, and, using his feet for takeoff, ran as fast as he could. Excitement fueled him. His heart pumped adrenaline-rich blood, his jaw clenched in concentration. He focused as the edge of the cliff came closer and closer. Reaching the brink, he pushed off with his legs, springing into the air with the strength and agility he'd developed through years of gymnastics.

Suddenly the onrushing wind caught the muslin wings and lifted the glider into the air. Swiftly, the little plane soared straight up—all of five feet—and then, much more swiftly, soared straight down again. Out of control, the wings funneled the air, sending Jimmy plummeting off the side of the cliff into the ground. The busted tail followed. Stunned and more than a little banged up, he lay still for a minute before untangling himself from the mess of wood, wire, and muslin.

"Are you all right?" Lawrence asked, running to Jimmy's side.

Jimmy poked his head through the debris. Strut wires and splintered spruce hung from his neck and shoulders.

"See that, Larry?" Jimmy asked. "Just need a little faster start, that's all. Wait till you see my next flight."

Salvaging as much of the glider as he could, Jimmy rebuilt his "baby." Analytical by nature, and fiercely determined, he decided that he needed more speed to make the glider fly. Luckily, he had a friend whose father owned a car.

Jimmy tied the rope to the bumper then walked back to the glider. Stepping into the contraption, he again strapped himself in and held on for dear life.

"Ready?"

"Ready!"

Gradually, the car took off and Jimmy started to run, pushing himself faster and faster until his legs couldn't keep up. Relying on his training as a gymnast, he vaulted into the air, willing the glider to lift off the ground.

Unfortunately, the glider didn't lift. By the time the car stopped, Jimmy's body and ego were equally bruised, and his glider was in shambles. Daunted, but not defeated, Jimmy again collected the pieces.

Determined to succeed, Jimmy returned to the drawing board. There weren't enough pieces left to rebuild the two-winged glider, so he turned to a monoplane designed by Alberto Santos-Dumont, from another issue of *Popular Mechanics*.

Convinced that installing a motorcycle engine would solve the speed problem, he set out to earn enough money to purchase one. The fastest way for Jimmy to earn money was boxing, so he arranged to enter a series of amateur matches. The prize for a winning match was a gold watch that the promoters bought back for $10.00. Jimmy entered three matches and won each bout, earning $30.00—enough for a used engine.

★ ★ ★ ★

A freak storm may well have saved Jimmy's life. Gusts of wind lifted Jimmy's "baby" off the ground, tossed it over the neighbor's fence, and smashed it into tiny bits of debris, before he could take it on a test flight. Discouraged, Jimmy accepted defeat and turned his attention to a new project—the wooing of Josephine Daniels.

CHAPTER 2

BAD BOYS—GOOD GIRLS

"To Neal Creighton: [We give you]
Clifford Biddleston's and Josephine
Daniels' power to do much and
say little."

—*The Artisan,* Manual Arts
High School, 1914

JOSEPHINE Daniels, nicknamed "Joe" after her favorite uncle, didn't consider herself particularly attractive. It wasn't a criticism or complaint, just the facts as she saw them. Instead, she counted on her intelligence, a quality she had in spades. Let her pretty little sister Grace flaunt delicate charms to woo the local lads. Joe, confident and in the top of her class, would depend on something much more substantial: a solid education.

Joe stretched under the soft lights of the school library, and settled back over her term paper. Her brow furrowed as she attempted to reorganize her words. Anything less than an "A" was unacceptable. A lock of dark hair pulled free from her bun and curled around the fair skin of her face. Frustrated, she crossed out a sentence, and then looked up just in time to see Jimmy Doolittle enter the library. What was it about some bad boys that made them so attractive? She watched as he approached the table, hair uncharacteristically slicked down, clothes freshly pressed.

"Anyone sitting here?" he asked.

Joe looked around the room at the sea of empty tables. A practical joker, Jimmy was usually found at the center of a crowd. She looked for his friends, but they were conspicuously absent.

"No," she replied.

Jimmy pulled out the chair next to her and sat down.

She usually studied at home, but lately Gracie, her younger sister, entertained a string of beaus and it was difficult to concentrate with the noise. Plus, working at the library got her out of the house and away from her parents' scrutiny.

"Aren't you going to study?" she asked.

Jimmy, with a sheepish grin and the signature twinkle in his eyes, picked up one of Joe's books, turned it upside down, and pretended to read.

Joe suppressed a giggle, retrieved her book and with mock anger asked, "Don't you have anything better to do?"

"Not better than coming to see you."

A blush stained Joe's cheeks. *All* the girls liked Jimmy Doolittle. Consequently, his statement surprised and secretly pleased her. However, she wouldn't be falling for someone like *him*. Smart as a whip, he was, but he never let on. No, Jimmy was content playing the class clown. Shyly, she looked back down at her term paper. "Jimmy Doolittle, I have work to do. And you should study a little yourself."

"Jimmy!" Frank Capra, the top man in the school's pyramid team and future Hollywood director, leaned his head in the library door and called out in a loud whisper. "We've got practice."

Jimmy pushed his chair back and stood awkwardly beside the table. "Can I give you a ride home after practice?"

"On your motorcycle?"

"Sure." Proud of his transportation, he pulled himself up to his full 5 foot 4 inches and grinned.

"Jimmy Doolittle, good girls do not ride on the back of motorcycles!"

"You sure?"

"I'm sure!"

Jimmy wasn't one to give up on something he felt worth pursuing. He continued to court Joe, bringing her candy on Valentines

Day and minding his manners in her presence. He even accepted the part of Ross Freshman in the school play "Strongheart" to spend time with her. Eventually his persistence paid off, and soon everyone acknowledged that Joe was Jimmy's girl.

Joe sat in her uncle's office, perched on the edge of the burgundy leather chair.

"Joe, have you given any thought to what you'll do after high school?" her uncle asked as he straightened a stack of papers on his desk.

"I thought I might get a job," she answered. Despite her resolve to not fall for Jimmy, she'd come under his spell months ago when he had stopped her in the hall and demanded a date. She was a quarter of the way through her senior year. No promises had been made, and as long as Jimmy boxed professionally, they weren't likely to make any. "Maybe take some classes in library science. I might like to work in a library."

Uncle Joe looked at her kindly. "Joe, you're intelligent. Smarter than any kid I know. Have you given any thought to a four-year college?

Joe dropped her eyes. Sure she'd thought about college, but seriously doubted her father would pay for such an extravagance. Maybe if she'd been a boy.

"How would you like to go to law school?"

Her heart jumped. A lawyer? Her?

"Father would never agree." She answered.

"He doesn't have to. I'll pay for it. But, when you graduate, I'd want you to work here, with me."

Joe knew that implicit in the offer was the understanding that she and Jimmy stop seeing each other. Her family disliked "that Doolittle boy." Sending her to law school would be a way of keeping them apart. Part of her thrilled at the idea. She knew that she was smart, and law school would be a challenge. One of the few people with a photographic memory, Joe would make an excellent attorney. On the other hand, was she willing to give up her relationship with Jimmy?

The next day dawned with clear skies, a welcome relief after the week of drizzling rain that threatened to postpone the big game. Manual Arts High School was playing football against its cross-town rival Los Angeles High School and this year, after years of crushing defeats and near misses, they were determined to win.

The two-thirty bell rang and the student body moved en masse toward the football field. Five thousand fans gathered on the sidelines, equally divided between the rival teams.

Jimmy cut through the crowd and slipped beside Joe as she sat in the stands with a group of friends.

She looked up, a smile starting at her lips and lighting up her eyes. Still, she felt torn over her uncle's offer. Although they'd been a couple for almost a year, she and Jimmy had never discussed marriage. Besides, like many "bad boys," Jimmy seemed to have a female fan club wherever he went. Joe knew she wasn't just one of the crowd, but she still believed she could be replaced.

The crowd roared as the teams flooded the field and began to warm up. With the players evenly matched, the ball made little progress in either direction. Halftime arrived and the score remained zero to zero.

Climbing down from the stands, Jimmy turned and offered his hand to steady Joe's footing. Holding tightly, a little longer than modesty allowed, Joe reluctantly pulled her hand from his, and placed it chastely on his arm.

"Jimmy," she said, struggling to find the words, "My uncle offered to send me to law school."

He grew serious, and the crowd around them disappeared into the background.

"Are you going?" he asked.

"I don't know," she said, almost holding her breath. When he didn't respond, she continued. "I'd be good, especially at the research."

"That's swell!" Jimmy said, the jovial tone forced. "Joe, you'd make a great lawyer! Really great."

They returned to the stands. The game resumed. A refreshed, energized team played for Manual Arts. With a beautiful passing rush, Thayer took the ball over the line and the spectators on Manual's side rose as one and burst into cheers. Hats flew into the air and the band struck up a victory tune. Joe and Jimmy joined the celebration, marching four abreast through the streets of Los Angeles. Neighborhoods for miles around heard the cheering students.

But the question of law school hung between them, unresolved.

Joe settled down at their table in the library. Her copy of the *Artisan,* Manual Arts' senior annual, lay open in front of her. Senior year drew rapidly to a close and the sweet melancholy of parting with friends engulfed her.

She leafed through the yearbook, pausing at the senior prophecy and read the "tongue-in-cheek" predictions of the yearbook staff. Most of them were humorous, and she smiled at the lighthearted fun poked at fellow students.

Her own prophecy made her laugh out loud: *Josephine Daniels is acknowledged by all to be the world's champion woman athlete. She has established new records in running and vaulting. We thought that she would get married and get out of public life, but the glamour of publicity was too attractive for her.* How funny!

Scanning the pages, she looked for Jimmy's name then read the entry.

Then you see this mean-looking lad, James Doolittle, he was such a wonderful discoverer. You know, he discovered the fifth dimension and then wrote a treatise on the subject, which showed it to be such a simple thing that now it is taught in the sixth grade at school.

She wondered if her fellow students weren't a bit blind. Surely, beneath the rough surface Jimmy projected to the world, others could see his qualities. Didn't they see his inquisitive mind? Or, recognize the discipline needed to excel in sports? Why, even as much as she detested his boxing, she acknowledged the discipline required to shine the way he did.

"What are you reading?" Jimmy asked from directly behind her, breaking into her musings.

"Just looking at the annual."

Jimmy pulled out the chair next to Joe and sat down. He reached for the book and read his prophecy. He laughed, but Joe could see that the humor didn't reach his eyes. She started to say something, then caught herself.

Jimmy continued to read, making comments about fellow students stopping at Joe's prophecy. He read it through twice.

"Have you given any more thought to your uncle's offer?" he asked.

"I've been thinking about it, but haven't decided yet."

Jimmy grew quiet, fidgeting with the pages of the yearbook. "How do you feel about getting married?" He looked down, then up into Joe's face. "To me."

"Jimmy Doolittle, you must think I'm out of my mind! I could never marry a man who wants to fight all the time."

She contemplated the yellowish bruise fading from his cheek and the split lip that had just lost its scab. She knew that he was still boxing professionally under the assumed name of Jimmy Pierce. She shook her head no, but her heart raced.

"I could give up boxing, and you could skip law school," he said hopefully.

"My mother would never approve."

"Darn it Joe, I'm marrying *you*, not your mother!"

A moment of silence lengthened between them. Jimmy shifted in his seat. Joe suppressed a grin.

"You'll quit boxing?" she asked.

"Yes."

"What will you do?"

"I'll go back up to Alaska, make some money, and then send for you."

The silence returned. Jimmy began to play with his hat. Joe absently ruffled the edges of the yearbook.

"Okay," she said.

"Okay?" Jimmy threw his arms around her and kissed her soundly on the lips.

Blushing, she pushed him away, glancing nervously around, hands flying up to straighten her hair.

"I'll take you through the Inside Passage," he promised remembering the beauty of Alaska's coastline. "It's the most beautiful place on earth!"

"And you'll keep me in the public eye like my prophecy promises?"

"Oh, yes," he said grinning. "I promise."

The summer of 1914 rolled around. Jimmy packed his belongings and caught a ship to Seward, Alaska, his head filled with visions of financial success. He spent little time thinking about the father he hadn't seen in more than five years. In Seward, Frank Doolittle had purchased two lots and offered his son apprentice wages to help him build a house. Leftover tensions from Jimmy's childhood lingered between them. Years of distance couldn't be breached.

"Do you remember what you said to me when I whipped you for something you didn't do?" Frank asked his son.

"Sure."

"Are you going to do it?"

Jimmy caught his father's eyes and, with icy resolve, held them. Positive that his years of boxing guaranteed easy success, he asked, "Do you figure I can do it?"

"I believe you can."

"Then I won't have to."

Conflicting emotions vied for prominence in young Jimmy's soul: fear that he never earned his father's love, shame that he couldn't reach out to his father, anger that his father never apologized for wrongly accusing him of lying, and an all-consuming sadness that his father had expressed so little faith in him.

When they finished the house, Jimmy packed his belongings, bought some provisions, and headed out to Six-Mile Creek in search of gold. But Alaska was in the throes of a deep depression. The boom days were over and the gold had almost disappeared. The miners who remained were mostly unemployed. Jimmy lived in a tent and ate salmon three times a day. As summer drew to a close, he packed his gear, hiked back to Seward and stowed away on the *SS Yale.*

By the time he left Alaska, Jimmy knew two things: he wanted to build things and he wanted to see the world. He returned to Joe, determined to fulfill his goals. He asked her to wait for him while he attended engineering classes at the local Junior College. Two years later, he transferred to the University of California's School of Mines at Berkeley, where he worked toward a degree in Mining Engineering.

By the summer of 1917, everyone was talking about the war in Europe and the possibility that the United States would send troops to fight the Germans. Jimmy stood in front of the recruiter. He had no desire to sign up for the infantry, but desperately wanted to join the Aviation Section of the Army's Signal Corps.

"Over 5,000 pilots will be trained immediately," the recruiter promised.

He shifted his weight from one foot to the other, impatiently waiting for his turn to sign. When it came, Jimmy intrepidly autographed the register for the Signal Corps Enlisted Reserve. He expected to be in uniform and on his way to flight school within days. The adrenaline pumped; he had always wanted to fly.

Days turned into weeks. Jimmy worked odd jobs and waited for his orders. They finally came—in October. Assigned to ground school at Berkeley, he was now designated a "Flying Cadet", making close to $50.00 a month.

★ ★ ★ ★

On Christmas Eve 1917, Joe, crushing a recently pressed white handkerchief between sweaty palms, stood facing her parents. Both she and Jimmy were twenty-one and had decided to get married. She knew her parents couldn't stop her, but she nevertheless wanted their blessing.

"Josephine Daniels, you can't be serious!" her mother wailed. "We raised you for a better life than traipsing after a soldier."

"He'll never amount to anything," her father added, glaring over the top of his newspaper.

Joe looked at her parents with sadness. The blessing she wanted would not be forthcoming. She tucked the hankie in her sleeve, turned away and walked out the door.

Her sorrow evaporated the second she saw Jimmy coming up the front walk. He wore his new uniform with pride, and she felt immense pride at the sight of him. In her heart, she knew that Jimmy Doolittle was someone special, and that life with him would never be dull. Without reservation, Josephine Daniels kissed Jimmy softly, and reached for his hand.

They emerged from City Hall a little dazed. The evening was crisp and clear with stars sprinkled across a canvas of deep blue. A frowzy woman wrapped in a worn coat approached them as they walked arm and arm down the front steps as Mr. and Mrs. Jimmy Doolittle.

"Have you got a spare dime?" she asked.

Joe, having paid for the license with her Christmas money, opened the clasp of her purse and pulled out fifty cents. With a warm smile, she pressed the coins into the woman's cold, thin hands.

"Merry Christmas," Joe said.

"Joe, are you crazy?" Jimmy asked as the woman shuffled away. "We haven't got twenty dollars between us, and here you go throwing money away."

But Joe just smiled, her full heart lighting her eyes.

"It'll bring us luck, Jimmy," she said softly, tucking her arm back in his, walking beside him into their future.

CHAPTER 3

A LOVE AFFAIR WITH FLIGHT

"As a lieutenant you caused me worry but as time passed, your real qualities came out. Your skill as an airman, your ability as an aviation engineer and finally your all-around knowledge brought admiration of all who came in contact with you."

—Gen. Henry H. "Hap" Arnold

JIMMY thought the Curtiss JN-4 "Jenny" was absolutely beautiful and he itched to climb aboard. But he stood patiently next to the airplane and listened intently as Charles Todd, his flight instructor, completed the first-day briefing. Slowly, Jimmy circled the plane, checking the tires, the fabric, looking for fuel leaks and obvious drops of fresh oil.

Satisfied that she was in good condition, and with Todd's nod of approval, Jimmy climbed into the cockpit and carefully followed instructions.

"Switches off?"

"Check."

Jimmy had dreamed of this day since childhood. He studied the dials and knobs in front of him. "Throttle advanced slightly," he repeated as he pushed the knob forward.

Taking a deep breath, he looked down at the mechanic standing next to the plane. "All clear?"

"Clear," answered the mechanic as he pulled the prop.

The Jenny's engine jumped to life. The grin on Jimmy's face spread quickly from one ear to the other. Slowly, he eased the throttle forward and the Jenny began to roll, first a little to the right as Jimmy leaned around the engine to check the runway, then a little to the left as he "spotted" from the opposite side.

Finally, they reached the end of the runway. Jimmy pulled back on the throttle and the Jenny coasted to a stop. Visually, he checked his surroundings, looking for traffic. He scanned the air, searching for incoming flights. The coast was clear. Taking a deep breath, he pushed the throttle forward allowing the engine to build up power and speed. Palms sweating, he gripped the controls.

Overhead, the sound of trainers drifted toward them, followed by a grinding crash. In slow motion, Jimmy saw the two planes fall from the sky, the twisted carcasses hitting the ground a few yards in front of their Jenny.

Todd cut the engine, and both he and Jimmy scrambled out of the plane and rushed to the downed aircraft. In the first plane, a student, flying solo, slumped over the controls. Dead. Both the instructor and student in the other plane sustained serious injuries.

Jimmy and Todd offered what assistance they could. An ambulance made its way across the field. Medics assisted the injured, loading them on stretchers and retreated to a nearby hospital. Eventually, ground crews removed the wreckage.

When flying activity on the flight line resumed, Todd carefully assessed Jimmy. He wanted his student to respect, but not fear, flying.

"We should get on with our business," Todd said.

Jimmy nodded in agreement.

Both men walked silently to the plane. A sober Jimmy repeated the visual inspection of the Jenny. He mentally reviewed Todd's preflight briefing, focusing on each detail.

They restarted the engine and revved it for takeoff. Within minutes they were airborne. The image of the twisted, downed planes faded into the background, and Jimmy Doolittle, for the second time in his life, fell in love. Flying made him feel more alive than he'd ever imagined, but underneath the love he felt a profound respect, as well.

Jimmy graduated from flight school on March 5, 1918, and was commissioned as a second lieutenant six days later. Eager to get into the fight in Europe, he awaited orders, but a European assignment never materialized.

In the meantime, Joe worked at the Terminal Island Shipyard in Los Angeles where she ran the Holowitz filing system and managed several hundred girls.

The money was good and, with the onset of WWI, Joe appreciated her job and its contribution to the war effort. While Jimmy transferred from station to station on the East Coast, Joe worked and saved for their future.

Stateside flying was not without its own risks, and many pilots were killed because of faulty equipment and pilot error. Aware of the dangers, Joe kept negative thoughts at bay by focusing on her work. She was working when the first reporter called.

"Mrs. Doolittle? Is this Mrs. James Doolittle?" the unfamiliar voice queried.

"Yes."

"What is your reaction to your husband's death?"

"Excuse me?" Joe said, reaching out to hold the side of the desk.

"Your husband, James Doolittle was killed today in a crash in Buffalo, New York."

"I think you're mistaken," Joe said, attempting to control her voice. "Jimmy isn't in Buffalo."

"It's true," continued the reporter. "I have the report in my hand."

"I don't believe it," Joe said, then calmly replaced the telephone receiver. She grabbed her purse and walked out of the shipyard to the nearest Western Union station. She didn't believe it. She was certain she'd know if anything had happened to Jimmy. But she had to be sure.

"I'd like to send a wire to the base commander at Gerstner Field near Lake Charles, Louisiana," she told the clerk behind the window.

"What would you like to say?"

"Received report that James Doolittle was killed in crash in Buffalo, New York. Stop. Please advise. Stop. Josephine Doolittle."

The clerk's eyes reflected pity as he took her money, assuring her that he would send the message immediately.

She walked back to the yard, a warm ocean breeze stirring around her shoulders and lifting her hair. She returned to her office, rubbing her hands together for warmth and silently praying to hear Jimmy's voice.

The phone rang, and Joe grasped the receiver.

"Hello," she said.

"Joe?" Relief flooded over her and she wiped away the tears that had gathered and silently spilled down her cheeks.

"Jimmy, are you all right? I got this call…"

"I'm fine. But there was an accident. A fellow by the name of James R. Doolittle was killed in a training flight to Buffalo."

"Thank God," she said, and then felt a twinge of guilt. Somebody's Jimmy had died today.

"I love you, Joe."

"I love you, too," she said before breaking the connection.

A few weeks later a hurricane swept through Gerstner Field, ripping apart buildings and uprooting trees. Several people were killed and many others injured. All three hundred planes were destroyed. The crews stationed at Gerstner considered themselves out of luck. None of them would fight in World War I.

Jimmy and his friends, posted back to Ream Field in San Diego, served as combat and gunnery instructors for the duration of the war. At twenty-one, Jimmy, anxious to see combat, was disappointed. His only consolation was his proximity to Joe.

Regulations prohibited pilots from taking civilians up in military aircraft. Jimmy, who, throughout his life, used rules as guidelines rather than steadfast boundaries, decided to share his love of flying with Joe. Borrowing a car from a friend, he took her to an orchard outside San Diego, and left her there, promising to return with a Jenny.

Joe heard the plane before she saw it. Excited, she moved to the edge of the orchard and waved to Jimmy. He put the Jenny down in an open field, stopping a few yards in front of Joe. He waited for her to join him. She made her way across the field and tried to pull herself up on the lower wing, but her pencil skirt restricted her movement.

"Come *on*, Joe," Jimmy yelled over the grind of the engine, "Before someone comes out to check on the plane."

Looking down at her tight skirt, Joe shrugged and grabbed the hem on either side of the seam and pulled until the threads gave way. She scrambled onto the lower wing.

"Here you go," Jimmy said and reached down to help her up into the plane. He handed her a leather helmet and goggles, and turned back to the controls.

Joe buckled the safety strap across her lap. She pulled on the helmet, fastened it under her chin, and then adjusted the goggles over her eyes.

Jimmy taxied to the end of the clearing and revved the engine. The plane bounced over the bumpy ground, building speed, then lifted like a large bird into the clear blue sky. Joe was exhilarated! The field receded and the orchard became a dark patch of green. Deep blue water stretched away from the ribbon of sandy beach, and miniature people sunned on blankets or paraded on sidewalks. Buildings shrank and tiny cars navigated the grid of roadways, as Joe watched from her perch in the sky.

Amazed, Joe reveled in the new experience. Jimmy, caught up in her excitement and encouraged by her smile, gestured with his hand, indicating that he would perform a series of stunts. Joe flashed an upturned thumb and held on while Jimmy eased the nose of the plane upward, then pushed it into a perfect barrel roll. Soaring. Looping. Rolling. Spinning. He put the plane through its paces, intent on impressing her with his ability and daring.

Joe squeezed her eyes tight, hoping that by avoiding the visual spinning of the earth she could keep from getting sick. Her hands gripped the side of the plane and she held her breath. Her stomach lurched up toward her throat as her head hung low toward the earth. Finally everything settled down into place and she opened her eyes.

Just when she thought she'd made it, Jimmy pulled the nose up again and the Jenny started a second roll. Even squeezing her eyes shut didn't help. She clutched the edge of the plane with both hands, and, fighting the wind, promptly lost most of her lunch over the side of the open cockpit.

Jimmy landed in a pasture on the far side of the bay. An unsteady Joe climbed down from the cockpit. Her feet now firmly planted on the ground, she promptly lost what little was left in her stomach.

"Stop you're grinning, Doolittle," she said as she handed Jimmy back his helmet and goggles.

He just laughed and waved. Joe stood at the edge of the pasture as Jimmy taxied the plane into position and took off.

Still a bit unsteady, her nausea exacerbated by the unpleasant smells emanating from the nearby potash plant, she made her way to a phone at the plant and called a cab to take her back to San Diego. Joe felt a lot better by the time the cab dropped her at the first streetcar stop. She paid the driver, then caught a streetcar to the Coronado Hotel. Feeling eyes upon her, Joe looked up and noticed the other passengers. Some stared—most smiled. Recapturing only the pleasant memories of her new experience, she smiled back.

Blue skies, dotted with soaring seagulls, framed the Coronado Hotel. A light ocean breeze, smelling lightly of seaweed and salt, lifted the stray strands of her dark hair. Her earlier mood of jubilance, fully restored by the time she entered the hotel lobby, lent a bounce to her steps. A woman in a bright red dress nodded and smiled. Joe returned the gesture. A man in a pinstriped suit tipped his hat. Joe waved. A small child hiding behind his mother's skirt watched Joe as she passed. Her smile widened.

By the time she reached Peacock Alley she was convinced that the other hotel patrons either shared her joy in the beautiful day or could read her secret on her expressive face. Footsteps light, she made her way down the long corridor to her room.

Stopping briefly at the mirror to straighten her hair, Joe stared in horror at her reflection. Her face, coated in black castor oil from the Hisso engine and eyes ringed in white from the goggles, stared back at her. How could he let her go out in public like that? Jimmy Doolittle may have survived flight school, but there was serious doubt that he would survive tonight with his wife!

★　★　★　★

Teaching men to fly was a dangerous occupation. Jimmy, who didn't want to embarrass himself in front of his students, spent hours perfecting his skills as a pilot. He took teaching very seriously, and wanted to impress upon his students the seriousness of flying. Accidents, frequently the result of pilot error, occurred on a regular basis.

Jimmy scanned the skies as his young student took the controls and held a steady course in the Jenny. Flocks of birds flew in formation across the clear sky and army regulars scurried like ants on the airfield below. Pulling the Jenny around in a smooth turn, they began their descent on the final approach for landing. Neither Jimmy, nor his student, saw the Thomas-Morse Scout cut across their path.

The sudden impact shook the plane and the wrenching of metal screeched over the pitch of the prop engine as the landing gear tore away. Jimmy, taking over the controls, fought to maintain altitude; he surveyed the weakened lower wing and damaged propeller. Positioning her over the runway, Jimmy eased the Jenny out of the sky, bringing her to rest on her belly on the far end of the field.

Uninjured, Jimmy and his student climbed from the plane and made their way to the downed Scout, which had plummeted onto the flying field.

The body of the decapitated solo pilot was still strapped in his seat. Shaken, Jimmy remembered his first flight and the casualties from the collision of the two Jennies. Recalling Todd's self-assured confidence in the face of tragedy, Jimmy insisted on taking his student up in another plane to continue the flying lesson.

As they flew, Jimmy thought about the dead student and wondered if there wasn't something he could have done to prevent the accident. Inwardly shaken, he talked his student through their final approach and landing.

They pulled up to the flight line and Jimmy climbed out of the plane.

"Next!" he hollered.

If any student refused, Jimmy planned to wash him out on the spot.

Later, as the last student left the field, Jimmy stood next to the carcass of the downed Scout.

"That was pretty heartless of you, Doolittle."

Jimmy turned to face his colleague, still wondering if there wasn't something he could have done to prevent the accident, but angered that a peer questioned his judgment.

"I want to impress upon them that flying is serious business and is unforgiving of carelessness, incapacity, or neglect." Jimmy answered.

The colleague broke eye contact first, and, without another word, spun around and walked away. Jimmy turned back to the wreckage.

"FLYER KILLED IN CRASH," the headlines screamed across the top of the paper catching Joe's attention as she rode the trolley home from a friend's funeral.

"Lt. Doolittle…" she read, before the passenger turned the page.

Stunned, mouth suddenly dry and eyes moist, she got off at the next stop and bought a paper. Leaning against a nearby building, she searched the pages, found the article, and resumed

breathing. Again Jimmy escaped death. She counted her blessings, and then wondered how many times her heart would stop
as the news of a flyer's death reached her.

The opportunities for disaster were ever-present. Jimmy took
chances other pilots avoided. He courted excitement and pushed
himself to the outer limits of his ability. But each new stunt, seen
by his peers as daring and risky, was calculated. Already, Jimmy
Doolittle was becoming the master of the calculated risk.

There were times when Jimmy Doolittle's size worked to his
advantage. Wing walking was one of those times. John McCullough
banked the plane to the right, and leveled off as Jimmy unbuckled
the canvas safety belt. Carefully, he climbed out of his seat and, with
the natural grace of a gymnast, lifted his body onto the wing. The
air pressure created by the moving plane tore at his clothes, ruffled
through his dark curls, and stretched the sun-baked skin of his face
toward his ears. His heart beat rapidly, but his hands were steady as
he reached his arms, shoulder height, to his sides. He pressed forward, into the wall of air that rushed around his body as he and the
plane sliced their way through the sky. Carefully finding his footing,
he inched his way to the center of the wing.

Coming to the end of their last low pass over the field, John
motioned Jimmy toward the plane, indicating his desire to land.
Jimmy edged his way back toward the fuselage, but, instead of
climbing into the cockpit, he reached under the plane and
grabbed the landing gear. Jimmy had five dollars riding on a bet
with a fellow pilot—a bet he planned to win. Gripping the struts,
and ignoring John's frantically repeated gestures, Jimmy sat on
the axle between the wheels and waited for John to land.

Fearing that the fuel might run out, John circled the field
one last time, and landed with Jimmy sitting on the landing gear.
After coming to a complete stop, John exited the cockpit,
chocked the wheels, and then, without a word to Jimmy, turned
and walked away.

Later that evening, Lt. Col. Burwell sat in his darkened office
at headquarters with his friend, the famous movie director Cecil
B. DeMille. Rushes from the days' filming flickered across the
white screen on the far wall.

The camera panned the sky, and then focused on a Jenny as she approached the field for her final descent. Burwell watched as the plane eased onto the runway. His breath caught in his throat as his mind finally registered the figure sitting between the wheels, holding onto the struts.

Burwell stormed across the room, threw open the door and hollered at his adjutant.

"Ground Doolittle for a month!"

The grainy image flickered erratically on the screen and DeMille felt it impossible to identify the culprit.

"How do you know it's Doolittle?" he asked.

"It has to be Doolittle," Burwell replied. "No one else would be that crazy!"

As Officer-of-the-Day, every day for a month, Jimmy was required to be in proper uniform, and forbidden to work on the planes or participate in any form of athletics. Only the hours spent on his motorcycle "inspecting" the field's boundaries broke the monotony.

Jimmy skirted the field, running back and forth on his motorcycle. The long hours of the morning stretched behind him, and the emptiness of the afternoon loomed blankly ahead.

The midday sun washed over the field and shadows hid under the string of planes parked along the flight line. Jimmy scanned the horizon, watching as the small dot grew larger and larger, finally materializing into a Thomas-Morse Scout. Swinging around in a wide circle, the little plane descended for its final approach.

Without serious thought, Jimmy turned the bike around, streaking down the runway in an uneven game of chicken. The plane continued on course, then pulled up and away. Banking left, it circled the field for a second pass.

Grinning, Jimmy waved at the retreating pilot before making a U-turn. He stopped to watch the Scout complete its turn and begin a second attempt at landing. Again, Jimmy darted forward into the path of the oncoming plane. Again the pilot pulled up, aborting the landing.

Finally discarding its approach, the Scout changed course and touched down at the other end of the field. Jimmy turned the motorcycle and raced toward the plane as it taxied to the flight line. He arrived just in time to see Col. Burwell descend from the cockpit.

Chances seemed excellent that Jimmy Doolittle would hold the post record for consecutive months as Officer-of-the-Day.

★ ★ ★ ★

The armistice, signed on November 11, 1918, demobilized hundreds of servicemen, flooding the private sector with unemployed, many of them pilots. Civilian aviation jobs, limited to the precarious practice of barnstorming, offered little future for a married man.

Jimmy enjoyed the camaraderie and structure of military life, and he loved flying. His decision to stay in the service was weighted heavily by his desire to stay in the cockpit.

The fledgling air service, seeking to carve out a permanent niche for itself in the nation's defense program, began to market air power through record attempts and air shows.

Jimmy, who perfected his skills as a pilot while serving as an instructor, won a position on a five-plane aerobatics team. On November 25, 1918, the air around San Diego reverberated with the shattering roar engines and the skies above were blanketed by 212 military planes flying in such tight formation that they seemed linked together in an enormous ceiling five thousand feet above the swarm of civilians lining the streets and sitting on rooftops. Below the massive backdrop, five pilots entertained the crowds, locked in a mock dogfight.

Jimmy relished the freedom of tumbling across the sky. By visualizing the maneuver, and then executing his vision, he put into practice the techniques learned in acrobatics from his childhood. That day, the few doubts he had about remaining in the service disappeared forever.

CHAPTER 4

THE PILOT'S LOUNGE

"Doolittle has always been a man around whom other men flocked. Mrs. Doolittle says that all through her married life she has never known how many friends he might show up with for dinner. (Note to young Army wives: She always fed them, unperturbed.)"

—Arthur Bartlett, *Los Angeles Times,* May 14, 1944

J O E stood on the porch as Jimmy opened the front door to their rented house in San Diego. After a year and a half of marriage, this would be the first home she shared with Jimmy. The decision to move had been a difficult one. Joe worked her way up into management at the shipyards and made more money than her young husband. But Jimmy's immediate supervisor, Lieutenant Robert "Bob" Worthington, felt that she would be a settling influence on her mischievous husband, who seemed to spend more and more time in Col. Burwell's doghouse.

Jimmy swept his wife up into his arms and carried her across the threshold of their new home.

"Doolittle! Put me down!" Joe blushed, as she scolded him.

Bob and his wife, Louise, followed them into the front room.

"The kitchen is this way," Louise explained, taking charge of the tour.

Joe stood in the doorway to the kitchen and her heart skipped a beat. She didn't know the first thing about cooking. Her parents had expected her to marry well. She could run a Holowitz, add a column of numbers, write and edit reports, but she couldn't prepare a meal. Her culinary skills were limited to chocolate cake and fudge.

"You don't like it?" Louise asked, noticing the look of dismay on Joe's face.

"No, it's wonderful!" Joe exclaimed as pink flushed her fair cheeks. "I just don't know how to cook."

Louise reached out and clasped her hand. "Don't worry Joe, I'll teach you."

★ ★ ★ ★

Brigadier General William "Billy" Mitchell, an outspoken advocate of aviation, encouraged pilots in the Air Service to share his enthusiasm. Pilots set, broke and reset records at an amazing rate. Military and commercial aviation began to move forward rapidly. By August 1918, even the Post Office had experimented with airmail delivery. Everyone wanted a piece of the action.

In the spring of 1919, Jimmy suggested to Col. Burwell that he and two other pilots fly three Jennys from San Diego to Washington, D.C., demonstrating how quickly important messages and personnel could be transported from the California coast to the nation's capital. Much to Jimmy's surprise, Burwell approved.

Jimmy checked the spare propeller strapped to the side of his Jenny. Satisfied that it was secure, he walked back to join Lieutenants Walter "Stump" Smith and Charles Haynes. All three were ready.

They consulted the out-of-date army maps one last time. There were few important landmarks in the desert to guide them, and the only charts available were unreliable. With the war over, many of the army airfields had been closed, forcing pilots to land in pastures for refueling with gas bought from local sources.

The three planes lined up, taxied down the runway, and lifted off into clear skies on their way to Indio, California, ninety miles northeast of Ream Field. They landed without incident, refueled, and immediately took off again.

The Jenny had a range of around 120 miles, the distance between Indio and Needles on the Arizona border. Feeling lucky, the three pilots decided to push the planes, and gas up in Needles.

As the town came into view, Jimmy looked for the field. Hanes pulled up beside him. Palm turned up, Hanes shrugged his shoulder as if to ask, "Where's the field?"

Jimmy searched the horizon. Desert stretched out in all directions, punctured with outcroppings of rocks. He shook his head and returned the shrug. The airfield, if it had ever existed, was no longer there.

Hanes again caught Jimmy's attention. He indicated that his fuel was low and pointed to the ground. They continued to search the landscape, but the desert offered little for the pilots. Jimmy pointed to the road that stretched across the desert, banked left and lined up with the highway outside the small town of Needles. Smith followed, landing easily.

★ ★ ★ ★

Both pilots turned as they heard the engine in Haynes plane sputter and die. The propeller rotations slowed, then stopped. Jimmy watched helplessly as the third Jenny crash-landed on the rocky landscape.

Jimmy and Stump jumped from their planes and ran across the sand. Uninjured, Charles and his mechanic climbed out of the damaged Jenny.

That evening, Jimmy called Burwell from Needles.

"Where are you?" Burwell asked.

"In Arizona, sir."

"Is everything all right?"

"Fine trip—everything's okay," Jimmy answered, "only one plane cracked up."

"What?"

"Proceeding, sir."

The men settled down in Needles for the night, then headed back to their planes early the next morning. Jimmy climbed into his Jenny. His mechanic primed the engine, and climbed into the second seat. They bounced over the field and onto the highway. After a short taxi, the little plane lifted off and circled, waiting for Stump to get airborne.

Stump's Jenny rolled down the highway, building up speed. The plane began to lift off the road, then, catching a wingtip on a telephone pole, spun around and stopped in a cloud of dust.

"Still in Arizona, Sir—very large state," Jimmy said into the phone.

"Is everything okay?"

"All's well, sir. Second plane cracked up, but I'm proceeding."

"Like hell you are!"

Jimmy held the phone away from his ear.

"Doolittle, you're a damned Chinese Ace!" Burwell shouted. "Make arrangements to ship the wrecked planes back to Rockwell by train, and then get yourself back here!"

"Yes, sir," Jimmy said.

Disillusioned, Jimmy climbed back into the Jenny with his mechanic and headed southwest, back to San Diego. Thick fog hid the land from view, and the Jenny bucked heavy headwinds that bounced her hundreds of feet in both directions.

Burning gas without making any progress, Jimmy dropped through a hole in the clouds and landed the plane in a freshly plowed field. The soft ground caught the front wheels, flipping the plane onto her back. Pilot and mechanic hung upside down for a minute before releasing their safety belts and dropping into the mud.

Jimmy climbed from the plane, snagging his pants on the cockpit and ripping a flap in the seat.

Farmhands, working in a nearby field, rushed over.

"Are you all right?" they asked.

"Fine," Jimmy said as he surveyed the belly of his plane.

Together, they turned the plane over and set her on her wheels. The propeller was split, but the spare was in good shape. Jimmy and his mechanic switched it out and made some minor repairs to the tail.

Finished, they climbed back into the cockpit, and limped back to Rockwell Field.

The landing at Rockwell went smoothly enough, but a message was waiting for Jimmy when he arrived.

"Colonel Burwell wants to see you immediately!"

Dirty and bone weary, Jimmy made his way into Burwell's office.

"Doolittle, you've got to be one of the most irresponsible pilots around!"

There was little Jimmy could say. Burwell was right. He should have planned better. Jimmy snapped to attention, saluted Burwell, then turned to leave the room.

The torn flap on his pants hung open exposing his posterior.

Livid, and taking the exposure as an implied insult, Burwell exploded.

"Doolittle, you're so stupid you can't even keep your ass in your pants!"

★ ★ ★ ★

Joe bustled about the kitchen, combining the flour, salt and pepper, rubbing it into the pot roast, making sure she covered the surface before browning it evenly on all sides. Circling the roast with fresh carrots, potatoes and onions, she added the thyme, tomato juice and Tabasco. Carefully reviewing her notes, she covered the meat and placed it in a slow oven. She checked the meringue crust on the counter. Humming to herself, she began beating the egg yokes, measuring and adding the ingredients to make lemon custard, stirring while it thickened.

When the filling was ready, she poured it into the crust, wiped her hands on her apron and turned to survey her new domain. Taking a second to check the meat, Joe removed her apron, hung it on the hook by the door, and then went to bathe and change.

When Joe returned to the kitchen the savory aroma of pot roast and vegetables, mingled with the sweet scent of Angel Pie, filled the air. She glanced out the window. Dark pinks swirled into golden pools as the sun made its way into the Pacific Ocean. She set the table for two and began to whip the heavy cream topping for the pie.

Knowing Jimmy would be along any minute, Joe lit the candles. She placed the roast surrounded by fall vegetables on the center of the table and waited.

Hours passed slowly. Joe returned to the window, pulling the curtain back on the black night, where stars vied for attention in the moonless sky.

Turning back to the table, she watched the candles flicker in pools of hot wax. A thin layer of fat isolated the vegetables like small islands in a newly frozen lake. Slowly, she walked to the table and blew out the candles then returned to her perch by the open window, a pair of tears tracking down her cheeks.

A lone figure rounded the corner and walked toward the Doolittles' small house. Joe recognized Louise Worthington, Jimmy's commanding officer's wife, as she came up the walk, and moved from her window seat to open the door.

"I've just heard from Col. Burwell," Louise said, taking in the cold roast and wilted whipped cream. "The boys are out on maneuvers. They'll be late."

"Where are they?" Joe asked.

"I don't know, and I don't expect to be told."

Joe nodded wordlessly, afraid her voice would betray her emotional state and embarrass her in front of Jimmy's commanding officer's wife.

"Joe," Louise said, voice stern but not without compassion. "Being an officer's wife is not an easy job. There will be many times that your husband will not come home, or an assignment will take both of you someplace you'd rather not go.

"You have a choice here. You can make the best of it and bloom where you are planted, or you can grow into a bitter woman who allows the bond between you to become a chain. The choice is yours."

It wasn't long before the little house near Ream Field became headquarters for lonely airmen in search of the comfort of a home-cooked meal. Joe, like Jimmy, made friends easily, and her home, no matter where it was, offered a hot meal, good conversation and lasting friendship.

Joe skinned and sliced the potatoes into a baking dish. She added ham to make it into a main entrée, stretching their meager supplies to feed the expanding group of pilots and mechanics who lounged in the front room.

Jimmy looked beat when he arrived home. She worried about him getting enough rest.

Bruce Johnson sat on the couch. His sock-covered feet rested on the coffee table.

"I thought Burwell would ground us for sure!" Brucey said, sipping a glass of Joe's home-brewed beer.

"What happened?" Joe asked, entering the room with a bowl of salad.

A sheepish look crossed Jimmy's face and Joe shook her head.

"Well?" she asked.

"We were flying around in the mountains when we spotted a flock of ducks." Bruce said. "This is particularly great sport, because the ducks and the Jenny fly at about the same speed."

"But the ducks can dive away faster than we can," Jimmy added.

"Anyway," Bruce continued. "We chased them into a canyon, but they took off and we lost sight of them."

"Unfortunately, they led us into a dead-end canyon and the walls were higher than the Jenny could negotiate." Jimmy added, rubbing the back of his neck with his left hand. "I couldn't turn in either direction, so I gave her full throttle and pulled back hard on the stick."

"We cleared the nose but the tail didn't make it." Brucey said. "She went smashing into the brush and rocks on top of the peak. Busted her up pretty good."

Joe looked at Jimmy.

"Neither one of us was hurt," he said. "But Brucey pretended to have internal injuries so the pretty widow would offer him a place for the night."

"And did you go with him?" asked Fonda Johnson, a young lieutenant who rented the spare room from the Doolittles'.

"Are you kidding?" Jimmy asked, remembering Burwell's endless lectures about how a pilot must stay with the plane in the event of a forced landing or crash. "We're in enough trouble with Burwell as it is! I spent the night huddled in the cockpit trying to stay warm, while Casanova over there entertained the widow's pretty maid!"

Later, when they were alone, Joe ran her hand down Jimmy's cheek.

"You're all right?" she asked.

"Fine. But Burwell is pretty upset."

"What did he say?"

"He reminded me that the taxpayers had to pay for my foolishness." Jimmy looked at her with tired eyes. "And he was right. I have no business wrecking their airplanes."

In the summer of 1919, the shrinking Army Air Corps cut the number of instructors at Rockwell Field to nine. Jimmy again received orders that would separate him from Joe.

The "pilots' lounge" at the Doolittles' closed its doors, and Jimmy kissed Joe goodbye. He and a few of his fellow pilots headed first to Kelly Field in Texas, then on to Eagle Pass on the Rio Grande. Their assignment: to patrol the Mexican border from Las Caeves to Del Rio, where bands of smugglers, following Pancho Villa's example, continued to cross the border, raid ranches, and slip back into Mexico with cattle, horses, and supplies.

The Texas sun blazed down on the city of Army pup tents housing the troops, but the melancholy suffocating them came more from the shooting death of Fonda Johnson by Mexican bandits than from the stifling heat. Their machine guns were loaded, but they were forbidden to return fire.

Spirits sagged as Jimmy and Bruce made their way to their de Havilland DH-4's. The heat rose off the dirt-packed field in waves as Jimmy taxied and took off. Bruce followed, close on his tail, and the two planes swung westward.

They flew above the Rio Grande, searching the desolate landscape for any signs of suspicious activity. The roar of the de Havilland engines gave advance notice of their arrival, allowing possible culprits time to find shelter. However, clouds of telltale smoke gave away hiding positions, if and when the intruders dared to fire at the American planes.

Jimmy banked the de Havilland DH-4 to the left, away from the short bursts of smoke that rose from the brush on the banks of the river. He headed north, away from the river, circling wide around a herd of Texas Longhorns grazing in an open field.

Bruce Johnson waved from his cockpit. Both men dropped their planes low over the grass, heading directly for the herd. Startled, the cattle bolted. Maneuvering the planes like trail-hardened cowboys, Jimmy and Bruce drove the stampede directly toward the thick overgrowth hugging the river.

The bushes began to quiver and shake, before spitting out a bevy of angry Mexicans, who jumped headfirst into the relative safety of the river. Turning away, Jimmy grinned as one last look revealed furious cattle rustlers shaking their fists and shouting at the retreating cowboys in their military airplanes.

★ ★ ★ ★

The house Jimmy found in Eagle Pass looked more like a shack than a house, but Joe was happy just to be together again. She ran her hands over the table and chairs, over the bed and hope chest. They felt solid, just like the man who had built them.

It wasn't long before Jimmy's friends found their way to the Doolittle house, and Joe was again cooking for the troops.

Gracie, Joe's younger sister, came out to keep her company, and Joe fussed over her as much as she did over Jimmy. Joe frequently smiled as a cadre of young soldiers vied for Gracie's attention, and felt secretly relieved when Gracie married Leland S. "Andy" Andrews, one of Jimmy's squadron mates.

The assignment at Eagle Pass lasted a year. In 1920, Jimmy received a transfer to Kelly Field. The Doolittles couldn't have been happier. Promoted to first lieutenant, Jimmy was assigned to the Air Service Mechanics School where he learned to take an airplane apart and put it back together.

The Doolittle household continued to be as popular as ever. The "pilot's lounge" shifted posts, but remained open. On January 16, 1920, the Volstead Act, better known as Prohibition, went into effect. It was illegal to manufacture for sale, transport, or sell alcohol, but it wasn't illegal to drink it. Joe's beer rivaled her cooking as a draw for the pilots. Many an inebriated soldier spent the night on the Doolittles' floor.

Joe hefted her swollen body off the bed. Her advanced pregnancy slowed her down a bit, but certainly didn't stop her. Careful not to wake Jimmy, she made her way across the dark bedroom, eased the door open, and, stepping over the bodies of sleeping troops, made her way to the bathroom. Startled by the soft rumbling snore coming from the dark bathroom, Joe switched on the light, only to find one of the bachelors sprawled out in the tub, sleeping like a baby.

On October 2, 1920, Joe gave birth to James H. Doolittle, Jr., at Fort Sam Houston Hospital. A little less than two years later, on June 29, 1922, John Prescott Doolittle was born.

PART 2

INSTRUMENT TAKEOFF

"Country. Job. Family. Because without my country I could not have a job and without my job, I could not support my family."

—Jimmy Doolittle

CHAPTER 5

COAST TO COAST

"It is not the critic who counts, not
the man who points out how the
strong man stumbled, or where the
doer of deeds could have done better. The credit belongs to the man
who is actually in the arena, whose
face is marred by dust and sweat
and blood, who strives valiantly,
who errs and comes short again
and again, who knows the great
enthusiasms, the great devotions,
and spends himself in worthy cause,
who at best knows achievement and
who at the worst if he fails at least
fails while daring greatly so that his
place shall never be with those cold
and timid souls who know neither
victory nor defeat."

—Theodore Roosevelt

BRIGADIER General Billy Mitchell led the vocal battle for a separate Air Service. He successfully demonstrated the destructive
power of air attacks by sinking the German battleship *Ostfriesland*.
The Army Air Service continued to encourage its pilots to seek
public support by displaying the potential benefits of aircraft.

Jimmy still believed that airplanes could be used for timely transport of troops from one coast to the other. This time, instead of three planes and six crewmembers, he sought and received permission to make a solo flight from Jacksonville, Florida, to San Diego, California. He planned to complete the flight in less than twenty-four hours, setting a cross-country record.

A recent graduate of Mechanic's school, Jimmy was anxious to put his new knowledge to work. After consulting Army engineers, he replaced the front seat with a 240-gallon gas tank and a 24-gallon oil tank. He installed a turn-and-bank indicator, newly developed at McCook Field, and modified the landing gear.

Comfortable with the capacity of the plane, he contemplated the more serious issue of pilot fatigue. He planned just one stop to refuel at Kelly Field in Texas. There would be no opportunity for rest. He would fly from one coast to the other, awake and airborne for almost twenty-four hours—with no one to talk to, no one to help fly the plane. A catnap could prove fatal. Still, he believed he could do it.

Dusk settled over the Florida coast, the vibrant colors of sunset faded, and the air stirred with excitement. Twenty-six year old Jimmy Doolittle sat in the cockpit of his de Havilland DH-4 and surveyed the large cluster of people gathered to witness his attempt at the coast-to-coast record. Flattered by the attention, he also felt success would create positive publicity for the Air Service.

He planned carefully, flying each leg of the route, from Florida to Texas, and then from Kelly Field to San Diego. He kept a detailed diary of each flight. In February 1921, Lieutenant Alexander Pearson lost his way and was forced down in Mexico while attempting to fly from Florida to California. Later that same year, Lieutenant William Coney was killed when his plane crashed in Mississippi while flying from the west coast to Florida. Jimmy studied their flights, and fine-tuned his own. He planned to take off at dusk, and fly all night. With one stop to refuel, he would complete the leg to San Diego in daylight.

Jimmy started the engine. He searched for Joe in the growing crowd. Finding her, their eyes locked in an unspoken embrace. He flashed a thumb up; she smiled. Adrenaline pumping, he waved to the spectators, pulled his goggles over his eyes, and began to taxi down the hard sand of Pablo Beach.

The crowd pressed forward, straining for a glimpse. The de Havilland bumped over the packed sand, building up speed. Nearing the end of the makeshift runway, the wheels caught in soft sand and the plane lurched to the left.

Instinctively, Jimmy tried to correct his course, but not before a wave caught the landing gear and flipped the small plane onto its back.

Salt water rushed into the cockpit, filling his nose and ears, sweeping his helmet forward over his eyes. Jimmy held his breath. Fighting his body weight, he struggled to release the safety belt from across his lap. Finally freed from the restraint, he grasped the fuselage and pulled himself up the side of the plane. Holding tight with one hand, he used the other to push the helmet and goggles from his eyes and then stretched his legs toward the ocean's floor. Finding the bottom with his boots, Jimmy stood up—calf-deep in cold water.

A wave of laughter rippled over the crowd once they realized only Jimmy's ego sustained injury.

"Are you hurt?" a woman asked, moving forward to offer assistance.

"No, but my feelings are," he answered.

He was soaking wet, and by the time Joe reached his side, embarrassed beyond belief. As the crowd dispersed, he and his mechanics turned the plane over. Jimmy surveyed the damage. The nose was crushed, the propeller and rudder broken. The de Havilland would have to return to Kelly Field by boxcar.

"Are you all right?" Joe asked when they were alone in their room.

He nodded, running a hand through his salt-matted hair. "This is the last time I'll make a public attempt at a record."

A sharp knock shook the door, interrupting their conversation. Jimmy answered it.

"Telegram for Jimmy Doolittle."

"Thank you."

Jimmy signed for the telegram then quietly closed the door. Failure weighed heavily on his shoulders. He turned the envelope over in his hands, fearing it contained his orders to return to base.

"Who's it from?" Joe asked, placing a warm hand tenderly on his arm.

"My guess is General Patrick."

"Well, open it."

Jimmy eyed the envelope, and then slid a finger under the flap. Reluctantly, he eased the telegram out. General Patrick wrote:

"REGRET UNFORTUNATE ACCIDENT PERIOD BETTER LUCK NEXT TIME PERIOD INSTRUCTIONS FOLLOW"

Flooded with relief, Jimmy lifted Joe and swung her around in a circle.

"Looks like we're good to go!" he said smiling.

Bolstered by the general's blessing for a second attempt, Jimmy set about planning the needed repairs. This time, even with the press pestering him, he kept his plans to himself.

★ ★ ★ ★

Once again, Jimmy eyed the deserted stretch of Pablo Beach. This time a row of lanterns, at fifty-yard intervals, marked a straight course over the hard-packed sand. Two mechanics from the base at Montgomery, Alabama, assisted him.

Breathing in the salt air, he made a trial taxi run, watching for soft spots in the sand. Satisfied that the runway was solid, he repositioned the de Havilland and revved the engines. Throttle full forward, the plane sprinted down the beach and lifted into the darkening Florida night.

With a heightened sense of awareness, Jimmy climbed to an altitude of 3,500 feet. A sprinkling of stars fanned out over an indigo sky. One thousand fifty miles stretched between Pablo Beach and San Antonio on the first leg of his journey. A full moon rose over his shoulder, and Jimmy settled in for the long flight.

Unpredictable weather plagued the southeast corner of the United States. Electrical storms accompanied summer's finale and ushered in the fall. September 4, 1922 held true to form. About two hours out of Pablo Beach, lightning split the night sky and thunder shook the de Havilland. The scent of ozone permeated the air. A curtain of darkness descended, erasing the horizon.

Jimmy consulted his gauges. Skirting the disturbance would put him off course and take too much time, so he plunged into the heart of the storm. Lightning cracked the sky, seemingly within hand's reach, and cast a glow on the land below. With each bolt, Jimmy scanned the countryside for landmarks, matching them to the Rand-McNally road map spread across his lap. Violent turbulence tossed the de Havilland like a small boat in a fifty-foot sea. Jimmy's arms strained to keep the tiny plane steady. Using his compass and turn-and-bank indicator, he held a true course.

The lightning died away and the black night enveloped him. Not a single star or speck of moonlight penetrated the cloud cover as Jimmy made his way across the southern sky. For sixty long minutes, without ground reference or celestial navigation, he flew on faith alone.

A second storm of gusting winds and icy rain waited for him over New Orleans. It reached past New Iberia and soaked the Texas border. Rain stung Jimmy's face. He adjusted his course slightly, guiding the plane northward around the eye of the new storm, but stayed as close to his route as possible. Finally, the angry sky quieted. The moon and stars reappeared.

Although Jimmy kept his secret, others were less discerning. News of his record attempt leaked out, and long before daybreak, a crowd gathered at Kelly Field. They waited, watching apprehensively for the "Lone Pilot." Dawn spilled golden light across the Texas sky, and poured it over the countryside. Anxious aviators climbed into planes and punched holes through the low ceiling of fog, searching. Spectators tensed, as one discouraged searcher after another landed. Soft voices discussed potential hazards between New Orleans and San Antonio. Still the crowd waited, hoping to witness history.

Shortly before 7:00 A.M., a lone plane dropped through a hole in the clouds. Joe held her breath. At 7:05 the wheels of Jimmy's de Havilland touched down at Kelly Field, successfully concluding the first leg of the coast-to-coast flight. The crowd roared! A jubilant

Jimmy climbed down from the cockpit, and waved. A group of handpicked mechanics surrounded the plane, refueling, oiling, and examining her from stem to stern.

Hungry, Jimmy and Joe, surrounded by fellow pilots and well wishers, ate a hearty breakfast at the field. One hour and fifteen minutes later, Jimmy climbed back into the cockpit for the second half of his trip.

Joe walked him back to the plane and passed Jimmy, Jr. up into the cockpit. A photographer snapped a quick picture. Jimmy passed the baby to Joe, kissed her, and taxied out onto the field, checked the windsock and took off into the wind.

From his days patrolling the border, Jimmy knew the terrain between Kelly Field and San Diego. Even so, he feared the second leg would be the more dangerous part of his journey. Tired, and with over a thousand miles to go, he knew the continuous drone of the engines promoted sleep.

The crowd surged forward, cheering as the de Havilland lifted off smoothly and, accompanied by a number of local planes, punched through the low ceiling.

The last escort plane pulled away at El Paso, leaving Jimmy solo on his journey to the West Coast. Vast brown deserts and droning engines had a hypnotic effect. Sleep would be fatal, but the aural and visual monotony brought on drowsiness. Jimmy fought to stay awake. Mile after mile of bleak landscape drifted by. Fatigue mounted, eyelids drooped, and Jimmy's head began to nod.

Luck, however, smiled on him. A light rain fell. The cold water rolled off the windshield and ran down his back. Jimmy's eyes flew open and the urge to sleep vanished.

Cold and tired, but awake, Jimmy crossed into Arizona. He had written ahead, asking two friends to escort him on the last part of his journey. As the de Havilland approached Yuma, Jimmy saw the two planes piloted by Captain William Randolph and Lieutenant C. L. Webber. His heart soared. The end of his journey was near; success was within his reach.

His friends' planes took up position on Jimmy's wings, flying escort on the final leg, landing one after the other at Rockwell. He had flown 2,163 miles, coast-to-coast, in just 21 hours, 19 minutes of flying time. A total of 22 hours, 30 minutes elapsed time. Jimmy Doolittle had set a new record.

Jimmy climbed down from the cockpit, adrenalin keeping him upright, the excitement of the crowd keeping him awake.

"How would you like a little snort?" a fellow officer asked, passing Jimmy a flask of whiskey.

Jimmy took a fair sized gulp. The whiskey burned its way down his throat, chasing away all ruminants of fatigue. As the rounds of congratulations came to an end, Jimmy was escorted to the field hospital where military doctors checked him thoroughly, analyzing the extent of physical and mental fatigue. A little chagrined, Jimmy kept to himself the slug of whiskey, hoping that it wouldn't skew the results too much.

Orders transferring Jimmy to the Air Service Engineering School at McCook Field in Dayton, Ohio, cut his stay in San Diego short. On September 8, 1922, Jimmy climbed back into the cockpit of his de Havallen DH-4 and returned to Kelly Field where a large crowd awaited his arrival.

A light breeze fluttered Joe's skirt as she and her mother, Margaret, scanned the horizon for Jimmy's plane.

Margaret brushed Joe's arm, and pointed toward the west.

"Is that him?" she asked.

The crowd on the flight line turned to watch the plane's final approach. The aircraft landed smoothly and taxied over to the ramp.

The crowd pushed forward as Jimmy climbed down from the cockpit. Joe, in her characteristically unassuming way, stood quietly to the side. A great deal of enthusiastic hand pumping and backslapping ensued; everyone wanted to talk to Jimmy.

Col. Howard, commanding officer at Kelly Field, took Jimmy's arm and, pulling him away from the crowd, stopped in front of Joe. As Jimmy took her into his arms, she studied his face. Worry lines from fatigue furrowed across his forehead; she soothed them with her fingertips.

Jimmy turned to embrace his mother-in-law, who, if not especially warm, at least tolerated him. Hustled into an awaiting car, the three of them led the parade of private automobiles from Kelly Field to City Hall in San Antonio.

The mayor of San Antonio greeted them, and gave a short speech about Jimmy's bravery and daring. A few words from Col. Howard followed.

Pressed into the spotlight, Jimmy thanked the crews at Jacksonville and San Antonio, and then quickly ended his speech. Rushed back to their car, they again led a caravan through the streets of San Antonio, in what ultimately became the first of many parades in Jimmy's honor.

Early the next morning, Jimmy was off again, taking the train to McCook Field. Several planes from his old 90th Squadron, in a salute from his peers, flew overhead as he left San Antonio. A few days later after closing up their quarters in Texas, Joe boarded a north-bound train with a two-year-old, an infant and all their worldly possessions.

CHAPTER 6

BACK TO SCHOOL

"These tests were put through with
that fine combination of fearless-
ness and skill which constitutes the
essence of distinguished flying ...
through them scientific data of
great and permanent importance
to the Air Corps was obtained."

—Army Citation: "Oak Leaf
Cluster for the Distinguished
Flying Cross"

ALTHOUGH he felt strongly about missing out on the "real"
action during WWI, Jimmy put his time stateside to excellent use.
He spent hours in the air perfecting maneuvers, and equally as
many hours on the ground in the company of mechanics, tinkering with the engines.

His assignment in 1920 to the Air Service Mechanics School,
followed by Parachute School, had deepened his understanding
of the mechanical side of flight. Few pilots had engineering back-
grounds, and even fewer engineers flew airplanes. Jimmy wanted
to merge the two fields. In September 1922, on the heels of his
successful coast-to-coast flight, Jimmy reported to the Air Service
Engineering School at McCook Field, Ohio.

Jimmy's transfer to McCook came pretty close to his idea of
heaven. After settling Joe and the boys into their new quarters,
he set out to fly every plane he could get his hands on. Believing

military and civilian aviation shared a symbiotic relationship, the school at McCook focused on research that benefited both. In an attempt to make mail delivery faster, safer, and more reliable, they developed a system of night lights, and encouraged pilots to make frequent flights between key cities at night, under various weather conditions.

Jimmy accepted any excuse to fly, and believed that by becoming familiar with the terrain, a pilot could push the limitations placed upon him by weather. Day in and day out, he flew his small plane low over the route between Dayton and Cleveland. In no time, he became so familiar with the countryside that he extended his daily flights to Middletown, Pennsylvania, often flying in weather that grounded other pilots.

Storm clouds blew across Lake Erie, rolling over the farmland, chasing Jimmy's plane south from Cleveland to Dayton. Raindrops whipped against the windshield, and pelted the back of his helmet. Jimmy looked over the side of the plane, located a familiar barn, lined himself up with the farm's silo, and settled back into his leather jacket. His hands felt cold and stiff on the controls, but he knew exactly where he was.

A full moon peeked out from between the clouds as Jimmy again checked his heading by locating familiar landmarks, making minor course adjustments when needed. Proud that he could fly in weather that kept other pilots on the ground, he pushed on to McCook Field. Jimmy's confidence in his knowledge and skill as a pilot, gave him an all-important sense of comfort in the face of any unexpected crisis.

The lights of McCook came into view. Jimmy, chilled and tired from hands-on flying, swung around the end of the field, headed into the wind, and landed. The plane bounced a couple of times, rain hitting the windshield, and rolled right through the deepening puddles on the runway. Jimmy taxied over to the hangar and cut the engines.

"Hey Doolittle," one of the mechanics waved a greeting.

Jimmy returned the wave.

"Doolittle!" Colonel Thurman H. Bane barked. Bane stood with a cluster of pilots at the end of the hangar.

"Yes, Sir?"

Expecting to be congratulated on a job well done, Jimmy joined the group. The rain tapped out a steady cadence on the tin roof. His smile faded when he saw the colonel's face.

"You don't have enough sense to be a good airplane pilot," Bane admonished. "You fly in weather that keeps rational men on the ground."

Dumbfounded, Jimmy tried to explain, but Bane didn't give him a chance. Without another word, the Colonel turned around and left the hangar.

Jimmy was still fuming when he got home an hour later. The boys were asleep. Joe stood in the kitchen wiping down the counters. She took one look at his face and put the cloth down.

"What's wrong?" she asked.

"Bane just bawled me out," Jimmy said. "Basically called me an idiot."

Joe waited.

The same tenacity that had driven him to run marathons as a young man in Alaska drove him as a pilot. Frequently the first to take off in the morning and the last to land at night, Jimmy put in more hours in the air than the other pilots.

"He doesn't understand." Jimmy complained. "I've memorized every farm, silo and house on that route. I know where I am all the time because I've flown it so often. It's not that I'm daring—I just know what I'm doing."

Jimmy paced back and forth in the tiny kitchen, his boots tracking rain on the floor. "There are times when I've been irresponsible. Quite a few, actually. But not this time," he said shaking his head. "I can fly when others can't because I know where I am."

Although Doolittle drew frequent criticisms from Col. Bane, he also received recognition for his skill and intellect. During his assignment at McCook, Jimmy continued to fly in air shows, both as a solo performer and in formations. Anything to stay in the air.

Upon completion of Engineering School, Jimmy applied for a Master's Degree in Aeronautical Engineering from Massachusetts Institute of Technology. Two of Jimmy's friends, Captain Eddie Aldrin and Lieutenant Samuel P. Mills, petitioned the University of California, Berkley on Jimmy's behalf, requesting that a Bachelor of Science degree be granted based upon his previous studies and work in engineering at McCook. Berkley agreed, and MIT promptly accepted his application.

The Doolittle family pulled up stakes, and moved to Dorchester, Massachusetts, where Joe found an apartment in a three-family house. Four-year-old Jimmy, Jr., and John, an active two, kept her hands full.

Joe looked in on the boys, who slept peacefully after a busy day. She bent down to pick up the mess of blocks that young Jim used to build a fort, and John loved to scatter in aerial attacks. Placing the last block in the toy box that Jimmy had built for the boys, she kissed them softly on their sleeping foreheads and pulled the door closed.

Sprawled on the couch in the small living room, Jimmy reviewed his notes from the day's classes. Joe walked over to him and placed her hand tenderly on his shoulder.

"Tired?" she asked.

Jimmy smiled. If anyone had a right to be tired, it was Joe— chasing after two rambunctious boys all day, and then helping him with his studies at night.

"Are these all for today?" she asked, taking the stack.

Settling down in front of the special typewriter equipped with mathematical symbols, she began to transcribe Jimmy's notes, stopping periodically to get clarification on a point. She had no trouble understanding the complex concepts, enabling her to quiz Jimmy, often studying with him into the wee hours of the morning before falling into bed, completely exhausted.

Their goal for Jim was to complete his Master's degree in two semesters, then use the remaining year to earn his Doctor of Science degree in Aeronautical Engineering. For his Master's thesis, Jim elected to study the amount of stress an airplane could take before it fell apart.

Jimmy documented the effect of stress on airplanes, but also the effect of G's, the multiple forces of gravity, on the pilots. His research led him to draw conclusions about the probable causes of "blackouts." Overall, the thesis was well received, especially in

Europe. His dissertation studied the effect of wind velocity gradient on airplane performance. Field experiments supported his conclusions, but the requirement of "scholarly" language, in Jimmy's opinion, hampered its potential usefulness to pilots.

Not everything at MIT meant work. Jimmy was still attached to McCook Field and routinely flew the aircraft assigned to the Air Service Reserve at Boston Airport. Although a hefty percentage of his flying tested his theories on stress and the effect of wind velocity gradient, it sometimes allowed him to relax and play, as well.

Captain Bob Brown, commander of the reserve unit, and a good friend, frequently gave Jimmy permission to fly the aircraft at Boston Airport. Jimmy and Jack Allard, a buddy from the Rockwell days, took advantage of the offer whenever they could.

Jimmy flew straight and true, pushing the Jenny over the lush fields between Boston and Lexington. Just above the City Green, known as the birthplace of the Revolutionary War, he rolled the Jenny onto her back and cruised the main street of the town in a low level inversion. Jack, playing follow-the-leader, entered the street and executed an identical barrel roll and inversion.

Shopkeepers—some cheering, others annoyed—stepped out onto the sidewalk as the planes regaled them with a second pass. Jimmy pulled up at the end of the street, passed over the small bridge, banked left and headed back toward Boston.

Taking over the lead, Jack followed the Charles River, swinging wide over Boston Harbor and into the bay. The intense sunlight shot a myriad of crystal patches across the surface of the water, and Jimmy could feel its warmth on his neck and shoulders. A sailboat drifted lazily off to his right, and a small fleet of fishing boats motored toward the harbor.

Jack swung around again, and Jimmy closed the distance, as they headed for Boston Airport.

The edge of the runway rose up before them, and Jimmy watched as Jack, unable to clear the lip of the airstrip, sheered off the landing gear.

Cold sweat broke out on Jimmy's upper lip as he pulled back hard on the controls. But the Jenny responded sluggishly. Her nose rose slowly as the steep edge of the runway loomed directly ahead. He pulled harder, resting the gears in his lap.

The piercing snap of metal stays breaking loose preceded the howling screech of the Jenny's belly as she skidded on the hard surface of the runway. Out of control, Jimmy watched helplessly as his Jenny finally ground to a halt next to Jack's plane.

An eerie silence prevailed. All motion stopped. Jimmy looked over at his friend. Jack's head, supported by his hands, rested between his arms. Jimmy jumped down from the cockpit and surveyed the damage.

"Didn't think I'd follow you, did you, Jack?" Jimmy asked, as he approached the other ship.

"I didn't mean to do this," Jack said, looking down at Jimmy. "How are we going to explain this to Bob?"

Before Jimmy could answer, the sound of a car engine drew their attention. Within seconds, Bob's staff car appeared.

Speechless, the men looked at each other. What possible excuse could they offer? They were playing around with government property. What justification could they give?

"Are you two all right?" Bob asked, as he emerged from his car.

Silently, he walked around the two airplanes. Coming to a stop next to Jack's plane, Bob rested his hand on the fuselage and looked up.

Jack stared back.

"Bob, I'm really sorry," Jimmy said, convinced that he could physically see his flying privileges evaporate into the late afternoon sun.

Jack, still sitting in the cockpit of the injured Jenny, opened his mouth to speak, but finding it difficult to locate the words, promptly closed it.

Bob looked from one plane to the other, then at his friends.

"You two have done me a great favor," he said, a smile reaching from ear to ear. "I've been trying to get rid of these two clunkers for months, but the Army wouldn't replace them with newer planes until these were unflyable." He looked again from one plane to the other.

"I'd say you two have definitely made them unflyable!"

CHAPTER 7

STUNTS AND SPEED

"Your splendid accomplishment in
winning the Jacques Schneider once
more proves America's position
among the nations of the world.
The victory was won through your
superior knowledge of aeronautics.
It is especially pleasing because of
the worth of your competitors. The
War Department is proud of you. I
am certain the entire personnel of
the American Army desires to add
its congratulations."

—Secretary of War
Dwight F. Davis

BY 1925, the western world basked in the glory of the Golden
Age of Aviation. Aviators, especially race pilots, rose to celebrity
status as role models for youngsters.

The United States spent a very small portion of its post WWI
budget on military aviation. The Army and Navy battled fiercely
for the limited funds. Hoping to increase their share of government dollars, commanders in both services ordered their airmen
to seek positive publicity. Pilots, exploring new territory, raced to
establish aviation "firsts." Lucrative purses for air races, coveted
by military pilots trying to live on their meager salaries, fostered
fierce competition.

Many considered the Schneider Cup, established in 1912 by Jacques Schneider and reserved for seaplanes only, the premier international air race. The trophy, awarded annually, helped inspire the growth of civil aviation, especially transoceanic travel. The race, held in the country of the previous winner, attracted participants from United States, England, France, Germany and Italy. Any nation winning three out of five years would be awarded the trophy in perpetuity. As national pride in aviation grew stronger, entrants received military backing.

General Mason M. Patrick, chief of the Army Air Service, believed in sharing the glory, and insisted that a diverse selection of pilots be offered the opportunity to compete.

In 1925, Baltimore, Maryland hosted the Schneider Cup Race. Patrick selected twenty-nine year old Jimmy as the Army Air Service primary pilot, and Lieutenant Cyrus Bettis as his alternate.

The Americans, anxious to recapture the world speed record from the French, entered three planes in the Schneider Cup. Lieutenants Cuddihy and Ofstie, flying for the Navy, had trained in seaplanes and held a distinct advantage over Doolittle, who flew for the Army.

Jimmy, inexperienced in seaplanes, reported to Anacostia Naval Air Station for training in August 1925. He had two months to practice.

Two tests were required to establish the seaworthiness of the planes entered in the Schneider Cup. For the "navigability" test, a pilot must taxi, take off, land and moor a seaplane. This is followed by the"watertightness" test where the plane must remain afloat for the next six hours.

The Curtiss R3C-1 idled as Jimmy waited to begin the navigability test. The biplane bobbed like a top-heavy catamaran on its twin floats, rocking with the movement of the Chesapeake Bay.

At the signal, Jimmy eased the throttle forward, increasing the RPMs as he began his taxi over the starting line. Feet pressed to the rudder pedals, he increased pressure, first to the right, then correcting left, easing the R3C-1 into a straight, controlled taxi, at a speed just exceeding 12 knots.

As his wings passed the second buoy, Jimmy pushed the throttle full forward and kicked up his RPMs for take off. When the engine was ready and the plane had gained enough speed, he pulled back on the stick. The pontoons clung momentarily to the water, then, with a final breaking of the surface tension, released. The plane popped up, surging forward. It hovered for an instant, before rising from the liquid runway, airborne, flying straight and true.

Jimmy pushed her forward, easing around the first pylon, then the second, before dropping steadily toward the bay. Holding back, he eased the controls forward, steadily approaching the surface of the water.

Unlike land-based planes, seaplanes lack landing gear equipped with brakes. Jimmy knew he needed room to gain full control of the plane before taxiing over the finish line.

Focused on the finish, he pulled back on the throttle and dropped toward the bay. The R3C-1 slapped hard against the surface and tried to bounce, but the pontoons were sucked back into the water. Jimmy worried about the hard landing, hoping nothing jarred loose. There would be no repairs. The engines, sealed at the beginning of the navigability trials, could not be worked on until after the final race.

Allowing the friction to slow the plane, he focused on the course. Finding a balance between the rudders, he dropped his speed to just over twelve knots, and taxied toward the finish line.

Alert to any changes in the sound or feel of the engines, he crossed the finish line and steered toward the assigned mooring. The test for water tightness began immediately. He shut off the engine. The plane bobbed on the surface, rocking gently, rolling in the wake of a passing speed boat. Small waves smacked against the pontoons, and the plane listed to the left, as Jimmy climbed down from the cockpit and stood on the pontoon. After helping to secure the plane, he climbed aboard an awaiting boat. His Curtiss R3C-1 would sit, unmanned, for the next six hours.

Threads of English, German, French and Italian wove a rich tapestry of sound, as excited spectators waited for the Schneider Cup Race to begin. Thousands of fans, including manufacturers and military brass from around the world, crowded onto the grass of Bay Shore Park in Baltimore, Maryland. Even Orville Wright watched from a patch of green near the far edge of the park.

Five planes qualified: three from the United States, one from Great Britain and one from Italy.

The weather was ideal—cool and sunny. A slight chop in the water broke the surface tension without creating a spray that might slow down the takeoff.

The course, three 31.07-mile legs, stretched out into the Chesapeake Bay. Each plane would make seven laps, flying 217.5 miles, before landing in the bay.

Joe, having left the boys with a friend at McCook, stood in the cool breeze, the fur collar of her coat pulled snuggly against her chin, the brim of her hat shading her eyes.

A squadron of Navy planes in tight formation circled the bay, then, with the roar of finely tuned engines, flew high above the crowd. Frank H. Constant, in an American pursuit plane, tumbled in controlled aerobatics, thrilling the spectators with breathtaking dives and rolls. But the crowd, although appreciative of the show, waited for one thing—the start of the race.

Joe shaded her eyes and turned toward the bay. At 2:30 P.M., the starting gun barked and Jimmy took off. Lifting easily from the water, he sped toward the first pylon. Herbert Broad, in a British Gloster-Napier, took off second, followed by Lieutenants Cuddihy and Ofstie in U.S. Navy planes. The fifth plane, an Italian Macchi, piloted by Giovanni de Briganti, took off last.

In the lead, Jimmy climbed rapidly under full power before approaching each pylon. He then made a tight, diving turn before leveling out on approach to the next pylon. Joe bit her lower lip as she watched Jimmy's steeply banked turns use gravity to gain a critical speed advantage.

The Army plane left the Europeans behind. Only the Navy, in matching R3C's, gave any real competition. Lap after lap, Jimmy led the pack. Cuddihy, pushing his plane, briefly closed the gap. Joe silently held her breath, until Jimmy finally pulled away.

"I think he's got it!" General Patrick said to Joe, as they stood side by side in the sun.

"I think you're right," she said, turning her warm smile on the General. Only Joe knew that Jimmy had practiced the pitch of his turns, over and over again, working out the math to shave seconds wherever he could.

"Come on, Jimmy!" the General shouted, as the Army plane streaked past them, well in the lead.

Trouble held off until the sixth lap, when the planes, stretched out single file, swept past the crowd. As they turned toward the bay, smoke poured out of Ofstie's engine, and the Navy pilot pulled out of the race, leaving Cuddihy as the only serious contender.

On the back stretch, over the water, Joe spotted flames and dark smoke pouring out of the engine of Cuddihy's R3C, and watched as the plane dropped toward the bay.

Joe said a silent prayer, first for Cuddihy, then for Jimmy as he sped across the finish line in first place, pulling out of the pattern before landing on the water.

Britain's Herbert Broad crossed second, followed by Giovanni de Briganti. But after Briganti crossed the line, he pulled around the pylon, and then sped out to sea where the Americans had gone down.

Joe could see the outline of the two R3C's being towed into the bay when she noticed that the Italian seemed to be experiencing trouble of his own.

"I think he's in trouble," she said to the general, pointing to the Macchi.

"Looks like he's out of gas," General Patrick said, as the plane drifted lower toward the horizon.

"Congratulations!" General Patrick said when a smiling Jimmy joined them a few minutes later.

"Thank you, Sir." Jimmy shook the General's hand before turning to kiss Joe. Just seconds later, an onslaught of well-wishers engulfed him.

Loud speakers crackled and the announcer's voice filled the air.

"First place officially goes to Lieutenant James H. Doolittle of the United States Army Air Service with a seaplane record of 232.573 miles per hour.

"Britain's Herbert Broad captured second with a speed of 199.169 miles per hour. And third to Italy, with Giovanni de Briganti finishing with a speed of 168.169 miles per hour. Congratulations, men!"

Although pleased with his victory in the Schneider Cup, Jimmy believed he could get even more speed out of the R3C.

Before flying the required three-kilometer course in front of observers from the National Aeronautic Association and the Federation Aeronautique Internationale, he changed the pitch of the propeller slightly, resulting in a higher RPM at full throttle.

On October 27, 1925, Jimmy set a new world seaplane record of 245.713 mph, 13.1 mph faster than the record he had set the previous day in the Schneider.

Following the race, the Doolittles returned to McCook Field, with Jimmy the newly appointed Chief of the Flight Test Section. His assignment gave him the opportunity to use his engineering background, and to verify his ideas in flight tests.

Winning the Schneider generated international attention. Jimmy, already recognized for his cross country record, quickly became a public figure. Recognizing this, and hoping to capitalize on his celebrity, Clarence Webster, of the Curtiss Aeroplane Exporting Company, and C. M. Keys, of the Curtiss Wright Company, asked the Air Service to place Jimmy on an extended leave, and allow him to demonstrate the Curtiss P-1 Hawk to potential buyers in South America. The Air Service gladly complied.

Traveling with Boyd Sherman, a mechanic from Curtiss-Wright, Jimmy arrived in Santiago, Chile in late April, 1926.

Laughter filtered through the cigarette smoke in the officers' club. Representatives from Britain, Italy and Germany joined the American in friendly, but spirited competition for airplane sales to the Chilean government.

Earlier in the day, Jimmy and Boyd had examined the planes, and sized up the competition. The English and the Italians presented no problems. The Hawk easily outclassed both. The German's 260-horsepower Dornier posed little threat to the Curtiss 400-horsepower D-12 engine, as well. But the German pilot, Karl Von Schoenebeck, a World War I ace from the Richthofen

Squadron, deserved their respect. Jimmy envisioned a mock dog-fight, knowing the outcome would depend as much on pilot skill as it did on maneuverability of equipment.

Confident that they would walk away with the sales, the two Americans stopped at the bar to refresh their drinks before joining a group of Chilean officers.

"Maybe Doolittle can answer our question," one Chilean officer suggested, as Jimmy and Boyd walked up.

"What's that?" Jimmy asked.

"Your American actor, Douglas Fairbanks," explained the South American. "Does he do his own stunts in the movies or does someone do them for him?"

"Ah," Jimmy said, his impish grin in place. "What Fairbanks does isn't so special. All American kids can do that."

The group of officers laughed.

"Surely you jest," said the spokesman.

Jimmy's grin widened as he handed his drink to Boyd.

"Here, move back," he said. "I'll need a little room."

Adroitly, he placed both hands on the floor and kicked up into a handstand. Balancing for a few seconds, he walked across the room on his hands, and then kicked back into an upright position.

"Bravo!" The group of officers cheered, and toasted Jimmy.

Encouraged by the attention, Jimmy took a running start, and crossed the room in a series of front handsprings.

"Ole!" they toasted, cheering and slapping Jimmy's back.

"This is fine, very impressive," said one of the pilots, "but in the movies Fairbanks does his tricks on a window ledge."

Retrieving his drink from Boyd, Jimmy drained the contents and made his way to an open window. A ledge, two feet wide, spanned a courtyard, fifteen feet below.

Jimmy set his empty glass on a table, and climbed onto the ledge. Planting both hands carefully, he eased himself up into a controlled handstand.

Cheers again rang out across the room.

Making sure he firmly planted his left hand; he shifted his weight slightly, raised his right arm, and balanced fully on his left arm.

"Bravo, mi amigo!"

"Fantastico!"

Jimmy recaptured vertical on his feet. Emboldened by the free flow of pisco sours and cheers, and feeling no pain, he reached inside the window. He grasped the inside ledge, planted his hands, and extended his body parallel to the brick courtyard one story below. Again, Jimmy raised his right arm.

The spontaneous outburst of cheers and applause almost masked the sound of crumbling plaster as it pulled away from the windowsill.

As if everything moved in slow motion, the sandstone ledge in Jimmy's hand broke free and he fell feet first. Air rushed past his face. He clutched at the side of the building, desperately seeking a handhold.

Crash landing directly on his feet, Jimmy felt sharp pains shoot up both his legs from his ankles. Unable to support himself, he slumped to the ground.

Excited expletives and murmurs of concern, mostly in Spanish, flooded through the window, breaking through Jimmy's haze of pain. The officers poured down the stairs and into the courtyard. Two of the larger men grasped Jimmy by the arms. Lifting him, they carried him to the parking lot and loaded him into a car. They sped down the rutted highway. With each bump, Jimmy gritted his teeth. Completely sober now, he silently cursed his own stupidity.

At the hospital, the two officers gingerly pulled him from the car and carried him to emergency room. Some of the officers from the party had followed Jimmy to the hospital. Together they waited—agitated, impatient, some still intoxicated: nevertheless, they waited, not wishing to abandon their comrade-in-arms.

Hours later, X-rays revealed a simple fracture in one ankle and a complicated series of small breaks in the other. Sympathetic moans erupted twice—once at the diagnosis, and again when the doctors kicked everyone out of Jimmy's room.

They left Jimmy sitting in his hospital bed, contemplating his situation. No hangover could be worse than the pain of embarrassment. No excuses—he had let people down.

What would Clarence Webster of Curtiss Aeroplane Exporting Company think? Or C.M. Keys of the Curtiss Wright Company? What would they say when they learned that their celebrated "salesman," through his own irresponsibility, rendered himself unable to demonstrate the P-1 Hawk? What would his friends at McCook, passed over on this assignment, say, when the story circulated back home?

What would Joe say? He could answer that for himself. She wouldn't say anything. She'd just look at him in that way she did, and he'd feel ashamed. Jimmy ran his hands through his thinning hair. He had let them all down.

His plaster-encased legs itched to high heaven, and the hard mattress pressed against his aching spine. Long hours of solitude allowed for long hours of introspection. He had no doubt that Von Schoenebeck and his Dornier would walk away with sales that should go to the Hawk. Jimmy knew he would be unable to face himself, much less anyone else, if he let that happen. The Curtiss-Wright P-1 Hawk was a superior plane, and he needed to find a way to prove it.

On the morning of June 24, Boyd Sherman showed up with a hacksaw. Sawing away, he shortened the casts to below Jimmy's knees, and then drove him out to the airport. They fastened clips to the bottom of Jimmy's flying boots, and eased the boots over his casts.

Jimmy scooted out of the car and, leaning heavily on crutches, hobbled over to the Hawk. Unable to climb up by himself, Boyd and another mechanic hoisted Jimmy into the cockpit.

They clipped his boots to the rudder pedals. Jimmy started the engine and taxied onto the runway. Giving the plane full throttle, he took off. Believing the snap roll to be the most taxing on his injured ankles, he decided to test his stamina. After reaching altitude and air speed, he briskly applied full rudder to the right, followed almost immediately by aft stick. As soon as the plane began its roll, he eased the stick forward to increase the rate of rotation. As the Hawk completed its roll, he gave her full rudder to the left with the stick forward of neutral, bringing her back into a straight line of flight.

Over and over, he practiced the maneuver, putting pressure on the rudder pedals with his injured legs. Small cracks appeared in the plaster of his casts, and in his imagination he could hear the snap as small pieces broke away from the strain.

Satisfied that he could withstand the discomfort, he landed. Jimmy and Boyd returned to the airport the next day, practicing the snap roll to the left, this time cracking his left cast.

"Jim, I think you're going to permanently damage your ankles if you don't replace those casts," Boyd said, as he helped Jimmy down from the cockpit.

"You're right," Jimmy said, looking down at the crumbling plaster.

They headed for the hospital. Pulling up in front, Boyd opened the passenger door and eased Jimmy from the car. Depending more on Boyd than on his crutches, Jimmy made his way up the walk and into the building.

"Crazy American!" the doctor said, shaking his head and turning them away. "No. Go home."

Jimmy's ankles throbbed and the splintered casts felt like tourniquets. Easing himself into a bathtub, he began to soak off the casts. Peeling off the last of the plaster, he examined his legs. Dark purple stained the swollen skin, and even his toes had lost all recognizable shape.

"Jim, you can't fly without protecting your ankles," Boyd said, after taking one look at Jimmy's misshapen legs. Supporting as much of Jimmy's weight as he could, Boyd practically carried his friend to the bed.

Jimmy winced as the pressure from the top sheet shot lightning bolts of pain up his ankles, and through his legs, settling in his hips. He almost welcomed the pain as punishment for his stupidity.

"We'll need to find someone who can engineer a cast," Jimmy said, his mind attacking the problem.

Their research culminated in the discovery of an old German who made prostheses for a living. Using flexible corset stays, he reinforced heavy plaster casts and fitted them to Jimmy's lower legs. Still dependent on crutches to navigate on the ground, the casts proved quite satisfactory in the air.

Rain falls sporadically from May to October in South America, but the morning of the exhibition dawned bright and clear. Bodies pressed against each other in stands filled to capacity. The President of Chile, surrounded by his cabinet, filled the first row. Chilean Army and Navy officers, like a starry backdrop, illuminated the stands behind him.

When Jimmy arrived, Von Schoenebeck dominated the sky. He pushed his Dornier through a series of loops and rolls, climbing high into the cloudless sky, then plunging toward the ground. The crowd held its breath, and then broke into wild applause when it looked as if the Dornier would crash into the ground, only to pull up and fly away again, at the very last moment.

Anxious to get to his plane, Jimmy lumbered on his crutches toward the Hawk. With Boyd's help, he scrambled into the cockpit. After running a quick instrument check, Jimmy took off and climbed into the transparent sky.

Following a closely choreographed routine, Jimmy put the Hawk through her paces. They tumbled in snap rolls to the left and the right, soaring toward the blinding sun, then dropping like a wounded bird, only to recover and fly away.

With increasing confidence in the functional performance of his casts, and his plane, Jimmy lined up for a pursuit pass.

Accepting the challenge, Von Schoenebeck leveled out, and headed directly for Jimmy. The two planes passed within feet of each other, then turned out in a roll. Jimmy brought the Hawk around behind the Dornier and kept on its tail.

The Hawk, with her 400-horses and superior maneuverability, performed flawlessly. After proving the Dornier incapable of losing the Hawk, Jimmy pulled off Von Schoenebeck's tail, zooming overhead to exhibit the Hawk's superior speed. He swung around to make a second pass, followed by a third, very close to the Dornier. Just as Jimmy lined up to make a final pass, Von Schoenebeck broke away. As the German descended, Jimmy noticed the frayed fabric on the Dornier's upper wing.

Satisfied that the Hawk had driven all competition from the sky, Jimmy rose into the sky for a final set of aerobatics. As he ended the routine, Jimmy approached the stands, and flipped the Hawk for an inverted pass, very low to the ground. The crowd went wild, cheering for the "Crazy American."

The applause thundered even louder when Jimmy landed. Spectators flooded the airstrip in front of the stands, surrounding the Hawk. Adrenaline pumping, Jimmy sensed no pain in his ankles. He waved broadly to the crowd before being helped from the cockpit and handed his crutches.

Not everyone applauded. A group of pilots around the Dornier, believing Jimmy had deliberately brushed Von Schoenebeck's upper wing on one of his passes, scowled at the American.

"No!" Jimmy explained when he finally understood their accusations. "I would never purposely damage another airplane in peacetime."

Hobbling on his crutches, Jimmy inspected the frayed wing.

"Here," he called to the others. "Look at this. It's obvious the stress on the wing damaged the fabric," he pointed to the frayed edge of the wing, "and here along this edge."

Bone-tired, but satisfied with the day's results, Jimmy returned to the hotel. The Chilean military acknowledged the Hawk's superiority with the purchase of several planes. The throbbing in Jimmy's ankles was no match for the satisfaction he felt in completing his assignment.

Bolivia followed Chile on Jimmy's itinerary. On August 18, after installing an extra gas tank, Jimmy stowed his crutches in the machine gun mounts. He took off from Santiago, stopped for fuel in Antofagasta, Chile, and continued to La Paz, setting a world record of eleven hours and twenty-five minutes.

The dispute between Bolivia and Chili over the mineral-rich coastal area of the Atacama Desert dated back to the mid-1800s. Social turmoil dominated the 1920s. A sagging economy, bolstered by U.S. loans, left the Bolivians resentful. When Jimmy landed in La Paz—tired, ankles aching—they greeted him with animosity. The Bolivian people wanted nothing to do with an American pilot who sold planes to their sworn enemies in Chile.

After checking into the Stranger's Club, Jimmy collapsed on the bed. Fatigue, from hours in flight, mixed with pain from his swollen ankles, and he dropped into a fitful sleep.

"Down with Gringos!"

The chant woke Jimmy from his nap.

"Down with Chile! Long live Bolivia!"

Jimmy, bracing himself, first on the bed, then using a chair back, and then the wall, made his way to the window.

He looked down on the street below. A huge mob carpeted the grounds in front of the club, spilling into the street, and flowing around the corner. Thousands of angry Bolivians stood looking up at his window and Jimmy felt a shiver of fear.

"Go home, Gringo!" they shouted.

Someone in the crowd spotted him and hurled a rock. Jimmy ducked back as the plaster next to the window crumbled and fell. A chill of panic raced up his back. In good health, he could run fairly fast, but with two broken ankles, he'd never outrun a mob. He pulled back from the window and balanced against the wall.

Angry epithets multiplied, as the mob became more volatile. A rock sailed through the open window and landed near his bed.

"Americano, go home!"

Police sirens whined in the distance, growing more intense as they approached. Shrill whistles and the sharp crack of rifles sliced through the din of rabble-rousers. Their chants dissolved into growls of confusion.

Eventually the crowd withdrew, receding like low tide. Twilight approached, and the light from the street lamps reflected off scores of broken bottles and other debris. The wrath and fury that, only moments before, permeated the air, dissipated into harmless, innocent night noises.

Jimmy hobbled away from the window and sat down on the bed. His ankles throbbed and cobwebs of fatigue threatened to pull him back to the pillows. By the time his hosts called him down to dinner, Jimmy had lost his appetite and begged off. He had the distinct impression that his hosts were relieved by his decision. He planned to demonstrate the Hawk in the morning. He sincerely hoped that the demonstrators would not be present.

He climbed into bed and pulled the light covers up to his chin. He wondered what Joe and the boys were doing. What would she say about his "reception"? He slept fitfully, waking often to see the hands slowly circle the face of the clock.

Dawn arrived. Although the litter from the demonstrators left tangible reminders of anti-American sentiment, none of the protestors remained.

Leaning heavily on his crutches, he joined a small group of Bolivian officers, and haltingly made his way to their car. Only a few military dignitaries and the Bolivian Secretary of War waited for Jimmy at the deserted airport.

Jimmy put the Hawk through her paces. But, obviously, the Bolivians weren't interested in buying the same plane that their rivals had just purchased.

"Very impressive," the Bolivian Secretary of War said, inspecting the Hawk.

Courteous, but disinterested, the other officers paid their respects and then left.

"They think you're a spy," the Secretary said, as they walked toward the awaiting car.

"They think what?" Jimmy asked.

"Well, you have just come to us from Chile," he answered smoothly. "Even our parliament has denounced you."

Jimmy shook his head in wonder. His legs ached from the pressure exerted on his ankles during his aerobatic routines. He felt exhausted from interrupted sleep. Now, he found himself the subject of suspicion in a country far from home.

"You know," the Secretary said. "If I were an American pilot on crutches, who couldn't run very fast, but had a very fast airplane waiting at the airport, I would get in it and fly home."

It didn't take much thought. Curtiss Wright didn't have any fans in Bolivia. Both the plane and the pilot were in danger. One day later, on August 22, 1926, Jimmy climbed back into the Hawk and returned to Santiago, setting a new record of nine hours and fifty-five minutes.

Jimmy's itinerary took him to Argentina next. Crossing the Andes by air presented considerable hazards, and a number of

1. *Jimmy and his father Frank Doolittle in Nome, Alaska.*

2. *Jimmy as a boy in Nome, Alaska.*

3. *Rosa Doolittle with her dog sled, the most efficient means of transportation in turn-of-the-century Nome.*

4. Jimmy's third grade class in Nome.

5. Jimmy Doolittle and Josephine "Joe" Daniels were high school sweethearts.

6. Jimmy was an excellent gymnast. Here he is performing the one-handed handstand that would later get him in trouble in Chile.

7. Jimmy and Joe as high school students with friends at the beach.

8. Joe mugging for the camera.

9. Lieutenant James H. Doolittle at Ream Field in San Diego.

10. Joe as a young Army Wife.

11. Jimmy grew a beard while stationed with the 90th Aero Squadron at Eagle Pass, Texas.

12. Jimmy, shown here at Pablo Beach, Florida, was the first person to fly coast-to-coast in under 24 hours. He set the record on September 5, 1922.

13. Jimmy with his son, James H. Doolittle, Jr. at Kelly Field just before setting out on the second leg of the cross country flight.

14. Jimmy was forced to crash-land the Super Solution when the landing gear failed to extend.

16. Joe typed Jimmy's thesis and dissertation on a special typewriter at Massachusetts Institute of Technology where he earned his master's and doctoral degrees in aeronautical engineering.

15. Jimmy talking with General Mason M. Patrick, Chief of Army Air Services. Jimmy was selected as alternate pilot for the Pulitzer Race.

17. *Jimmy took first place in the 1925 Schneider Cup with an average speed of 232.573 miles per hour.*

18. *Joe and General Patrick congratulate Jimmy after he won the Schneider Cup.*

20. *Jimmy visited Germany in 1930.*

19. *Jimmy broke both ankles while performing a hand-stand on a second story window ledge in Santiago, Chile. He flew the Curtiss Hawk in demonstrations with both ankles in casts and strapped to the rudder peddles.*

21. *Jimmy crash-landed the Corsair in thick fog on March 15, 1929 in Elizabeth, New Jersey by hooking a wing on a tree to break the momentum. He believed that had he been flying the Consolidated NY-2, equipped with instruments, he could have landed safely.*

22. *Jimmy flew the Consolidated NY-2 trainer, fitted with instruments created by the Guggenheim Foundation, for the first blind flight on September 24, 1929.*

pilots had died attempting the feat. Jimmy clipped his boots to the rudder pedals and prepared for takeoff. Knowing that he wouldn't be able to free his feet in time and doubting that a man with two broken ankles would be very successful at survival in the Andes, he eschewed the wearing of a parachute.

He taxied, revved the engine, and lifted from the runway. Coaxing the Hawk to 18,000 feet, the city of Santiago faded into the lush foothills. The rugged peaks of the Andes, colors muted by the thin haze, rose majestically from the landscape. Six hours and forty-five minutes later, in another city-to-city record, Jimmy landed in Argentina. Demonstrations went well and Jimmy sold a number of Hawks to the military. Satisfied with a job completed, if not well done, Jimmy left the airplane in Argentina and headed home by boat.

Anxiously, Joe scanned the passengers as they streamed down the gangplank. The crisp bite in the air held the promise of the approaching fall colors. Joe wrapped her sweater close to her body.

"There he is, Mom!" young Jim announced. At seven, he had assumed the role of man-of-the-house during his father's absences.

"Where is he?" five year-old John asked, pulling on Joe's skirt.

Joe searched the departing travelers, and then spotted him.

"There he is, John," she said, kneeling down to his level and pointing at Jimmy. She fought to keep the expression on her face from showing concern. Four months after the accident, Jimmy still hobbled on crutches. Pain etched deep groves in his forehead. She saw his struggle to hide it.

"Welcome home, Doolittle," she said, slipping into his arms.

At Joe's insistence, their first stop after arriving at McCook was the base hospital. The base physician immediately ordered Jimmy to Walter Reed Hospital in Washington, D.C.

X-rays revealed that his ankles had not healed properly. Jimmy's doctor prescribed new casts, and sent him to bed for a month. His recovery proceeded slowly. Joe and the boys moved to an apartment near-by. For six months, Jimmy was confined to the hospital and underwent intense physical therapy. Released on April 5, 1927, he returned to duty at McCook.

The months of confinement at Walter Reed gave Jimmy long hours to contemplate questions of physics and flying. While working on his Masters at MIT, he had studied not only the effects of stress on airplanes, but also on pilots. He knew that the maximum acceleration a pilot could withstand depended on the length of time the acceleration continued. It also depended on the physical condition of the pilot.

Pilots routinely performed an inside loop during aerobatic demonstrations. Questions of pilot safety and airplane durability kept most pilots from attempting the more dangerous outside loop. Believing the negative effects on the body could be lessened by conditioning, he began working out on the parallel bars.

Armed with the results of his studies at MIT, and spurred on by insatiable curiosity, Jimmy climbed to 10,000 feet and began preparing for an outside loop.

Over and over, Jimmy accelerated in the P-1 Hawk, pushing down at high speed, keeping steady pressure on the stick, holding it forward as the blood rushed to his head. Each time he experienced unpleasant pressure, but it cleared shortly after he righted himself. Again and again, he pushed over the top, then around and under, holding on a little longer each time, before pulling out.

Finally Jimmy reached altitude and speed, then pushed over the start of the loop, holding the stick forward. The plane rolled over the top and continued to cling to the imagined circle, turning Doolittle upside down at the bottom of the loop. Still exerting pressure, he continued to push the stick forward, believing and hoping that he had enough speed to complete the loop. The pressure in his head made him dizzy, but he resisted the urge to pull out. Continuing with the stick full forward, Jimmy felt the plane return to the top. Grinning, he believed he had just completed the first outside loop. He straightened out and allowed himself to regain all his faculties before returning to the field and landing.

Jimmy went over the plane from propeller to rear rudder, examining all pressure points, paying particular attention to the wing joints and fabric. Satisfied that the Hawk had survived without damage, and convinced that he had no lasting negative effects, he allowed himself a moment of satisfaction. Had he really completed an outside loop? He needed confirmation to know for sure.

A couple of days later, Jimmy asked his friend, Lieutenant James T. "Hutch" Hutchinson, to watch while he climbed into the Hawk and ascended to the required altitude. Checking his gauges, and scouting for other aircraft, Jimmy pushed the plane down, over and around in an awkward outside loop. Again, he allowed himself to fully recover before landing.

"You did an outside loop, Jim!" Hutch bellowed as soon as Jimmy landed.

"It was a little sloppy. I can do better." Jimmy's signature cockeyed grin lit his face.

"Listen, Hutch," Jimmy said, "I don't want this to get out yet."

Reluctantly, Hutch agreed and Jimmy returned to the sky, day after day, until he could execute a perfect loop. When finally satisfied, he invited six fellow test pilots to witness his stunt. Word spread that Doolittle was going to attempt "something," and spectators crowded the flight line.

On May 25, 1927, Jimmy again climbed into the Hawk, and while his friends watched, pushed the P-1 over and around into a perfect outside loop. His ecstatic friends congratulated him. Reporters crowded around. Jimmy Doolittle had established another aviation first.

"What made you try an outside loop?" one reported asked.

"Don't know." Jimmy answered, his eyes bloodshot, but otherwise in fine shape. "Just thought of it on the spur of the moment."

The next morning Joe looked at Jimmy over the morning paper.

"You're in the news again," she said, shaking her head. "Jimmy, what were you thinking when you said that? The press already has you labeled as a daredevil. They have no idea how many hours you spent perfecting the outside loop. They'll never take you seriously if you continue to wisecrack."

He looked at her with a sheepish grin. As usual, Joe was right. But regardless of whatever the press reported, his "high jinks" proved that military planes had reached the point where a pilot could depend on the strength of his plane in a high stress maneuver.

In January 1928, Curtiss-Wright asked Jimmy to make a second trip to South America.

"Be careful, Doolittle," Joe said, as Jimmy prepared to leave.

"I'm always careful in airplanes," he answered grinning.

"Oh, I don't mean in airplanes," she replied, with a grin of her own. "I mean in officers' clubs where they serve pisco sours!"

Jimmy's second tour of South America earned him the National Order of the Condor of the Andes from the Bolivian president. This time, unlike his visit in 1926 when he was greeted by protestors and encouraged to leave, Bolivia welcomed him with open arms.

He demonstrated planes, flew passengers, delivered medical supplies, and set speed records between cities. South American ambassadors dubbed him a "one man good will tour."

By the time he returned to McCook Field five months later, Jimmy entertained serious questions about his future. Thirty-one years old and still a first lieutenant, he worried about the lack of opportunity for promotion in the Army Air Corps.

Other factors contributed to his dilemma. John and Jim attended school and Jimmy didn't want to uproot them every few years. In addition, he and Joe supported both their mothers, straining their meager budget. As much as he enjoyed his military career, he needed to consider what would be best for his family.

CHAPTER 8

FLYING BLIND

"This chap [Doolittle] has the
advantage over any of our Navy
people of not only a lifetime of flying, but a technical education that
has given him a distinct advantage
in the development of new equipment."

—Captain Emory S. "Jerry" Land

BY 1928, civilian aviation had blossomed in the United States.
Commercial airlines carried passengers and mail on routes established by the Post Office. More reliable and faster planes flew
longer distances, but only in good weather.

Daniel Guggenheim, recognizing the potential for aviation,
established a fund of 2.5 million dollars in January of 1926, "to
promote the advance of the art, science and business of aviation."

Guggenheim's son, Harry, served as the fund's president.
Particularly interested in studying flying in fog, Harry established the Full Flight Laboratory in 1928 at Mitchel Field in New
York, and asked U.S. Navy Captain Emory S. "Jerry" Land, the
fund's vice-president, to recommend someone to run the blind
flight laboratory. Land recommended Army Air Corps pilot
Jimmy Doolittle.

Jimmy, who had been considering a well-paying job offer as
a test pilot for Curtiss-Wright, promptly accepted Guggenheim's

offer as head of the Full Flight Laboratory. Remembering his own experience on the 1922 coast-to-coast flight, and knowing that his success hinged in part on the turn-and-bank indicator he'd installed in the de Havilland, he firmly believed that future flight would_depend on instruments. He couldn't resist the opportunity to put his education and experience to work on a project that could potentially revolutionize commercial aviation. Detached from the service and on loan to the Guggenheim Fund for a year, Jimmy moved his family to base housing at Mitchel Field on Long Island in New York.

"Ain't she sweet," Joe sang softly as she moved around the small kitchen of their new home. Cranking the handle of the grinder, she ground chunks of leftover ham into a bowl, adding curry and diced pickle. Setting that aside, she stirred honey into a fresh pitcher of lemonade.

Their quarters, one of four two-bedroom units in a long-vacant, termite-ridden wooden barracks, would be home for the next year while Jimmy headed the Full Flight Laboratory. The family didn't notice the termites or the aging wood in the cramped unit. Within hours of arriving, Joe had unpacked their possessions and established a home filled with family and friends.

She looked out the kitchen window. John and young Jim ran across the expanse of lawn, swashbuckling, brandishing makeshift swords and attacking trees, imaginary foes, and of course, each other. Images of Jimmy, suspended from a window ledge in Chile, came to mind as she watched the boys. Like father—like sons.

Fall leaves, turning brilliant shades of red, orange and gold, clung tenaciously to the trees, resisting the pull of pending winter. Joe dried her hands on a dishtowel, and tucked her short white hair behind her ears.

Intense conversation from the dining room drifted into the kitchen. She filled two glasses with homemade lemonade and arranged a plate of toasted squares with deviled ham. Straightening her apron over her dress, she carried the tray into the dining room.

Jimmy, meeting with Elmer A. Sperry, Sr., head of Sperry Gyroscope Company, leaned over a drawing on the dining room table. Convinced that instruments played an important role in safe flight, he discussed his ideas with Sperry's top man. The two men, huddled over Jimmy's sketch, hardly noticing her presence. A gentle breeze billowed the white sheers and stirred the papers on the table.

"The turn-and-bank indicator is fine for measuring the rate of turn and whether it is coordinated or not," Jimmy said. "But it's useless for take-offs and landings."

Jimmy studied the picture, then added, "What we need is an accurate, reliable, easy-to-read instrument that shows the exact direction of heading and precise attitude of the aircraft, particularly for take-offs and landings."

"The artificial horizon will duplicate the orientation of the natural horizon, showing if the aircraft is flying straight and level, climbing, diving or banking." Jimmy continued pointing at the drawing. "And the directional gyro will show heading."

Sperry studied Jimmy's rough draft of a directional gyro superimposed on an artificial horizon.

"We could build a single instrument like this," Sperry said, "but, for simplicity of construction, I'd recommend two separate instruments."

"You're probably right," Jimmy replied.

"I'll have my son, Elmer, Jr., design and construct a prototype." Sperry said, still studying the sketch. "He'll work directly with you."

The afternoon sun dipped beneath the horizon and Joe kept busy in the kitchen. She chopped the florets off the broccoli and peeled the stocks, slicing them into a small saucepan. She ground the remainder of the ham, and put white potatoes on to boil.

The group, assembled by the Guggenheim Foundation, soon became close, and Jimmy was able to build a team that worked well together.

The front door opened and Professor William G. "Bill" Brown of the Aeronautics Department at MIT entered. His wife Betty and Jack Dalton, the team's mechanic, followed him into the house.

Bill popped his head into the dining room, and then headed directly for the kitchen. He came up behind Joe and gave her a kiss on the cheek.

Smiling, Joe turned around.

"Hops," Bill said, holding out his offering. "So you can stay in the brewing business."

"And I've brought along some fresh tomatoes," Betty said entering the room behind Bill. "May I give you a hand?"

"Of course," Joe said, passing her a paring knife. "Please slice those tomatoes and I'll serve them with the deviled ham."

The glass windows shook with the percussion from a small cannon. Joe wiped her hands on her apron and opened the back door.

"Hutch," she called out to her neighbor. "You're going to get the boys in trouble with the base commander again!" She wasn't sure who was more ornery: Jimmy, the boys or Jimmy's friend from next door.

Alexander "Sacha" de Seversky, an internationally known speed pilot and very fine aeronautical engineer, and Sachinka Toochkoff, the former Russian chief of naval aviation, joined the group in the kitchen. Both White Russians and survivors of the old Moscow regime had adopted the United States as their home after the revolution in Russia. Joe handed them each a cold beer.

"Beer have I had in Moscow," Sachinka said, seizing Joe's hand and kissing it. "Beer have I had in Leningrad and in Copenhagen and in Vienna and in Munich, and in every damn place. But, Joe, there is no beer like your beer."

"Hear. Hear," the others chimed in, clinking glasses in a toast to their hostess.

Laughter bubbled from the kitchen and flowed into the living room. An eclectic menagerie of friends—scientists from the Guggenheim project, pilots and mechanics from Mitchel Field, and civilians from the local community—filled the quarters and spilled into the front yard. It was business as usual at the Doolittles'.

Jimmy firmly believed that to live to an old age, a pilot must define his limitations and stay within them. With constant practice, he can expand them, but prudence requires that he respect them.

The Guggenheim Fund purchased two planes for testing at the Full Flight Laboratory, a Navy Vought Corsair O2U-1 for cross-country flights, and a Consolidated NY-2 Husky, equipped with instruments for the blind flying experiments.

Occasionally, the O2U filled in for the Husky. On March 15, 1929, Jimmy decided to establish weather limits for the Corsair. He took off from Buffalo, New York, and headed back to Mitchel Field.

The fair weather held through the early part of his flight, and he cruised over recognizable landmarks at Rochester and Syracuse. By the time he reached Schenectady, however, the skies began to cloud up.

Banks of white cotton candy brushed against the Corsair's windows and wrapped around her wings. Jimmy looked out the window. Conditions were deteriorating, but still flyable. He'd passed the turn back point, and decided to press on.

By the time he reached Albany, the clouds had thickened and visibility had dropped. Jimmy descended beneath the ceiling, searching for recognizable landmarks. Far below, he spotted the bright lights of a passenger train. Dropping, he flew just above tree level, left wing hovering over the train as it wound through the New York countryside. Smoke from the locomotive drifted up, blending into the clouds. With the brightly lit train as his only companion, Jimmy flew south, parting company only when the mountains reached skyward, blocking his path, and the train burrowed deep into the tunneled earth.

Jimmy turned to the Hudson River, flying low over the water, below the blanket of clouds. The moisture penetrated his flight suit leaving him cold. His fingers were stiff on the controls. Unhappy with the deteriorating weather conditions, he considered landing on the parade grounds of West Point. In the distance to his left, he could see the solid mass of Michie Stadium. He vacillated for a few minutes, considering his options, but conditions remained flyable—barely. He decided to push on.

The ceiling improved as Jimmy approached New York. The profile of the city emerged from the mist. Close to home, he continued south to the Battery, planning to land at Mitchel Field. But billowy pillows of white surrounded the plane, laying thick blankets over the banks of the Hudson, and obscuring recognizable landmarks. For the first time, Jimmy questioned his judgment. If he had flown the Husky, equipped with instruments for poor visibility, landing would not present much of a problem. But the

Corsair lacked the proper radio equipment and instruments. He checked the fuel; the gauge was near empty.

Circling back, he headed for Governor's Island. He planned to land on the drill field, but fog clung to the water's surface, completely shrouding the island. He checked the fuel gauge again and the needle dropped closer to empty. Fearing he had reached his limitations, Jimmy turned back toward Yonkers Golf Course. His knowledge of the area made it his best chance in zero visibility.

Again turning south, he prepared to land in Battery Park. He circled the park, dropping through an opening in the overcast. Jimmy braced himself for a rough landing. Just as he prepared to set the Corsair down, a lone figure ran on to the field, frantically waving Jimmy away. Frustrated, he pulled up.

The gauge eased closer to empty, and Jimmy eyed the icy waters of the Hudson River. He removed his parachute so he could swim ashore and prepared to crash land in the water. But the dark gray river, capped with white peaks, looked cold. He shivered at the thought of ending up in it. Clutching at the last straws of hope, he headed again for Newark Airport, praying for a break in the weather. As he crossed the river, the lights of Jersey City filtered through the overcast. Looking at his fuel gauge, Jimmy realized that he did not have enough fuel to reach Newark, and to try would put the unsuspecting population below him at risk.

Convinced now of the impossibility of a safe landing, he pulled up through the clouds. A crystal clear night, populated by a mass of stars, waited above the thick layer of fog.

Realizing he might be forced to bail out, he headed west, away from the lights of Jersey City. He eyed the fuel gauge, the needle dipped below zero. The O2U skimmed the top layer of fog as Jimmy searched for a break in the clouds.

Remembering his abandoned plan to ditch in the river, he reached for his discarded parachute. A beacon of light punched through the clouds. Hoping to find an emergency landing field, Jimmy turned on his landing lights and dove through the hole to scout the area.

Bands of fog hovered close to the ground as Jimmy flew just over the tree tops. The plane shuddered as the landing gear brushed against the upper branches. Snagged, the fabric tore away from the lower wing. Heart pounding, Jimmy pulled back at the controls, lifting away.

Out of gas and knowing that the damaged wing would only get worse, he searched for the best possible place to crash. Hoping to minimize the impact, he wrapped the left wing around a tree trunk near the ground. The Corsair skidded across the field and wedged between two scrub oaks.

Unhurt, Jimmy stood next to the shattered wreckage of his plane. Belly up, wings smashed and landing gear ripped away, the O2U presented a pitiful sight.

★ ★ ★ ★

Jimmy declined an invitation to fly an exhibition at the 1929 Cleveland Air Races. His schedule at the Full Flight Laboratory commanded most of his time and all of his attention. Orders from Major General James E. Fechet and permission from Guggenheim surprised and irritated him.

He walked around the loaner Hawk, shaking his head. The plane needed a major overhaul.

"The radiator cowling is cracked and leaking," he told the mechanic, pointing to the damage. Fastidious about his own planes, he was uncomfortable flying something so poorly maintained.

After requesting that a plate be riveted onto the cracked cowling, Jimmy took the plane up for a test flight. The plane overheated. He landed and approached the hangar.

"Does the Hawk need some Prestone in the radiator?" Jimmy asked an Army mechanic.

"The radiator is too small for this plane," the mechanic said, while adding a half-gallon of Prestone. "She always runs hot."

Still concerned about maintenance, Jimmy strapped on his parachute and flew the plane to a deserted area about seven miles from the field. He performed the first half of an outside loop, and then rolled out of it.

Climbing to 4,000 feet, he leveled off, and then slowly pushed into a dive. At about 2,000 feet, he heard a sharp pop and the broken wings began to peel back from the fuselage. They remained attached but useless. Jimmy throttled back. Thrown clear of the plane, he plunged toward the field. Air rushed past him, billowing his flight suit, pushing at his goggles. Within seconds of clearing the plane, he pulled the rip cord; the chute did not open. His body gained momentum and the ground came closer.

Small moth wings of fear beat in his chest as he spiraled downward. At around 1000 feet, he yanked the cord again, this time using more force. The 'chute released, jerking him hard before dangling him by the harness. The loud stream of rushing air grew silent as he floated toward the field. He thought about the experiments underway at the Full Flight Laboratory, many nearing completion. He silently cursed the politics that brought him to Cleveland.

He landed hard, feet first on still-tender ankles, about twenty feet off a back road near Olmstead Falls. Controlling his temper, he gathered up the parachute and hitched a ride back to the Air Corps headquarters.

Business as usual greeted him when he returned. Pilots and mechanics, mingling in the stuffy room, looked up as Jimmy entered.

"What happened to you?" one of them asked, when Jimmy dumped his parachute in an unoccupied chair.

"The plane broke up," Jimmy said, unsnapping the harness.

"Did you get out all right?"

Jimmy thought the answer obvious, but bit back a sarcastic retort. No reason to take his bad mood out on the guys.

"I'm fine," he said. "I just need another plane."

The second Hawk was in better condition and the demonstration later that afternoon went well. In addition to Jimmy, the headliners included Charles Lindbergh and Al Williams, who put on a spectacular show in a specially equipped Curtiss pursuit plane.

Jimmy declined several invitations to celebrate after the air show, opting instead to fly directly back to the laboratory on Long Island. Cleveland had left a bad taste in his mouth, and he was itching to spit it out.

The next morning, Joe smiled across the table at her husband. It was obvious that his usual good humor had not returned. The morning's headline, "TWO OLD AIR DOGS THRILL RACE FANS," hadn't helped.

"The trip to Cleveland was nothing more than a publicity stunt designed to get me in the air with Lindbergh and Williams," Jimmy said, perusing the article.

"It seemed to work," Joe said. "The crowd loved the show."

But she knew Jimmy's heart wasn't in stunting. Experiments for the Guggenheim Fund monopolized his attention and he resented any outside intrusion on his time.

"It's no wonder the Air Corps suffers so many accidents. Maintenance on the planes is almost nonexistent," Jimmy said, as he set the paper down on the table. "Appropriations for the Air Corps must be increased. If we are to be effective, the Air Corps needs to have more resources."

Jimmy continued to stew over the Cleveland Air Show and the condition of the Air Corps equipment. He submitted a report to Major W. O. Ryan, recommending that, like Williams' Curtiss, the planes should be specially prepared for stunting, and that any time the Air Corps was to perform in front of a large audience, "Army pilots should have the best possible equipment and training, not only to permit the Army pilots to show to better advantage, but for greater safety."

He also submitted a report to the Irvin Parachute Company, simply stating, "Airplane failed. Parachute worked."

With more conviction than ever, Jimmy returned to the lab, determined to solve the problem of flying in fog.

Equipping the NY-2 with specialized equipment and instruments, Jimmy went up time after time, refining the instruments and mastering their use. In addition to equipping the planes, the Full Flight Laboratory worked on techniques to disperse fog in the area around airports. Believing that private industry offered possible solutions, the scientists investigated their developments. One fog dispersal system, discovered by Harry Reader of Cleveland, Ohio, seemed particularly promising.

Reader used a large blowtorch heater to dry gravel and sand at his gravel pit. He discovered that even thick fog seemed to dissipate during this process. Hoping that Reader's discovery could help solve the visibility problems at local airports, the Guggenheim Fund asked him to install his equipment at Mitchel Field.

For several months, the weather remained clear and Reader's equipment sat idle. However, on the morning of September 24, 1929, Jack Dalton pounded on Jimmy's door.

Immediately awake, Jimmy pulled back the bedroom curtain. Thick fog pushed against the glass. Pulling on the trousers laying on top of the hope chest at the end of their bed, Jimmy made his way to the front door.

"It's a go!" Jack said grinning.

"I'll meet you at the field." Jimmy headed back down the hall.

"Who was that?" Joe asked.

"Jack. We're going to test Reader's equipment."

Joe finished dressing and went into the boys' room.

"Hurry!" she said, gently waking them. "We're off to the flight line."

Excited, John and Jim pulled on their clothes and headed for the car.

Reader met them at Mitchel Field and fired up his equipment. Captain Land and the rest of the team arrived. They huddled together, blowing on their hands for warmth.

The fog began to melt in front of the blow torches. Excited anticipation rippled through the gathering. However, minutes ticked by, and the fog still clung to the runway.

Jimmy looked at Joe, shaking his head. It didn't take long to figure out that Reader's machine would not produce the desired result. As patches of fog burned off, new fog rolled in to replace them.

Disappointment hung as heavy as the fog.

"I'm going to make a real fog flight," Jimmy said to Joe.

"Dalton, let's push out the NY-2, I'm going up."

The grin returned to Dalton's face.

"Yes, Sir!" he said with a salute. They both headed off to the hangar.

At the sight of the NY-2, everyone snapped to work, manning the radios and turning on the beacons.

Jimmy taxied out and took off, punching through the fog at about 500 feet. Following the fifteen-mile course he'd flown hundreds of times, he swung wide over the countryside, then around into landing position. Moments later, he dropped back through the fog, landing in front of the assembled crew and observers.

As he taxied back toward the hangar, Guggenheim arrived with a small contingent of people. Confident that both he and the plane were ready, Jimmy signaled Jack Dalton.

"Get the hood," he said. "Let's make this official."

As Jack headed back to the hangar, Jimmy walked over to Guggenheim.

"Good morning, Harry," he said, reaching out to shake hands. "I'm taking her up for a blind flight."

Excitement rippled rapidly through the spectators.

"Good Luck, Jimmy," Harry said, firmly grasping Jimmy's hand.

Jimmy climbed back into the cockpit and Jack Dalton pulled the hood over the cockpit windows and secured it. Jimmy would take-off, fly and land the plane on instruments alone. Ben Kelsey, acting as safety pilot, climbed into the other seat and placed his hands on the upper wing of the NY-2.

Once again, Jimmy taxied the plane onto the west facing runway and took off. Gradually climbing to about 1,000 feet, he leveled off, and then made a 180-degree turn to the left. He flew several miles before turning left again. Studying the visual indicator, he adjusted the plane so that both reeds vibrated through the same arc. Secure that he was lined up properly for landing, he leveled off at 200 feet and watched the fan marker. A single reed began to vibrate.

Jimmy decreased his speed to about 60 miles per hour, and then flew directly to the ground using the instruments developed by the laboratory. Despite his numerous smooth landings, the plane touched down hard and then bounced. Jimmy was disappointed with the sloppy landing, but the crowd on the ground was ecstatic.

Jack Dalton was first to congratulate Jimmy when he pulled the hood back, but he wasn't the last. Guggenheim shook his hand, and Captain Land clasped his shoulder. Photographers crowded around the plane, snapping pictures of the instruments and catching Jimmy in the cockpit.

That evening, the Guggenheim gang and their families gathered in the Doolittles' quarters to celebrate their victory. As usual, Joe prepared mountains of food and the home brew flowed.

Jimmy raised his glass and toasted the assembled group.

"We've got a long way to go, but we're on the right track," he said.

Joe looked around the room. History had been made today, and these were the people who had made it happen. From scientists to mechanics, executives to ground crews, each had contributed. Wanting to commemorate the event in her own special way, she pulled her best damask tablecloth from the hope chest.

Starting with Jerry Land, she asked everyone to sign the cloth. All together, she collected over five hundred names, each hand embroidered later by Joe, in black DMC thread over the original signatures. Eventually, the cloth became a virtual Who's Who in aviation history and was given to the National Air and Space Museum in Washington, D.C.

With work at the Full Flight Lab ending, the Doolittles again faced the question of employment. At thirty-three years old, Jimmy still wore a first lieutenant's bar. As much as he loved flying and testing every type of airplane owned by, or offered for sale to, the Air Corps, he had a growing responsibility to his family and the financial responsibility of both his own mother and his mother-in-law.

Curtiss-Wright filled the test pilot position while Jimmy worked for Guggenheim, so Jimmy accepted a job with Shell Oil Company in St. Louis. Reluctant to completely sever ties with the service, he applied for and received a commission as major in the Special-Reserve, skipping the rank of captain.

His contributions to the Guggenheim Foundation did not go unrecognized. In January, 1930, he received the Harmon Trophy, *Ligue des Aviation,* for his ground breaking work in instrument flying.

CHAPTER 9

THE SHELL YEARS

"It was during his earlier Army
service, of course, that he made his
name as the country's No. 1 test
pilot. But his most daring stunts
were always to prove something
about the plane, not about Doolittle.
A typical Doolittle report told first
what happened to the plane, then
what happened to Doolittle: 'Wings
broke off. Thrown out.'"

—Arthur Bartlett, *Los Angeles*
Times, May 14, 1944

JOE allowed a few seconds to observe the party before rejoining
the group from Mitchel Field. Dear friends filled the room, touching her beyond words. The guests at the party, like those who
frequented the Doolittles' home, came from every walk of life: military and civilian, fellow pilots, mechanics, scientists, industrialists,
businessmen, and, of course, a number of reporters. All came to
say goodbye.

Candles flickered on tables set for dinner. Drinks flowed
freely and Joe held back a flood of emotions. They had been a
part of the military community for more than a dozen years. The
tight-knit group provided comfort and shared experience.

Like other oil companies who hired well-known aviators to promote their products and establish themselves in the growing aviation market, Shell asked Jimmy to head their aviation department in St. Louis. Jimmy hired on at three times the $200.00 a month paid by the Army.

Joe watched Jimmy as he circulated. He would miss many things about the service—the camaraderie, flying and testing various airplanes, the knowledge that he contributed to the progress of aviation. But in her heart, she knew he'd find the same things in his new job.

Jimmy had always attracted people with his wit and charm. But, over the years, something had changed. She looked around the room. Not only had Jimmy gained their friendship, he'd also earned their respect. He was no longer the class clown, or the daredevil pilot who sat between the wheels during a landing just to win a five dollar bet. He'd grown up and she was proud of him.

A new layer of snow coated the field the following morning and the wind gusted, wrapping itself around legs and working its way under coats.

The new, fully-loaded Lockheed Vega, with its 425-horsepower Pratt and Whitney Wasp engine, waited to take the family to their new home in St. Louis.

Both John and Jim, Jr. hung on Hutch. Joe thought about how close the boys had become with their next-door neighbor. The way Hutch had taught them to fence like Douglas Fairbanks, the little cannon he had brought them, the hours spent playing in the yard, all the little things that meant so much.

Joe embraced Del, Hutch's wife.

"I'll miss you," she said.

Squeezing tighter, Del replied, "I'll miss you, too." Then, fighting a wave of tears, she looked over at Hutch and the boys. "And Hutch is really going to miss those boys of yours."

Joe knew that he would, and that the boys would miss him as well.

The circle of friends grew, wrapped in their winter coats against the wind. They rubbed their hands together and stamped their feet against the cold.

Joe noticed the reporters with their cameras and notebooks. She bit back a wave of resentment. Rarely could Jimmy do anything anymore without their presence.

"Let's go." Jimmy called to Joe and the boys, as he headed to the Vega.

The boys piled into the plane. Joe gave Del another hug, and then climbed into the back, next to the boys.

Jimmy, opening the bulkhead door, checked the safety belts.

"Everyone ready?" he asked.

With their faces plastered to the windows, the boys waved frantically to Hutch, who, standing behind Del, surrounded her with his arm.

Joe settled back into her seat as Jimmy started the engine. Wind whipped flurries of snow against the windows and across the air field. The Vega rolled forward, bouncing over the uneven ground.

She listened to the boys chatter over the increasing engine noise. Pulling her coat tight against the draft, she felt the shift in momentum as Jimmy released the brakes. The Vega surged forward.

"Are your belts fastened?" she asked, leaning over to make sure the safety straps were tight across her sons' laps.

Joe felt the jarring to the left, just seconds before Jimmy fell backward into the cabin.

"What happened?" she asked, as soon as Jimmy righted himself.

"The wheel caught in a snow drift," he snapped raising his voice. "I told you never to open this door without warning me."

"I didn't open it," Joe said, biting back her own anger. "I think something's broken."

"Nothings broken, and please let me fly this airplane!"

She watched as Jimmy climbed back into the cockpit, and began the second takeoff run. But, before she could settle back, the wheels caught a second time. Joe felt the gear give way, as the plane plowed into the ground. Skidding sideways on the icy runway, the wing snagged and the plane rocked forward into a ground loop—a nose first somersault into the snow.

★ ★ ★ ★

Shaken, Joe turned to the boys. Stunned into silence, both John and young Jim hung upside down, their eyes wide with surprise.

"Everyone okay?" Jimmy asked, as he crawled back to his family.

Suitcases and boxes littered the cabin, and snow pushed up against the windows. Joe struggled to release her safety belt, and then helped Jimmy release the boys.

The smell of gasoline filled the cabin, and Joe worried about fire. Jimmy tried to open the door—it wouldn't budge. He used his shoulder, shoving with his full weight, but snow packed it in. The gasoline fumes grew stronger.

Spectators and friends rushed over. Digging the snow away from the Vega, they released the door. The Doolittles tumbled out.

"God damn it, Joe!" Jimmy stormed, looking accusingly at Joe. "What the hell were you thinking?"

Joe held his eyes and remained calm, not responding to his public tirade. Jimmy, who usually treated Joe to long periods of icy silence when angry, lashed out.

"I can't believe you brought all this junk!" Arms folded across his chest, he surveyed the jumbled pile of luggage and household goods.

Understanding his embarrassment and obvious anger at overloading the plane, she held her tongue.

John and young Jim, having sufficiently recovered from their shock, jabbered excitedly. Joe looked appreciatively at Jim McCullough, as he corralled the boys and led them away.

"Are you kids okay?" McCullough asked.

"Oh, sure," young Jim said as they moved away, "but you should have heard what my father said to my mother and it wasn't her fault he cracked up the plane!"

Jimmy inspected the wreckage, and then called Shell to report the crash. He made arrangements to have the Vega crated and shipped back to Burbank for repairs. His spirits plummeted. Not only had the crash been his fault, the entire incident had been recorded by the press. The repairs would cost around $10,000, almost half the original cost of the plane.

The *New York Times* headline blared the news. "Doolittle's First Civilian Hop in 12 Years Fails—Ex-Army Pilot Crashes in Snow Before Start." Even more embarrassing was the fact that the new pilot for Shell Oil was forced to travel to St. Louis by train.

After the cramped quarters of military housing, the house at 6311 Washington in St. Louis seemed huge—five bedrooms, large kitchen, formal living and dining rooms, plus a private yard for the boys.

Joe unpacked the boxes and set the house in order. She hung family pictures on the walls and displayed treasured gifts from the boys. The hope chest that Jimmy built for her as a wedding present sat open at the foot of the bed. She removed freshly pressed white sheets and smoothed them over the mattress, making a pocket at the foot of the bed to reduce the pressure on Jimmy's ankles. Within days, the nomadic family settled into their new home.

By April, Joe and the boys found themselves on their own again. Jimmy, accepting an offer from Jack Allard, his friend from Ream Field and current president of Curtiss-Wright, took off on a 21-country tour of Europe.

Shell jumped at the opportunity to display their company logo and Jimmy joined a team of five pilots and two mechanics. His first stop—Athens, Greece.

Aviators share a camaraderie that cuts across national borders. The American team, invited by fellow pilots, inspected aircraft in every country they visited. Impressed by the advancements in European aviation, Jimmy studied their planes.

He found the French Farman a notable machine and felt that the Dutch Fokker exhibited many interesting innovations. But, the German Dorniers and Junkers impressed him the most. Built for speed, and the forerunners of military fighters, Jimmy believed these planes warranted concern.

The Treaty of Versailles after WWI strictly prohibited German development of military aircraft. In Jimmy's opinion, the German planes foreshadowed a violation of that treaty. But more importantly, he felt American aviation was falling behind.

Part of Jimmy's job on the tour included socializing. Dignitaries, in many countries, hosted parties in honor of the Curtiss team. The Hungarian dictator, Admiral Miklós Horthy, threw a formal reception for them. The American ambassador reciprocated with a dinner party.

Always up for a challenge, Jimmy's mischievous side got the better of him in Budapest. Flickering candles burned low as a silent contingent of waiters removed china and white linen from the American Embassy's dining room. The American ambassador, J. Butler Wright, shared a final glass of brandy with the Hungarian dictator. Strains of Vivaldi's *Summer* filled the air as the dinner drew to a close.

The American pilots, who had thrilled the Admiral earlier in the day with their display of Curtiss airpower, fascinated his twenty-year-old son.

Nicholas Horthy offered to introduce the aviators to the Hungarian night life. He led the boisterous group from the room and into a waiting automobile.

The Danube flows through the center of Budapest. Old buildings line the river's edge and a series of low, ornate bridges connect the two halves of the city. The ancient architecture, unlike anything in the United States, intrigued the Americans.

"Could your airplane fly under these bridges?" Nicholas asked Jimmy.

Jimmy studied the bridges. "There's nothing the Hawk can't do," he answered.

Jimmy, called upon to prove his claim, was dropped at the airfield. He warmed up the Hawk's engine and checked out the gauges. The night, clear and windless, stretched before him. He taxied into position and lifted easily from the runway. The Hawk, like its namesake, soared into the night sky, turning to follow the river into the city.

Budapest lay glittering before him. The moon reflected off the rippled surface of the Danube. Within minutes, Jimmy spotted his friends on one of the bridges. He dropped lower, and, for the first time, realized just how tight the fit would be for the Hawk.

Dropping steadily, his wheels skimming the surface of the water, he passed under the bridge without a mishap. He pulled away, and perched above the city, watched as his friends waved and cheered. It probably wasn't the smartest thing he'd ever done, but he felt confident that he'd caused no real harm.

By morning, Budapest buzzed with discussion of the American aviator's daring prank, prompting a less-than-flattering letter from the British minister to the American ambassador, criticizing the stunt.

Jimmy returned to the States, believing it imperative that the United States invest more in research and development to keep up with European aviation. Racing would lead to faster planes, better engines, lubricants, fuels and safety.

Joe met him at the airport. While he was away, his mother, Rosa, had taken a turn for the worse. She died shortly after he returned. A deep sadness settled over Jimmy and he threw himself back into his work.

★ ★ ★ ★

It never took very long for the Doolittle home to become a hub for social activity. In the small aviation community, everyone knew each other well. St. Louis, located in the center of the nation, frequently hosted aviators on their trek across the country. Most of them found their way to the Doolittles'. Joe made them all feel at home.

For the first time in their marriage, they had a little extra money. Jimmy insisted that Joe hire a housekeeper to help with the boys and allow her to travel more often with him. Mary Bryant became a part of the family.

However, the kitchen remained Joe's domain.

Looking out the window, Joe observed both young Doolittle boys facing the bushes along the back fence. Wiping her hands on a white flour-sacking dishcloth, she walked to the back door.

"What are you boys doing?" she inquired.

"Piddling," John answered, as he finished his business and turned to face his mother.

"Why on earth are you piddling in the yard when you have a perfectly good bathroom?"

"That's what all Dad's friends do," young Jim answered.

Joe suppressed a smile. With five bedrooms and only one bathroom on the first floor, it was perfectly true that during a party many of the men used the yard. However, she knew she needed to put an end to this behavior right away.

"Be that as it may," she looked from one boy's face to the other. "You two are to use the bathroom, not the bushes!"

Jimmy kept Shell's name before the public. He did so with a series of sales, aerobatic exhibitions and good-will flights. He flew in many of the air shows and races around the country. However, to date, Jimmy had never owned his own airplane.

When Jimmy Haislip wiped out the Shell Travel Air Mystery Plane in a crash landing, Jimmy decided to purchase the wreckage and rebuild it.

Using the bulk of their savings, he bought the plane from Shell, and installed a Pratt and Whitney Wasp, Jr. engine. He redesigned the wings and fuselage, encasing the connecting struts, and putting the landing gear in "pants."

On June 23, 1931 Jimmy took the Doolittle 400 on her first test flight. Word spread that Doolittle was "going up" and an audience, including his ten-year-old son Jim, Jr., gathered at the field.

Jimmy taxied out to the runway and took off. The plane climbed swiftly from the field, and Jimmy released the breath he'd been unaware of holding.

Systematically, he tested the plane's response to the controls, and with each test the plane responded perfectly. Satisfied with the controls, he climbed to a safe altitude and completed a simple aerobatic routine. The plane danced through the sky, responding effortlessly, rolling, tumbling, and looping with ease.

The engine throbbed as he completed a final roll and plunged into a dive toward the field. He pulled out of the dive at 100 feet, leveled off and raced past the spectators.

Exhilarated, Jimmy glanced at the airspeed indicator. The needle hovered just below 300 miles per hour. But he had no time to celebrate. Just as he began to climb for a final pass, he heard the crack of metal over the roar of the engine, followed by violent vibrations. Fighting to control the plane, Jimmy barely had time to get the Travel Air away from the crowd.

He pulled back hard on the stick, flipped her into inverted flight and prepared to jump. The wings began to disintegrate. The ailerons snapped off and fluttered away in the slip steam.

Struggling to release the second of his two safety belts, Jimmy pulled himself from his seat and rolled over the side of the cockpit. Acutely aware of his proximity to the ground, he immediately pulled the ripcord. The chute opened and within seconds, Jimmy landed feet first on the field.

Jim, Jr., rushed up to where his father stood, draped in his chute, gazing sadly upon the wreckage.

Jimmy turned to his son, expecting an outburst of filial solicitude.

However, instead of asking after his old man's well being, young Jim surveyed the busted plane, then asked, "Dad, how much dough did we have wrapped up in that crate?"

"All of it," Doolittle replied.

"Whoo Whee!" young Jim added, shaking his head, "Mom is going to be mad!"

Joe no longer wondered why her hair had turned white at twenty-five. The loss of their savings meant nothing compared to the potential loss of her husband.

She said nothing. Jim's belief that his design had caused the demise of the Travel Air punished him enough. She, on the other hand, privately rejoiced that he had again escaped death.

Still convinced that the pursuit of speed would contribute to the development of better airplanes, systems, and fuel, Jimmy contacted E. M. "Matty" Laird about flying one of his planes in the Bendix Trophy Race.

On September 4, 1931, Jimmy stood beside the Super Solution, a sleek biplane with a 500-horsepower Pratt and Whitney Wasp engine, enclosed landing gear, and tiny wings. She looked like a fast plane.

Seven other pilots waited in the fog at United Airport in Burbank, California. The Bendix, scheduled for a midnight takeoff, got a late start. The starting flag flashed and Lou Reichers, in a modified Lockheed Altair, took off. Jimmy, sixth in line, waited his turn. As soon as Beeler Blevins left the runway, he pushed his throttle full forward and released the brakes.

The Super Solution raced ahead, lifted from the runway within 400 feet, and sped past Blevins' plane. Jimmy landed in Albuquerque, New Mexico, and a team of Shell mechanics jumped to work, refueling the Laird with 140 gallons of Shell fuel, and Jimmy with a glass of milk. Within eight minutes, the Super Solution took off again, this time headed for Kansas City, Missouri.

Clear skies prevailed as Jimmy watched the grid of cities and the patchwork of rural areas pass below his wings. The pit stop in Kansas City took ten minutes. He was airborne long before any other plane approached.

Averaging 228 miles per hour with favorable tail winds, Jimmy sped across the country. A slight drizzle beaded on the canopy, and a scattering of dark clouds hung over Cleveland.

When Jimmy landed in light drizzle, only a few diehard fans waited at the airport. First place was based upon elapsed time, so even though Jimmy landed first, with an elapsed time of 9 hours 10 minutes and 20 seconds, he wasn't sure he'd won. Believing he commanded a healthy lead, he turned down Joe's sandwiches and jumped back into the Super Solution. Within minutes, he was in the air, on his way to Newark and a new transcontinental record.

Deteriorating weather churned on the horizon with a series of squalls directly in his flight path. Hunkering down, Jimmy headed into the storm. The Laird, buffeted by high winds, bounced in the turbulence. After pulling his collar up around his neck, Jimmy kept his hands firmly on the controls. Flurries of rain spit across the canopy and ran off the wings. The bad weather persisted as he climbed above the Allegheny Mountains. It began to lighten once he cleared them. Spotting the outline of Newark in the distance, he dove at high speed for the runway, landing a little before 5:00 P.M. eastern time.

Nine years earlier, to the day, Jimmy had set a transcontinental record breaking 24 hours. He had just cut that time in half. He'd flown from Burbank to Newark in eleven hours, 11 minutes.

With a few hours of daylight left, Jimmy, waved goodbye to the crowd and returned to the sky, retracing his flight to Cleveland, where Joe waited with the boys.

Tired but jubilant, Jimmy climbed out of the Super Solution. He had captured first place in the Bendix with a purse of $7,500, and another $2,500 for his new transcontinental record. Pleased with the day's results, he swept Joe and the boys into a family hug.

"Good job, Doolittle," Joe said, as she returned his embrace.

"Thank you," he said, pulling her closer and kissing her.

Finding his way to a phone, Jimmy called Shell Headquarters in St. Louis to report on the day's flying.

"Congratulations, Jimmy!" Vice President Alexander Fraser's voice crackled over the line.

"Thank you, sir," Jimmy replied, still grinning.

"We're hosting a little party here in your honor," Fraser said. "We'd like you to join us."

Jimmy could hear the sounds of celebrating in the background. Still pumped up by the day's events, he readily agreed.

"I'll get there as soon as I can," he said.

Weaving back through the growing crowd at Cleveland airport, Jimmy spotted Joe.

"I'm headed back to St. Louis tonight," he said. "I'll see you tomorrow."

Within minutes, he climbed into the company Vega and took-off. Joe and the boys watched him go.

CHAPTER 10

THAT SPEED PILOT

"People often think of Doolittle as 'that speed pilot.' He's much more than that. Actually, he is a somewhat shy, dignified man with a background rich in research. He has pioneered much of the flight path that has made America the world's out-standing air power today."

—*Liberty Magazine*

T o keep Shell Oil's name before the public, Jimmy continued to set city-to-city records across the United States. His accomplishments, regularly reported in the media, added to his popularity, and fans of all ages followed his career closely.

Toward the end of 1931, Shell's Public Relations Department came up with a new publicity event—connecting the three capitals of the Western Hemisphere in less than twelve hours.

In mid-October, Jimmy flew the Laird Super Solution to Ottawa, Canada, where he picked up two messages from Canada's Premier Richard B. Bennett: one to President Herbert Hoover in Washington, D.C.; the second to Mexican President, Pascual Ortiz Rubio in Mexico City.

The Super Solution climbed into the cloudless sky from Ottawa. The city's riot of fall colors retreated from view as Jimmy turned the plane south. He flew over the heavily forested acreage of southern Ontario, across the Saint Lawrence River into New

York, then along the eastern edge of Lake Ontario. Clear skies gave way to sporadic turbulence within patches of bad weather that hovered over the Appalachian Mountains and reached to the coast.

As usual, the newspapers publicized the flight. A welcoming committee of dignitaries and fans crowded the airfield in Washington, D.C. to greet Jimmy on the first leg of his venture. He stepped from the plane to the rousing music of a local marching band and the snapping shutters of both professional and amateur photographers. Escorted by an honor guard, Jimmy made his way to a platform facing the stands. An aide for President Hoover accepted the message from the Canadian Premier.

Like a swarm of bees, Shell mechanics surrounded the Super Solution and within minutes, prepared the Laird for take off. Jimmy, anxious to complete his flight, stood restlessly next to the welcoming committee. Dignitary after dignitary delivered speeches. Jimmy felt the minutes cut into his schedule, and wondered if he could make up the time. At long last, the ceremony ended with the band playing an exuberant rendition of "Happy Days Are Here Again." Only half an hour had elapsed, but for a pilot on a mission, it seemed much longer.

Long after the Shell trucks refueled the Laird and mechanics completed last minute checks, Jimmy climbed back into the cockpit and took off for Mexico City.

He flew south, landing at Birmingham, Alabama. His ground crew refueled and serviced the plane in seven minutes. At Corpus Christi, Texas, the Shell crew met him with fuel and lunch. Sixteen minutes later, he was back in the air heading for the Mexican capital and a new record. As he headed south, he knew that he would miss both the Shell team and Shell gas. The fuel in Mexico would not meet the needs of the Laird's engine, so he carried a can of tetraethyl lead to increase the octane level. Not an ideal solution, but it worked. Perhaps, he thought, he should pitch Shell products to the Mexican government.

He flew along the coast of Texas, crossing the U.S. border at Brownsville. The turquoise waters of the Gulf of Mexico shimmered under his left wing. To his right, the Sierra Madre Mountains, which had long served as a barrier to east-west travel, rose from the barren hills south of the Rio Grande. Dense, humid patches of vegetation clung to their coastal slopes. The silhouette of the Laird skimmed over the white sand, disappearing in dark shadows only to reappear on uninhabited beaches.

At Tampico, on the Mexican Coast, he began the climb over the Sierra Madres to Mexico City. The vegetation grew sparse, and small mining towns dotted the landscape. Permanently snow-covered peaks stretched toward the Laird and the air became thin.

Jimmy was a veteran when it came to crossing mountains. He'd crossed the Rockies more times than he could count, and in 1926, he crossed the Andes with both ankles in casts clipped to the rudder peddles. He was, therefore, rather surprised when he felt queasy and light-headed at 18,000 feet. He had bolted down a sandwich in Corpus Christi and wondered if he'd gotten a piece of bad meat.

He kept his eyes on the eruption of ice-capped peaks below. To clear them safely, he knew he had to maintain altitude, but increasing nausea and dizziness made the task difficult. He wasn't positive, but he didn't think food poisoning caused dizziness.

He dismissed the notion of too few hours of sleep. He knew fatigue. He shouldn't be suffering from altitude sickness either. If he were moving around or in poor physical condition, *maybe*, but he wasn't. Still the symptoms were undeniable—he battled to keep his wits.

He looked again at the rugged landscape with deep, steep-sided canyons. Nothing appeared flat enough to land on.

With the monotonous drone of the Laird's engine adding to his discomfort, Jimmy knew he was in trouble. His brain felt as if it were wrapped in cotton. The likelihood of a blackout intensified. His vision narrowed, and his stomach churned.

"What year did Columbus discover America," he asked himself, believing mental exercise would help keep him alert.

"1492."

He scrutinized the landscape thoroughly. Jagged peaks and deep valleys threatened perilously. No friendly tree reached out to break his momentum if he was forced to crash land the plane.

"When was the Declaration of Independence signed?"

He held tight to the controls, forcing himself to feel each finger. He deliberately looked at every instrument, repeating aloud the readings, and forcing himself to register their meaning.

"July 4, 1776."

He looked out the window at the ragged terrain of the Sierra Madres. To pass out meant certain death. He dug through the cotton, searching for a question.

"When is John's birthday?"

He thought about Joe and the boys; Jim, Jr. celebrating his eleventh birthday just last week; the house filled with neighborhood children; John, with his infectious laughter and inexhaustible reserves of energy, commanding center stage; and Joe, who never seemed flustered by the activity, calmly reigning in the heart of little boy chaos—unperturbed, tranquil—Just Joe as she'd always been. He wanted to see his boys grow up. He wanted to grow old with her.

"June 29, 1922."

Fear gripped him, and despite the cold temperature in the cockpit, beads of perspiration dotted his forehead and upper lip. He decided that if he reached a point where he couldn't answer simple questions, he would bail out. He tasted the salt of sweat on his lips. He prayed that a search party would find him if he had to bail.

"Subtract 164 from 321."

He struggled with the math. The easily solved problem eluded him. Mentally, he tried to picture the numbers stacked one above the other. Slowly, they came into focus. He borrowed a one and slipped the seven below the line. Then he borrowed from the three. He counted backward from eleven to six and put the five next to the seven. Taking a deep breath, he tackled the two. Two minus one is one. Slowly the figures fell into place.

"157."

He took another deep breath and opened his eyes. The nose of the Laird had drifted down. Jimmy, heart thumping, pulled back on the stick, easing her up. Sweat rolled down his neck and his hands felt sticky on the controls. He'd lost all sense of time.

Finally, the land below him began a gradual descent and flat-tened. The peaks leveled out into a plateau at about 7,200 feet. He could see the patchwork of Mexico City in the distance. He started the letdown, hoping his dizziness and nausea would disappear as the supply of oxygen-rich air increased. They didn't. His head pounded, and the lunch he'd eaten in Corpus Christi rumbled and churned in his stomach.

Jimmy's signature arrival into a city included snap rolls and loops, dives and inverted flight, sometimes even an outside loop. Always a master showman, he liked to "give them their money's worth." Today, there would be no show.

Feeling that pure luck or divine intervention had kept him alive, and drained of all energy, he set the plane down on the run-way. He taxied over to the reviewing stands filled with members of the Mexican government and military, set the brakes, and cut the engine.

A group of dignitaries approached to a lively strain of Mariachi music. Jimmy used sheer force of will to pull himself together. He climbed down from the cockpit, still battling light-headedness and nausea. He surmised that he could keep it together just long enough to deliver Premier Bennett's message.

When his feet hit the ground, lingering fumes from the Laird assaulted him, and Jimmy lost control. Nausea tore at his stom-ach, and he doubled over, vomiting onto the runway. Wave after wave of contractions kept him there, until only dry heaves racked his body.

Weak and embarrassed, Jimmy peered up into the reviewing stands that framed the startled welcoming committee. A capacity crowd, stunned into silence by the American pilot's obvious illness, looked on, anxiously.

"Fine entrance for a representative of the United States," he thought. The sun melted into the horizon, the day drew to a close, and Jimmy felt completely drained. As unobtrusively as possible, he looked at his watch.

A smile tugged at his lips and crinkled his bloodshot eyes. He had made good time. Eleven hours and forty minutes from Ottawa to Mexico City—well within the advertised goal. Still functioning on automatic, Jimmy maintained vertical just long enough to deliver Premiere Bennett's message to President Rubio, then asked to be taken to his hotel.

The next morning, somewhat recovered, but puzzled by the mysterious illness of the previous day, Jimmy took a cab to the airport. He had spent long hours the night before mentally searching for answers to the dilemma. At the airport, he searched the plane. The only logical explanation was an exhaust leak spilling fumes into the cockpit. Inch by inch, he examined the lines. There were no cracks, no pinholes, no leaks. Everything checked out.

Still perplexed, he searched the cockpit. Nothing rested on the floor or under the instrument panel except his parachute. He opened the compartment behind the seat where he stored his leather jacket; only a screwdriver and crescent wrench were in the pockets. He pulled out his extra flight suit and noticed a damp area on the leg. Sniffing it, he smelled the sharp metallic bite of lead. His eyes watered and his abdominal muscles contracted painfully. He set the flight suit down, reached back into the compartment and pulled out the can of tetraethyl. A small hole in the ruptured seam had leaked the highly toxic lead. The soldering had burst at high altitude. Poisonous fumes still lingered in the cockpit, and Jimmy's stomach ached anew, partly from inhaling the lead again and partly from the realization that his physical demise had been imminent.

Once again, sweat beaded on his forehead and upper lip, and he shivered from nerves. Lady Luck had surely smiled on him. Had he not been in excellent condition, he would either be perched on a peak in the Sierra Madres hoping for rescue, or buried within them. He eyed the offending can. It was standard practice to carry the additive for high performance engines, but there had to be a better way to add octane to fuel. He filed the thought away for future research. Changing mental gears from practical to spiritual, he offered up a silent prayer of thanks for his safe landing.

A few days later, on October 26, 1931, Jimmy returned to the States, setting a record of six hours thirty-three minutes, linking Mexico City with his home in St. Louis.

Home, sweet home. As he taxied to the Shell hangar, he searched the grounds for his family. Jim, Jr. inspected the fleet of Shell planes. John entertained the mechanics. And Joe, eyes bright with unshed tears, waited for him to come home.

It wasn't long before Jimmy's job took him on the road again. The boys kept Joe busy during the day, but to avoid being idle during the long evening hours, she wrote letters to her friends across the country. Sitting at her writing desk, Joe picked up a pen and started a letter to Ethyl Craig, a friend from California:

December 11, 1931
Dear Ethel:

Upon noting the date on your last letter to me—I was overcome with shame. Somehow I find but little or no time for personal correspondence in my busy schedule—yet feel very badly when the postman passes me by. Guess Old Man Procrastination has me in his clutches for I see no startling results following my efforts.

Young Jim and I went to the Air Races—John having failed to make the grade was forced to remain home with a tutor. So far this year—John has improved and Jim, Jr. has slumped. Only last week showing his first spurt of interest.—Hope it lasts.

Jim has been out of town about seventy-five per cent of the time—and is en route to NYC—Due to weather yesterday was forced down in Buffalo.

We've had a long lovely fall. The color was gorgeous. As the result the boys and I have had almost every weekend in the country—friends of ours have two country places—one about a hundred fifty miles away in the Ozarks. The other only about forty-five miles distant. They have been so kind in taking us along on trips to these places. Nearby the Ozark Cabin is a canyon wherein Dame Rumor has some of the Jesse James stolen treasure buried. We took the boys picnicking there one day—and they went around with pick and shovel searching all day in vain—finally hot and tired young Jim—fully dressed—accidentally fell head long in the stream. John soon followed—thus ending the possibility of untold wealth for us.

On one trip down there—some of the officials of the Missouri Southern Rail Road took us out for a hundred and fifty mile jaunt over their system. We traveled on schedule—side tracking for trains, etc. Extremely interesting and a new experience for all of us. Young Jim found it particularly enjoyable as he was permitted to drive over the level stretches.

Jim flew down to Dallas and brought back Lawrence Tibbitt here for his concert. They came in the afternoon before about five and we dashed to a tea for Lawrence—then to another for Mario Chamlee who had just had a concert a day or so before. To dinner with Lawrence and Mario—and then to two parties—Much too late to bed—but had to be up early as I had eight in to dinner before the concert—after [the concert] we were included on an after theatre supper for Lawrence and the next morning he came out for breakfast—bringing his manager and accompanist before they left for Toronto. A bit strenuous but fun never-the-less.

We've had so many out of town guests this winter. So much fun to have people pop in from all ends of the earth. Begins to seem like New York.

No cards—again this year—so I'll add our greetings for a Merry Christmas—and may the New Year bring you health—happiness and prosperity. Our love.

Always,

Joe

New Year's 1932 heralded new adventures in aviation. The addition of Mary Bryant to the Doolittle family permitted Joe the freedom to travel with Jimmy. More than a housekeeper, Mary had become a part of the family. The boys loved her and Joe enjoyed her company as much as she appreciated her help around the house.

In January, the publicity department of Shell came up with another idea to promote aviation products and to demonstrate the safety of flight.

On the 3rd of January, 1932, Joe Doolittle, Bill Downs, and Louis A. J. Michener, postmaster of St. Louis, joined Jimmy on a leisurely flight to Miami. Joe pulled her coat tight against the bitter cold of St. Louis as she climbed aboard the Lockheed Vega. Bill, a close friend from high school days, had changed little over the years and Joe appreciated the company.

The cabin remained cold and Joe watched her words come out in puffs of white. Most of the heat had been shunted to the carburetor to avoid icing. She figured the trade off for safety was worth it.

Joe looked out the window. The Mississippi, frozen over, curved through St. Louis and wound south. She searched the landscape until she located the dot that represented their house. Joe mentally blew kisses to the boys, and again thanked Mary for coming into their lives.

Gradually, the air in the cabin grew warmer and Joe could feel her toes again. A few hours in the sun would be a welcome change.

As they descended toward the airport at Jacksonville, Florida, Joe looked down on the crystal blue waters of the Atlantic. Clear skies and warm breezes greeted them when they deplaned.

The warmth of the sun felt wonderful and Joe turned her face upward. Having spent most of her childhood in Los Angeles, she missed California's temperate climate. Sometimes it seemed as if the icy cold of St. Louis had penetrated her soul and left her shivering well into the spring.

A number of reporters snapped pictures as they made their way to the car provided by Shell. The restaurant, with its crisp white table linens, opened onto the beach. They took a table close to the window, overlooking the ocean.

"You look like you've finally thawed out," Jimmy said, as he pulled out her chair.

"I think I have," she said smiling.

Seagulls spiraled over the white sand, and a lone beachcomber lingered at the water's edge. For a brief moment, Joe was homesick for the west coast, but chased the thought from her mind.

By the time their waiter served their Eggs Benedict, all traces of melancholy had fled. Joe cut into her perfectly poached egg. She closed her eyes and relished the tang of lemon and the zing of cayenne in the Hollandaise sauce. "Ah, a taste of heaven!" she thought.

Joe savored every wonderful bite of breakfast as she listened to Jimmy and Bill entertain Michener with tales of their post high school adventures in the mines of Virginia City.

Comfortably full and thawed by the Florida sunshine, the four travelers climbed back aboard the Vega and taxied out to the runway. They lifted over the ocean. Joe watched a fleet of sail-boats dart over the surface of the water. She saw fishing boats trolling for dinner. Flying down the coast of Florida, she watched the surf break on beaches below her, and enjoyed the realization that ice did not, in fact, encase the entire globe.

"We're passing over the Keys," Joe told Bill, as they flew over the chain of islands strung into the Straits of Florida.

A short time later the white sands and dense green foliage of Cuba jutted out of the turquoise water.

The greeting committee in Havana fluttered about the plane. The swarthy good looks of the Cuban people and the soft rolling Spanish language welcomed them.

A private car whisked them away from the airport, and delivered them to an outside café. Their waiter piled plate after plate of Cuban delicacies on the table. Joe bit into the *Camarones Alajillo*. The large, plump shrimp dripped with garlic. *Platanos Maduros Fritos* accompanied every dish, and they enjoyed a healthy helping of *Dulce De Leche* for dessert. Joe rolled a cinnamon stick over her tongue, savoring the sweetness. She was so full, she couldn't imagine ever eating again.

Cuba expected them to earn their keep. They returned to the airport where Joe, Bill and Louis received an escort into the stands with the Cuban dignitaries and officials while Jimmy climbed back into the Vega.

Joe watched as Jimmy ascended into the clouds then dropped into the skies directly in front of the stands. Like a prima ballerina, the Vega twirled and looped, dipped and climbed, plunging toward the earth, and lifting within feet of "certain death."

Joe never tired of watching Jimmy perform. His love of airplanes translated itself into routines of both daring and beauty. She took in the people around her. Collective "oohs" and "ahhs" followed his every move. Shouts of "Bravo!" rang out when the stunt proved particularly impressive.

As soon as he landed, spectators flooded the field. Joe stood on the sideline, as she frequently did, observing exuberant congratulations from the men and brazen flirtations from the women.

The band launched into a festive tune. Enthusiastic fans swarmed around Jimmy. Joe thought of the young man she'd known in high school, friendly, engaging. He'd come into his own.

The celebration drew to a close. Glad to be out of the Cuban sun, the foursome climbed into the Vega, circled the city of Havana and headed north to Florida.

The sun began to set, painting the sky with flaming shades of pink and yellow. The Vega dropped swiftly and made a smooth landing at the Miami airport. They ordered dinner at a local restaurant. Still stuffed from lunch, Joe picked politely at the beautifully presented plate of braised Halibut with steamed vegetables. When dinner was over, the foursome made their way back to the Vega. Landing on the snow covered runway in St. Louis, both Joe and Jimmy felt completely sated. With deliberate casualness, they had eaten three separate meals in three different cities in one day.

The press, still following the flight, praised the agility of the airplane and the freedom it granted to businessmen. Newspapers predicted that company-owned planes would save valuable time for busy executives.

Joe reached over and placed her hand on top of Jimmy's as they drove home.

"It was a good day," she said. "Thank you."

It *was* good, she thought, to spend time together. And, even better to come home.

1932 celebrated the bicentennial of George Washington's birth and the 157th anniversary of the United States Postal Service. When the Aeronautical Chamber of Commerce suggested a symbolic flight uniting the two anniversaries, Shell Oil Company jumped at the opportunity.

Jimmy, flying the Shellightning, a bright yellow Lockheed Orion 9C Special, invited Anne Madison Washington, George Washington's great-grandniece, and Alphius F. Maple, editor of Shell's magazine, on a dawn-to-dusk commemorative flight.

They lifted off at 4:35 A.M. on July 25 from Boston Airport. Jimmy headed northeast to Kittery, Maine, the northern most point of Washington's travels. Circling the city, Jimmy dropped to tree level over a park near the post office.

"Drop the first bag now," Jimmy's voice crackled over the headset.

Maples opened the door and Miss Washington let the first bag go. They all watched as it fell to the grassy park below.

Jimmy pulled the plane back to cruising altitude, and headed south to Providence, Rhode Island, where they repeated the drop. Throughout the day, they dropped bags of mail at many of the places that held significance for the first President.

As the sun began to set, Jimmy turned the plane toward New York. The final drop at West Point concluded a fifteen hour, forty minute day. More than a publicity stunt, the anniversary flight proved the practicability and reliability of a regularly scheduled mail service, bringing the Postal Service to the attention of the Congressional Appropriations Committee.

Between publicity flights for Shell and Curtiss-Wright, Jimmy spent time with his family in St. Louis. The parade of guests at the Doolittles' home included many foreign personalities. If they were a part of the international aviation community, they were most likely friends of the Doolittles.

Alexander "Sacha" de Seversky was born a Russian nobleman and served in the Russian naval air force under the Czar. Although he lost one leg below the knee after his plane was shot down by the Germans, he continued to fly and became one of Russia's top aces from WWI.

Sacha arrived in the United States in March 1918 as an assistant naval attaché at the Russian Embassy. When the Bolsheviks took over, he remained in New York, becoming a US citizen in 1927. Pilot, inventor, designer, businessman and author, Sacha's path frequently crossed Jimmy's. The two men shared a passion for the advancement of aviation and quickly became good friends.

As a frequent visitor to the Doolittles' home in St Louis, Sacha became very close to both John and young Jim. He entertained the boys with stories of his adventures and even taught them to swim.

In the early spring of 1932, Sacha attended a dinner party with Joe and Jim. The party went late into the evening, and it was past midnight when they returned home.

"Would you like some coffee?" Joe asked after dropping her purse and wrap on the dining room table.

"None for me," Sacha said, yawning.

Jimmy slipped his arm around Joe's waist. "I'm off to bed," he said, kissing her softly on the cheek before heading upstairs.

Joe turned off the light Mary Bryant had left on for them and followed Jim up the stairs. Stopping at the boys' room, she turned the handle and quietly opened the door.

The curtains shivered in the cold breeze and the full moon illuminated the empty beds. Specters of the Lindbergh kidnapping intruded before she could chase them away. At 10 and 12, she found it difficult to imagine that anyone could have taken the boys. Surely, she thought, Mary would have heard something.

Joe climbed the stairs to the third floor and knocked firmly on Mary's door.

"Have you seen the boys?" she asked.

"I tucked them both in bed hours ago," Mary said peering at Joe from under the thick layer of a down comforter.

"They're not in bed," Joe said, attempting to keep the growing panic from her voice.

Within minutes, Jimmy, Joe, Sacha and Mary Bryant fanned out over the neighborhood. Flattened grass around the drainpipe under the boys' window indicated recent activity. Jimmy headed across the yard to the pigeon coop. He spotted them first, cutting across the neighbor's backyard. Young Jim boldly led the way, followed by John, his jacket bulging on his skinny boy frame.

Jimmy waited silently in the shadows beside the pigeon coop, watching as the boys approached. Joe, crossing the yard, stopped short next to her husband.

"Care to tell us where you've been?" Jimmy asked when young Jim reached for the screened door of the coop.

Both boys stopped dead in their tracks and turned slowly toward their father's voice.

"What have you got there, John?" Jimmy asked indicating the bulk under the boy's jacket.

"Squabs," John said, meeting his father's eyes.

"I see. And where did you get them?"

"Well," John said, squirming just a little, "from their nests."

Jimmy was well aware that pigeons liked to build their nests high above the ground, and the most popular nesting area was a quarry not far from the house.

Jimmy looked directly at young Jim.

"And how did you reach their nests?"

"With this," young Jim extended a length of clothesline about the thickness of Jimmy's little finger.

Jimmy blanched.

Drawn by the voices, Sacha and Mary Bryant joined the Doolittle family in the back yard.

"Explain," Jimmy commanded his sons.

"Well, I tied the rope around Johnny's waist and lowered him over the edge."

Jimmy eyed the clothesline and pictured his youngest son dangling over the steep 30-foot drop to the quarry floor below. John, mistaking his father's silence for interest, piped in.

"He let me down to the nests then I'd grab the squabs and stick them in my coat. See!" John said, unbuttoning his jacket. The fluffy faced babies squawked with indignation.

"Put the pigeons away," Jimmy said, shaking his head, "and head up to your room. We'll discuss this in the morning."

"No question that they're your boys, Jimmy," Sacha said with a grin when the boys disappeared into the house. "Sounds like your first stunt with a glider!"

Now fully recovered, Jimmy had to agree.

For young Jim, restriction to his room was an easy punishment. He'd lose himself in books and games. But for the gregarious John, the punishment was torture. The only relief from the long hours locked away with his silent brother was the occasional plate of cookies and glass of milk Mary Bryant sneakedup to his room.

After extracting promises from the boys to curtail their little nocturnal expeditions, Jimmy turned his attention back to flying. Although Jimmy enjoyed the publicity flights he did for Shell, a piece of his heart still belonged in the laboratory. He loved tinkering with the airplanes, discovering their limits. He applied this curiosity to the Super Solution.

Jimmy believed, with a few modifications, the Super Solution could be much faster. He discussed his ideas with Matty Laird. In addition to installing a more powerful engine and new engine cowling, Matty and his mechanics strengthened the wing trussing and developed a controllable pitch propeller. Retractable landing gear would significantly reduce drag in flight. The engineers raised Jimmy's seat ten inches so he could see over the wing. They added a slide door to the cockpit so he could stick his head and shoulders out to see during landings. And, they increased gas capacity, pushing the distance that the Super Solution could fly without stops.

By the time they finished, Laird's people had addressed all the Super Solution's stability problems. The new design incorporated modifications for pylon racing. The improvements readied the Super Solution for the 1932 Bendix Race and Thompson Trophy Races. Many believed she couldn't be beaten.

On August 24, four days before the Bendix, Jimmy took The Super Solution up for her first test run. He could taste victory. Everyone believed that the modifications to the Laird would give him 50 to 60 miles per hour more out of the engine.

Jimmy taxied out and took off. The Laird performed perfectly. He flew over the flat patchwork quilt of farms that dotted the central plains of Kansas. She responded beautifully. The new engine gave her superior power, and the air speed indicator confirmed their highest expectations. Exuberant and confident, Jimmy swung around on approach to the air strip in Wichita, Kansas. He cranked the lever to put down the landing gear. It turned three and a half times, and then stuck.

Jimmy pulled out of the approach and cranked the lever again. Again it stuck at three and a half turns. Figuring the gears might be hung up on something, he attempted to shake them loose by banking hard to the right, then equally hard to the left, followed by a steep dive and pull out. No luck. He tried a second time. Then a third.

Unaccustomed to the landing system and hoping for help from the ground crew, Jimmy wrote a note and dropped it to the engineers on the field below.

"Something wrong landing gear. Can get 3 1/2 turns each way. If any suggestions, write on side of plane and come up. Otherwise, I will run out of gas and stall in."

Jimmy flew around the Kansas countryside, emotionally torn up. The Super Solution was the perfect racer. Fast and maneuverable, it would handle beautifully on both the distance runs of the Bendix and on the tight pylon turns of the Thompson. He had no doubt that she could take both trophies. He needed only to get the landing gear down and locked in place. The thought of a belly landing made him sick.

Eventually, a plane taxied out and took off. It gained altitude and pulled up beside Jim—close enough for him to read the instructions.

"ZOOM LEFT. ZOOM RIGHT. POWER DIVE."

Jim waved in acknowledgement to Preston Kirk, the pilot of the other plane. He'd already tried that, plus a series of other maneuvers. Nothing worked. Disheartened, he put the Super Solution through the suggested maneuver again. He zoomed left, zoomed right, nosed over into a power dive, and then cranked the lever. It turned three and a half times, then stuck, only this time it locked in a partial down position and he couldn't pull it up.

With a heavy heart, Jimmy climbed into the clouds, allowing the Super Solution to dart forward. He banked a turn around an imaginary pylon before, again surging full speed ahead. Savoring her power, he ran the imaginary course of the Thompson Race. After two hours of flight, his gas ran low.

He couldn't bring himself to abandon Matty Laird's creation, so he lined up on a grassy section of the runway and set the little racer down on her belly.

He heard the snap of the single wheel that had partially locked down. He shuddered at the crunching sound of the propeller as it bent. He felt physically ill at the screech of the fuselage on the grassy runway. The Super Solution ground to a lurching halt, resting on her belly in the middle of the field.

Uninjured, Jimmy climbed from the plane and surveyed the wreckage. The Laird team couldn't possibly repair the extensive damage in time for either race.

He placed his hand gently on her upper wing and struggled with his emotions. Minutes later, news cameras flashed, recording his picture beside the damaged Super Solution for release to the press.

Not since the destruction of the Travel Air, had Jimmy felt so badly about losing a plane.

Newspapers nationwide covered the crash, and immediately offers poured in from other manufacturers, hoping Jimmy would race their product.

The most interesting offer came from Zantford D. Granville, eldest of the five Granville brothers, who built a line of small racers called Gee-Bee Sportsters. The brothers had two planes, the Gee-Bee R-1, and the Gee-Bee R-2, and they wanted to know if Jimmy would like to race the R-1.

The remains of breakfast littered the table, and the boys flew out the door to play with the neighbors. Joe sat quietly, listening to Jimmy's assessment.

"Each plane is hand built, and designed for maximum speed," he explained. "Lowell Bayles won both the Goodyear and the Thompson in the Model Z Super Sportster last year."

"The same Lowell who was killed in the Z last December?" Joe asked.

Jimmy didn't need to answer. They both remembered the newsreel of the fiery crash and Bayle's flaming body flying through the air.

"Wasn't Russell Boardman supposed to fly the R-1?"

Jimmy looked sheepishly over his glass of orange juice.

"How *is* Russell?" she asked. "Has he recovered from his last Gee-Bee accident?"

"No. He's still in the hospital." He didn't add that Russell aborted a flight in the R-1, believing it to be too dangerous. Jimmy didn't have a death wish, but he truly believed, based on his understanding of the science of flight and his history as a test pilot, that he battled fewer limitations than many other pilots.

Joe sipped her cooling coffee and held her other questions. There was no need to discuss it further. She knew Jimmy lived on the edge. That was part of the man she married.

"Will you be home tonight?" She asked, as Jimmy left the table.

"I expect to," he answered. "I'll check out the Gee-Bee and make my decision."

The August sun beat down on Bowles Airport in Springfield, Massachusetts. The Granville factory, located in an abandoned dance hall near the city dump, stood at the edge of the makeshift airstrip.

Hot, humid currents of air swirled around a crowd of aviation buffs, including a number of youngsters gathered at the field, hoping to catch a glimpse of the famed racing pilot.

But Doolittle was all business. Seriously calculating the risk inherent in the Granvilles' design, and weighing that against its potential to win the Thompson, he walked to the hangar.

The gleaming red-and-white R-1 held his undivided attention. Inch by inch, he studied the bird, from her pitch-controlled propeller, down her seventeen- foot, nine-inch bomb-like body, to the stubby, almost non-existent rudder. The R-1 had a twenty-five foot wingspan and a 750-horsepower Pratt and Whitney Wasp Sr. engine. To counterbalance the powerful engine, Granvilles had located the cockpit far to the back, fared into the vertical stabilizer.

Jimmy walked around the plane, trying to predict what she would do in flight. He thought about the crash that had taken Bayle's life. The Gee-Bee appeared to snap out of control, flip over and smash into the ground at full speed. He examined the rudder; the tiny surface offered little stability.

Jim ran his hand down the side of the fuselage, and then stopped to study the 7-11 dice painted on the engine cowling. He knew from the size of the engine to the size of the rudder that the Gee-Bee would be fast, but touchy. For a brief moment he allowed himself to miss the Laird, then turned to conduct business with the Granville brothers.

The tall grasses swayed in the hot afternoon breeze. The spectators helped push the R-1 from the hangar, than a half mile across a dusty hayfield.

One of the Granville brothers climbed up on the Gee Bee and unscrewed the hatch. Jimmy took one last look at the racer, then, without another word, climbed into the tiny cockpit. Granville secured the hatch before climbing down.

Jimmy started the engine and let it rev. The little racer strained against the chocks wedged tight against the wheels. Granville and several of the spectators took hold of the wingtips as Jimmy opened the engine to full capacity.

The Pratt and Whitney roared. Grass, dust and pebbles flew everywhere. Jimmy felt the excitement of every racing pilot in control of so much power. Satisfied, he throttled back and signaled to Granville that he was ready to go.

The ground crew pulled the chocks from the wheels and released the wingtips. Jimmy waited until the controls felt comfortable in his hand, and then gave her full throttle.

The Gee Bee bolted across the dry hayfield. Daisies and buttercups lay prostrate as the plane filleted a section of the high grass, the tail never lifting more than an inch or two, as it bounced across the field.

Jimmy confirmed his calculations as he lifted from the makeshift airfield. The hot little R-1 required constant piloting. Not wanting to spend any more time than necessary in the little monster, he skipped the traditional circling of Bowles Airport, and set a course straight to Cleveland.

A few days later, Jimmy stood next to the R-1 at the field in Cleveland. The Thompson Trophy required qualification tests, and the timed trials had begun. He examined the Gee Bee from stem to stern.

"She's the touchiest plane I've ever been in," he told the Shell mechanics who stood in the hot sun next to him.

"Flying the Gee Bee is a bit like trying to balance an ice cream cone on the tip of your finger," he continued, touching the hot metal with the flat of his hand.

Jimmy thought about the test flight he'd taken the day before. Thankfully, he'd gone up to an altitude of 5,000 feet to practice pylon turns. The R-1 had completed two snap rolls before he could get it under control. A shiver ran down his spine. Had he not taken her up that high, he'd be dead. He ran a hand over the back of his neck. She would require every ounce of his attention every second that he stayed in the air.

He clocked the qualifying lap at 293.19 miles per hour, a new world's speed record, but discovered that the airfield lacked the proper equipment to confirm the record.

"I thought such details were handled by the race officials in case someone did set a record." Jimmy told the press.

"That's their business, not mine," he said, later. "A pilot has all he can do to fly his ship."

Disappointed, Jimmy returned to the Gee Bee to inspect her. Multiple indications of deterioration caused immediate concern. A few of the fastenings on the engine cowling had split, and the cowling had begun to pull forward, stretching the brackets. The prop had begun to vibrate, as well.

The mechanics set to work on the R-1, and Jimmy prepared to make a second attempt at Florentin Bonnet's 8-year-old, world record of 278.48 miles per hour. He won the $1575 purse for the fastest qualifying time on his second attempt, but failed to break the record.

On Saturday, September 3, he decided to try a third time. Jimmy warmed up the engine, and took off on the speed runs. Heavy cross-winds threatened, but the R-1 whipped over the course with an average speed of 296.287 miles per hour—a new world's record. Triumphant, Jimmy felt that he and the R-1 had passed muster for the Thompson Trophy.

He taxied to the hangar and completed another post-flight inspection. Both Jimmy and the mechanics inspected the plane, checking fastenings and brackets, tightening and stabilizing the propeller.

"Watch out!"

Jimmy turned toward the voice just in time to see the R-2 heading directly for his plane. They couldn't move the R-1, so he watched helplessly while one of the Shell mechanics darted between the two planes.

Frantically waving his arms, the mechanic ran to the side of the R-2, shouting up to the pilot. Lee Gehlbach, unable to see over the engine, looked down from the cockpit.

Making a cutting gesture with his hand across his throat, the mechanic finally got his message through to Lee.

Gehlback cut the engine. Shell mechanics, joined by pilots and mechanics from the other pits, grabbed the stubby wings, slowly turning the R-2 away from Jimmy's plane. When the racer finally came to a stop, she rested only eight feet from the R-1.

The line-up for the 1932 Thompson Trophy included many of the best pilots and planes: Jimmy Wedell flew his Wedell-Williams No. 44 with a qualifying speed of 277.057; Roscoe Turner piloted the Wedell-Williams Gilmore Red Lion at 266.674; Jimmy Haizlip flew Wedell-Williams #92 at 266.440; Bob Hall in the Hall Bulldog clocked in at 243.738; Ray Moore in Keith Rider R-1 at 237.738; Bill Ong in the Howard Ike at 213.855; Les Bowen in Gordon Israel Redhead at 202.490; and Gehlbach in the Gee Bee R-2 at 247.339.

The Gee Bees enjoyed a definite speed advantage, but behaved unpredictably. It was anyone's race.

Jimmy fired up the Pratt and Whitney. Flames shot out from under the cowling, whipping along the fuselage. The Shell team attacked them with fire extinguishers, while Jimmy cut the engine. Climbing down from the cockpit, he inspected the plane. Apparently, gasoline in the carburetor had flared up in a backfire. The short-lived fire left no serious damage.

He climbed back into the cockpit and restarted the engine. The Pratt and Whitney roared to life. Satisfied with the plane's relative safety, Jimmy taxied to the starting line.

Joe stood under the canvas tarp covering the R-1's pit area. Fifty thousand spectators crowded the field and filled the stands. Young Jim and John anxiously watched the planes taxi up to the starting line.

"There's Dad!" John yelled, when the flashy red and white Gee Bee pulled into position.

Joe looked across the pits to where the R-1 sat waiting with her husband inside. Heat rose in waves from the airfield, and the heavy smell of gasoline fumes singed her nose and burned her eyes. The hum of fifty thousand voices grew louder as the start time drew near.

She felt restless. The Gee Bee worried her; it had a reputation as a killer. Jimmy expressed concern over how "touchy" she handled. Joe couldn't get the image of Bayle's fiery crash from her mind.

Hall took off first. Ten seconds later, Jimmy's R-1 roared down the runway and vaulted into the sky. The crisp white and candy apple red Gee Bee looked like a shiny toy in the electric blue sky. In no time, Jimmy passed Hall, and, unchallenged, held the lead for the entire race.

Joe split her attention between Jimmy and the boys. Neither John nor young Jim could sit still. They ran to the edge of the field, excited that their father held such a commanding lead.

Scanning the crowd, Joe recognized many familiar faces in the sea of spectators. She noted the huge number of reporters covering the race, and thought of the chilling crashes recorded on news film clips. Shivering despite the heat, she turned her attention back to the boys. A camera-toting reporter stood next to them.

Moving from the shade of the tarp, Joe crossed the pit area and joined her sons. A second cameraman followed her. With a wave of nausea, she realized that their cameras were focused, not on the race, but on the family.

Uncomfortable with the media scrutiny, she shepherded the boys back to the R-1's pit area to watch the race from behind the roped off area.

The cameras followed. Odds favored a spectacular crash, and they wanted to catch the family's reaction on film. Sheltering the boys as much as possible, Joe bit back her anger and responded as graciously as possible when reporters asked her questions.

One hundred miles later, Jimmy's R-1 streaked across the finish line with an average speed of 252.686 miles per hour, a new course record for the Thompson.

Once Jimmy landed safely, the reporters abandoned the family death watch and ran to greet him. Joe, with gracious smile fixed in place, waited in the pit area. She believed that the risks of racing were no longer worth taking, and although she would never presume to make life decisions for Jimmy, she would certainly answer honestly if asked.

A feeding frenzy engulfed Jimmy as he pulled up on the flight line. Reporters swarmed the plane, pushing and shoving. Joe watched as Shell mechanics removed the canopy. Even from a distance, she saw relief etched on Jimmy's face. His eyes watered from hay fever, and she could see signs of fatigue, but a smile stretched from one ear to the other as he joked with photographers and reporters. Today's purse totaled $4,500: the Thompson Trophy, considered by many to be the most prestigious of the racing prizes, in addition to the Clifford W. Henderson Trophy, for winning the Thompson and achieving the fastest qualifying time, and the Lowell Bayles Trophy, for setting a new world's speed record. Not a bad day.

A shocked press listened a few days later as Jimmy Doolittle announced his intention to retire from racing. He was still fuming with anger from Joe's tale of photographers following her and the boys around at the Thompson Trophy Race. Joe hadn't asked him to quit, but he knew she worried every time he climbed into a racing plane. The Gee Bee, although the fastest airplane to date, underscored the danger of the sport.

"Mrs. Doolittle has made our minds up for us," he said playfully to one reporter. Catching Joe's eye, Jimmy winked.

Slipping his arm through Joe's, Jimmy steered her through the shocked mob of reporters. Closed circuit racing, he believed, had served an important purpose in the development of aviation, but the cost in pilots and planes far outweighed the benefits.

CHAPTER 11

★ ★ ★ ★

DOOLITTLE'S FOLLY

"There are countless ways of
achieving greatness, but the road
to achieving one's maximum potential must be built on a bedrock of
respect for the individual, a commit-
ment to excellence, and a rejection
of mediocrity."

—Francis "Buck" Rodgers

MANY people, including the press, doubted that Jimmy would
truly retire from air racing, but Joe knew he had made up his
mind and would not go back on his word.

"Air racing as a spectacle has outlived its usefulness," Jimmy
said. "It originally did promote safety in aviation through testing
of materials used in construction of planes and engines, and
probably still does. But lately it appears that the value received is
not commensurate with the personal risk involved."

The press stirred in the gallery behind her, and she could
hear a couple of reporters discussing Jimmy's statements. She
knew they would not take his opinions lightly, and that many of
his friends still involved with racing would not appreciate his
views, but she was glad he had decided to stop racing. The crash
of the Travel Air and Jimmy's lucky bail out still haunted her like
a specter whenever she let her guard down. Her stomach turned
when she thought about the reporters during the Thompson
Race following her and the boys, hoping to capture their grief if

Jimmy crashed. Jimmy acknowledged the risk he'd taken by flying the Gee Bee. The science of aviation would gain nothing from his death.

Jimmy slipped into the gallery beside her and briefly covered her hand with his own. She looked at him, and smiled a smile that lit her eyes and showered him with warmth. She knew he felt deeply that racing had served its purpose. She also knew that a part of him would miss the excitement and thrill of competition.

When the meeting adjourned, a flock of reporters mobbed the Doolittles as they left the building.

"Mrs. Doolittle, how do you feel about your husband retiring from racing?" a reporter shouted, as flash bulbs went off, recording the moment.

"I believe Jimmy has done his share of speed flying," she answered.

"Jimmy, do you really feel racing has outlived its purpose?"

"Racing planes are the guinea pigs of aviation," he answered, shooting Joe a quick look, and squeezing her hand. "I think the time has come to give attention to safety and reliability so that commercial aviation can develop for the common good."

With that, Jimmy grasped Joe's elbow and steered her through the pack of reporters to their car.

"You've really done it now," Joe said, when the doors closed and the reporters could only be seen in the rearview mirror. "The folks running the National Air Races will have your head."

Jimmy, eyes twinkling, looked fondly at his wife and grinned.

"Oh, well," she thought, settling back into her seat. "He always did enjoy a good scrap."

In 1933, Jimmy turned his attention to the safety and reliability of commercial aviation. His near death from lead poisoning on his 1930 flight to Mexico City still concerned him. Pilots still carried tetraethyl to beef up fuel performance, but the mixture proved undependable. Too much lead would burn up the pistons and too little did no good. The practice remained inefficient, unreliable, and very, very dangerous.

Every experienced aviator wanting to win knew he should get his fuel from California rather than Pennsylvania. Shell studied the components of oil harvested in different areas, and developed no less than eighteen different leaded and unleaded fuels, ranging from 65-octane used in Army trainers, to 95-octane used by the Curtiss-Wright Corporation for special test work.

Jimmy firmly believed that the fuels being produced should be standardized. His ties to the Army as a reserve officer kept him apprised of the super planes being tested at Wright Field. The new planes required 100-octane fuel to reach maximum potential.

Jimmy looked across the desk at Alex Fraser, Vice President of Shell Oil Company, the man he needed to convince.

"Who would buy such an expensive product?" Fraser asked.

Jimmy met his eyes and held them. Alex Fraser had zeroed in on the dilemma. Why should airplane manufactures build engines of superior quality when no fuel existed to operate them? And, conversely, why should oil companies develop fuel without engines requiring it?

"Larger planes are being built," Jimmy said. "I've seen them. There are bombers and fighters on the drawing boards and flying experimentally at Wright Field. However, they'll never get built without the right fuel."

"But Jimmy, this country is in a deep depression. You want to spend millions of dollars on a product with no guarantee of a market."

"Alex, no one else is doing anything about this. Shell should be ready to meet the demand when it comes, and it will come. We'll be ahead of the game if we just put some dollars into research."

Alex eyed Jimmy as he weighed the proposal. Jim believed this was a calculated risk worth taking. He believed that more powerful planes would never go into production without better fuel.

"If we develop this fuel, then I'll work on convincing the Army to standardize its requirement to 100-octane." Jimmy said. "The airlines will follow."

"I hope you're right, Jimmy." Alex said, ending the meeting. "This could be a million dollar blunder."

Shell built a plant to develop 100-octane fuel at Wood River, Illinois. Company petroleum engineers, Dr. Tydeman and Dr. Tymstra, listened as Jimmy explained his ideas and the requirements of the new engines. It wasn't Jimmy's credentials as dare-devil racing pilot that convinced them; it was his earned doctorate from MIT.

Satisfied that they were on the right track, Jimmy set out to convince the War Department to buy into Shell's new product. Word leaked to the press and they quickly labeled his project, "Doolittle's Million Dollar Blunder" and "Doolittle's Folly."

Jimmy ignored the bad press. Shell had more to gain than just profit. It was also competing for technical prestige and excellence.

In the meantime, Shell and Curtiss-Wright teamed up again, sending Jimmy on a promotional trip around the world. The five-month itinerary called for stops in Japan, China, the Philippines, Dutch East Indies, Burma, India, Iraq, Egypt and Europe. Joe, comfortable that Mary Bryant would take excellent care of the boys, decided to join her husband. Toting along her portable typewriter, she became the unofficial secretary for the trip.

They flew from St. Louis to San Francisco in early 1933, and boarded a ship ultimately headed for Shanghai, China. Joe stood at the stern of the ship watching the coast of California fade into the mist. Jimmy stood beside her in a comfortable silence, his hand covering hers on the rail.

Later that afternoon, as the ship sailed toward their first stop in Japan, Joe returned to the deck. A strong breeze swept across the grey-green Pacific, coating her face with a fine mist of salty spray. Her clothes, sculpted by the wind, clung to her body.

Resting her hand on the railing, she turned into the wind, allowing it to ruffle her short white hair. She scanned the deserted horizon, and wondered what the boys were doing. Did they miss her? She knew Mary Bryant would watch over them, but a little piece of her heart had stayed home with them.

She filled her lungs with the fresh ocean air. She had missed the calming peace of the ocean. Turning away from the breeze, she rested her back against the rail. Her hair whipped around her face, and she brushed it away with the flat of her hand.

A man stood alone, shrouded in gloom. She watched him. He wore a steward's uniform, the crisp white jacket just a shade too big. Sad dark eyes looked out over the water. She wondered why he looked so unhappy.

Feeling her eyes upon him, he turned toward her.

"Good afternoon," Joe said, smiling.

"*Buonaserra, Signora.*" The letter he held in his olive-skinned hand fluttered in the wind.

"Is everything all right?" she asked.

Embarrassed, he folded the letter. "*Sì.*"

She looked kindly at him. He was just a boy really, not much older than young Jim, fifteen or sixteen at the most. "Sergio" his name tag read. Italian, surely.

Perhaps something in her eyes reminded him of home. The genuine interest, the kindness.

"My mother is not well," he said, in heavily accented English.

"I'm sorry," she said and laid a warm hand on his arm. She offered no other words of comfort. Together, they watched the water, lost in their own thoughts.

He placed the folded letter in his breast pocket, beneath his name tag.

"*Graci,*" he said, with a shy smile.

"You're welcome." She smiled back.

That evening the salon filled with travelers: women in silk and fur, men in black ties. Laughter rose above the melodic strains of "Embraceable You." Smoke from dozens of cigarettes filled the air. Joe and Jim, surrounded by their colleagues from Curtiss-Wright and Shell Oil, sat near the piano, and the open windows.

"*Buongiorno* Signora," Sergio greeted Joe, as he navigated the crowded salon. He stopped at their table.

"Good evening, Sergio," Joe replied, then turned toward Jimmy. "This is Sergio, the young man I told you about."

"Good to meet you," Jimmy said.

"Good evening, Sir." Sergio bowed slightly from the waist, and then turned back to Joe. "Does the Signora prefer pheasant or partridge?" he asked.

"I like them both," she answered.

The cacophony of music and voices prevailed, uninterrupted, as the waiter escorted them into the dining room. The executives from Shell and Curtiss-Wright, along with Jim and Joe, sat at the captain's table, Joe on the captain's immediate right.

Candles in small glass votives cast soft haloes on the white linen. Crystal, silver and china reflected the flickering light. Soft strains of piano music drifted in from the salon. Waiters in dress-white uniforms bustled about the room.

Unobtrusively, a plate appeared in front of Joe. Both a partridge and a pheasant nestled in a bed of steamed vegetables. Flushing pink, Joe looked up. Sergio, shy smile lighting his face, bowed slightly, then blended into the background.

"Someone must be very taken with your wife," the captain said to Jimmy.

Joe's blush deepened. She had received a double portion, much more than anyone else at the table.

The following day, Sergio served her breakfast. Again, she received double portions. After two days, she feared her clothes wouldn't fit without a little exercise, and decided to walk around the deck.

In the brisk breeze, Joe walked first into the wind, feeling its resistance. She turned the corner, allowing it to push against her back. The endless gray water blended into the sky at an indistinguishable point in the distance. Her pulse beat rapidly in her neck, and she felt a slight burn in her calves. Perspiration dotted her forehead and arms, but evaporated quickly as she faced the ocean's breeze. After a dozen laps around the deck, she rested against the rail.

"*Buonjiorno*, Signora" Sergio said, appearing at her side. He held a tray laden with sweet rolls, butter and coffee.

Tension in the Far East made visiting Japan risky for an American aviator selling airplanes to China. The State Department advised Jimmy to avoid visiting Japanese cities and to be careful when docked in Japanese ports-of-call.

When the ship pulled into Yokohama, Japanese Customs officials boarded, and insisted that all passengers show their passports.

"Passport," the middle-aged official said to Joe, his hand extended for her documents.

Joe handed him her passport and sat quietly on the couch as he examined it. The official's black eyes, magnified by thick glasses, darted between Joe's face, the picture on her passport, and back again.

Finally, after a soft exchange in Japanese with a second official, he returned Joe's documents and asked for Jimmy's.

The two officials studied Jimmy's passport and Jimmy.

"Oh, American aviator," the first official said. "What do in Japan?"

"My wife and I are on a trip around the world."

"Oh, go to China?"

Jimmy nodded. There was no way to deny it—the boat was heading for Shanghai.

The official, still clutching Jimmy's passport, turned to his partner. They spent a long time discussing something in their soft voices, looking up frequently at Jimmy, then back at his passport.

They deliberated for some time before they returned Jimmy's passport and left the ship. Obviously, they suspected Jimmy of collusion with the Chinese, but to date, they had no proof.

In Tokyo, Jimmy and Joe, attempting to be as inconspicuous as possible for two Caucasians in Japan, slipped ashore. They visited temples and ate lunch at the Imperial Palace Hotel. For the first time in ages, Joe had Jimmy to herself. Almost like newlyweds, they explored a wealth of foreign sights, tastes and sounds. Nevertheless, a small part of their attention focused on spotting overly interested officials.

After days of overeating, and merciless teasing from her husband, Joe decided that walking the deck only added to her problem, and that she needed a trip to the ship's gym.

Joe poked her head out the cabin door, looking first one way, then the other. Convinced the coast was clear, she threw a towel over her shoulder and made her way down the corridor into the gym.

Jumping rope, lifting weights, running in place, she struggled to burn a few calories. Finally feeling that she had accomplished a fairly complete workout, she wiped the perspiration from her neck and face, and stood in front of the little porthole, allowing a breeze to skim over her warm skin. With damp, flushed skin and hair sticking to her neck, she opened the door.

Sergio stood in the hallway, dish towel over his arm. The aroma of strong fresh coffee and buttered sweet rolls rose from the tray in his hand.

Famous men attracted predatory women, a fact that Joe knew but did not dwell on. But, Sergio's infatuation, however harmless, made Joe the center of attention, a highly uncomfortable position for her.

"Perhaps I can speak with the Captain and employ Sergio for the duration of our trip." Jimmy said over breakfast, enjoying the discomfort the young Italian caused his wife. "I'm fairly certain I could convince him to follow us to St. Louis."

Joe raised her spoon to her eye, as if using a lorgnette. "Doolittle, watch your step," she said, and their tablemates burst out laughing.

Seventeen days after leaving San Francisco, they pulled into the port of Shanghai. Sergio stood anxiously outside Joe's stateroom, offering to carry their luggage. As they readied to debark, Jimmy turned to the lad, offering him the customary tip.

"No. No, Senior," Sergio insisted, obviously offended. "Is not necessary."

"Please, you've been so helpful, especially to Mrs. Doolittle."

Sergio looked over to Joe, his eyes dark and warm.

"Senor, my feelings would be hurt if you insist on offering me money. The only thing I ask is for the flowers in your room."

"You're welcome to them," Jimmy said. He returned the bills to a money clip and put them back in his pocket.

Jimmy marveled over his wife's effect on people. Not only was she genuinely interested in them, but she had the ability to communicate that interest. She did the thoughtful thing automatically, instinctively. In all the years he'd known Joe, she had never intentionally said or done something unkind, and, to the best of his recollection, he'd never known anyone who didn't take to her immediately.

Sergio bowed to Joe. "*Ciao, Signora.*"

Resting her hand lightly on his arm, she smiled. "Good bye, Sergio. I'll keep your mother in my thoughts."

★ ★ ★ ★

The unpredictable weather in Shanghai forced Jimmy to work out several sets of flight plans to demonstrate the Hawk's agility, including aerobatics for wet weather. He felt strongly that if the Chinese people wanted to come out in the rain to see them, then he would give them a show.

The first demonstration took place on April 13, 1933. Generalissimo Chiang Kai-shek's advisor, Dr. H.H. Kung, stood beside the runway, watching as Jimmy took off in the Hawk.

Clear skies prevailed, as the Hawk climbed to altitude. Like a gymnast in an aerial floor routine, Jimmy put the little plane through a series of precise movements, choreographed to a silent symphony that held the audience spellbound.

A smiling Dr. Kung greeted Jimmy when he landed.

"Could anyone fly like this?" Kung asked.

"Sure," Jimmy said, "With the right training."

After Kung and his party left, Jimmy helped the mechanics tie down the Hawk.

"What do you suppose they're doing?" he asked Joe, indicating a group of Japanese with cameras.

"It looks like they're taking pictures with a telephoto lens," she answered. "They photographed you in the air, too."

"That camera equipment looks pretty sophisticated." Jimmy ran his hand over the Hawk's fuselage. "They seem pretty interested in the Hawk."

The Japanese "tourists" continued to take pictures as the Shell team secured the plane.

"I'm glad we won't be going back to Japan," he said. "Our reception would be less than friendly."

Two days later, members of the Chinese armed forces crowded the flight line for another demonstration of the Hawk's agility.

Jimmy revved the engine and released the brakes. The Hawk soared into the sky like her predator namesake. Jim pushed above the clouds, and then dropped into a steep dive.

The Hawk began to shudder as the cowling slipped forward into the propeller. Quickly pushing back on the controls, Jimmy pulled out of the dive and began to climb. The cowling shifted back, away from the propeller. Jimmy began a gradual descent, landing as quickly as prudently possible.

He shut off the engine as soon as he hit the ground, and allowed the Hawk to roll to a stop. He jumped from the plane and examined the cowling and propeller. The cowling could be reattached, but it had damaged the propeller beyond repair.

Jimmy ran his hand over the cowling. Every fastener was undone. There was no way that had happened by accident.

He looked across the field. Again, a group of Japanese men stood on the sidelines, toting sophisticated cameras and taking pictures.

On April 16th, Jimmy returned to the airfield and inspected the Hawk. Today's audience would include T. B. Soong, a Harvard man, and Madame Chiang Kai-shek's brother. Jimmy had planned a spectacular show and was anxious to get started.

Satisfied that the cowling fasteners showed no signs of sabotage, he climbed into the Hawk and soared into the deep blue sky. He felt the air as it rushed over the windshield and lifted the flaps of his leather helmet.

Easing forward on the stick, he pushed the Hawk into a steep dive. He could hear the satisfied growl of the engine over the rush of air. Exhilarated, he pulled out of the dive into level flight. The engine stopped cold. For the second time in as many days, Jimmy abandoned the exhibition, gliding without power into an emergency landing.

Forced to look deeper for the source of the Hawk's trouble, Jimmy removed the cowling and opened the engine compartment. He needed to search no further. The fuel pump drive shaft, bent beyond repair, had been hammered in such a way that the pump would fail in flight. Again, the plane had been sabotaged.

He couldn't, however, explain this to the Chinese. It would sound like the Americans were making excuses for their products.

Setting to work with the mechanics, Jimmy replaced the faulty pump and went over every inch of the Hawk—wing-tip to wing-tip, propeller to rudder.

That night, and every night thereafter, an armed American sat with the plane, guarding the Hawk and the American image.

Two days later, Joe took her seat in the dangerously overcrowded stands. The exhibit, held outside Shanghai in a polo field, was open to the public. The grandstands swarmed with humanity, like ants on an anthill. Hundreds of Chinese spectators covered the roof, and Joe, feeling somewhat suffocated by the proximity of so many bodies, feared that the stands would collapse from the combined weight, crushing them all.

Overcast skies kept Jimmy's aerobatics low. He plunged toward the ground in death-defying dives, tumbled in a playful ballet and, flying close to the airfield, almost brushed the tip of his rudder in inverted flight.

Even though someone from the Curtiss team guarded the plane at all times, the nagging fear of overlooked vandalism worried Joe. Coupled with Jim's low altitude show, and apprehension about the overloaded stands, she had trouble enjoying the afternoon.

The crowds, however, did not. They were mesmerized by "Doo-rittle" and his little airplane. In unison, they alternated between holding their breaths and cheering. At one point, as Jimmy flew low over the field, the crowd stood, leaning forward. Joe held on for dear life, certain that the stands would give way.

She was glad—very glad—when the Hawk's engines shut down, the crowds dispersed, and Jimmy returned with her to their little hotel room.

On days when Jimmy wasn't flying, they explored China as tourists. She filled her memory with shrines and pagodas, fascinated by the variety of lifestyles in the little cities and towns.

Before leaving, China National Airways Corporation invited them to visit Peking. Jimmy flew in the co-pilot's seat on the small Chinese airliner.

Settling down in the back, Joe joined General Linson E. Dzau, from Chinese military headquarters; Mrs. Jack H. Jovett, wife of the former commander of the Chinese aviation school at Hangchow; and film producer Mark E. Moody.

The rapidly deteriorating weather cloaked the sky with dense clouds and shook the little plane, tossing it around like a toy. The pilot, aware of Jimmy's experience with instrument flight, eagerly turned over the controls.

Forced off course by the turbulence, they flew low over areas where the population had never seen an airplane before. People flooded out of their homes, staring into the air at the loud bird overhead.

Finally, Jimmy spotted an airfield, and decided to land long enough to refuel. The passengers piled out of the plane onto the dirt runway. Both women needed bathroom facilities.

As coolies, carrying five-gallon cans of gasoline on their heads, refueled the plane, Joe overcame her modesty and communicated their personal needs to a local official. Smiling at the two women, he led them to a screened off area with a series of holes in the ground.

The smell of human waste overpowered them, but so did their need. Adjusting their garments, both women squatted over the open holes. The instantaneous relief caused a huge sigh to escape from Joe; she allowed herself to relax and close her eyes. The sound of chattering brought her back to her surroundings. She looked up and immediately blushed a deep red. All along the top of the screens, the eyes of Chinese men gawked in amazement at the Caucasian women.

The group took off again, clinging close to the coastline. The weather continued to worsen, turbulence shoving the plane around. Dark clouds hovered above them, and rain pelted the windows. Joe looked around the cabin at the other passengers, then out the window at the long stretches of clear beach, and decided to ask Jimmy if they could land and wait out the storm.

Bracing herself on the backs of the seats, she made her way to the cockpit. The plane bucked and dipped. Her stomach had trouble keeping up with her body. Holding tight to the door of the cockpit, she raised her voice above the engine noise.

"Jimmy, why don't we set down on one of those beaches below us?"

"That would be imprudent," he answered, his knuckles white from gripping the controls.

The plane bucked again, and Joe barely held herself upright in the door.

"This area is controlled by warlords," the Chinese pilot added, when the worst of the turbulence had passed. "We would likely be held for ransom."

Not sure who would be willing to pay ransom for an American pilot and his wife, Joe worked her way back down the short aisle to her seat. She'd been up in smaller planes in worse weather with Jimmy, and they'd always made it. She was confident this would be no different.

They pushed on to Tsingtao. Joe watched out the window as they made their approach. A wheat field, a substantial portion in knee-deep water, served as an emergency airport. The motley crew, tired and sore from the long ride, climbed out of the plane, thankful to be back on solid ground.

At the end of June, Jim and Joe left the Hawk in China and continued by ship, first to the Philippines, then southward to the Dutch East Indies, where the Dutch military asked Jimmy to put on an exhibition in one of their planes.

Jimmy took off in the hot, thin air of the airdrome and climbed to 1000 feet. Testing the performance of a borrowed Hawk, he put her through a series of maneuvers, beginning with a 360-degree corkscrew-like roll, leading into an Immelman, followed by a full Cuban-eight. Building confidence in the plane, he pulled on the top of the loop, and then nosed down into a steep dive. Unlike the Hawk he'd left in China, the Dutch plane had a heavier engine, and plummeted toward the earth. He hadn't made adjustments for the thin air, nor allowed for the heavier plane's difference in response. When he pulled back on the controls, the plane did not pull out of the dive, but continued plunging toward impact.

Immediately realizing his miscalculation, Jimmy pulled the stick into his lap. Finally responding, the Hawk's nose pulled out of the dive. Just as the plane leveled out and reached skyward, Jimmy felt a sharp bump as the wheels struck the ground. Recovering from the jolt, he again pulled up hard and completed his tumbling routine. He landed without further incident, and taxied to the hangar. A group of Dutch officers, including a number of pilots waited, for him.

"That was the most delicate piece of flying I have ever seen," one officer told Jimmy as he joined the group.

"That was downright stupid flying," Jimmy answered, shaking his head in disgust.

"We knew," the officer said, clasping Jimmy on the back. "We just wondered if you'd lie about it."

★ ★ ★ ★

They played tourist during the remainder of their world trip. At Batavia, they boarded the *S.S. Valentine*, and sailed to Siam. From Siam, they took Royal Dutch Airlines to Burma, India, Iraq, and Egypt.

They visited Greece, Yugoslavia, Hungry, Germany, Holland and England. It felt like a second honeymoon. In every city, they visited tourist attractions, ate ethnic food, and strolled historic paths.

During his brief stint as a tourist, Jimmy became aware of two very important facts. First, public air transportation in Europe far surpassed America's. Scheduled flights took off on time, safely and dependably. Secondly, and much more disturbing, he noticed the exponential advancement and superiority of European military airpower. Even Germany, supposedly restricted by the Treaty of Versailles, had developed extensive civilian airlines and pilot training programs—planes and pilots easily converted for military use.

Countries in the Far East, some considered backward by US standards, were building air forces with substantial numbers of planes. The Japanese, in particular, had already turned aviation into a military force, with their invasion of China and their domination of Manchuria and many Chinese coastal areas.

The United States, however, had spent little money on defense after WWI, with just a small fraction reaching the Air Corps. He feared that American aviation was falling far behind the rest of the world.

More than ever, Jimmy believed that a strong air force was the key to military strength. He felt Shell should produce 100-octane fuel, and that the manufacturers should be goaded into designing and building planes that would use it. He vowed to speak his mind when he returned to the States.

They left London in late August, 1933 and sailed to New York. From there, they flew home to St. Louis. Mary Bryant and the boys waited for them. Although Joe had thoroughly enjoyed the trip, she couldn't wait to see her two sons, and she couldn't stop hugging them.

Weary from traveling, she warmed at the sight of their home. She kicked off her shoes as soon as she walked through the doorway. The boys talked over one another, attempting to catch her up on their activities, summer break, and the pending school term. The four Doolittles sat in the living room until the sun began to set, and the shadows reached across the hardwood floors, and up the walls.

Bushed, Joe climbed the stairs and headed down the hall to the master bedroom. Assaulted by an awful stench when she opened the door, Joe wrinkled her nose in protest and brought out a white handkerchief to cover the lower half of her face.

Turning, she made her way back downstairs. Jimmy continued to answer a barrage of questions from the boys.

"What's that awful smell in our bedroom?" she asked.

John and Young Jim exchanged looks, sheepish grins on their faces.

"Well?" she prompted.

"We needed a place to keep the babies." John volunteered.

"What babies?"

"The squabs. We were afraid if we left them outside they might die," young Jim explained.

"Ok," she said calmly. "But why didn't you keep them in your own rooms?"

"Because they smell too bad!" John answered, before Jim could stop him.

★ ★ ★ ★

Jimmy returned to work, but images of German aviation plagued his mind. His concern intensified in October, when German flying ace Ernst Udet traveled to the United States to purchase two Curtiss Hawks.

Representatives from Curtiss-Wright refused to allow Udet to fly the Hawk until they received payment. Udet refused to pay until he flew the plane. Curtiss called Jimmy to settle the dispute. By mutual agreement, Jimmy demonstrated the Hawk's capabilities, and an impressed Udet completed the transaction.

Udet, who shared a similar build with Jimmy, also shared a fierce sense of humor, and the desire to push an airplane to the edge of its performance capability.

From the start, the two men enjoyed each other's company, respected each other's skill, and became fast friends.

★ ★ ★ ★

When controversy over government airmail contracts triggered a congressional investigation into allegations of scandal among the large airlines and brought to light resentment on the part of small entrepreneurs, President Roosevelt cancelled all airmail contracts and asked the Army Air Corps to deliver the mail. However, only a few Army test aircraft were equipped with blind flying instruments and only about a dozen military pilots were trained in their use. In the following weeks, four Air Corps pilots were killed during airmail flights and another six died while training or ferrying aircraft.

In response to the public uproar, the President authorized new commercial contracts and appointed a 12-member board to study all phases of military air operations, including technical flying equipment and training. The board, known as the Baker Board, was headed by Newton D. Baker, former secretary of war during World War I. Jimmy was invited to participate.

Jimmy paced the small office assigned to him, furious with the members of the Baker Board. Surely they realized from the series of fatal accidents that the Army Air Corps lacked sufficient training and were flying antiquated aircraft. Anyone with half a brain recognized that the Air Corps, as an unloved stepchild of the Army, floundered from neglect. The nation needed an independent air force with sufficient funding to purchase equipment and train pilots. Although many in aviation felt Billy Mitchell went too far with his attacks on Washington, most agreed the United States needed a powerful Air Force.

Jimmy returned to the pages on his desk. He missed Joe, and her ability to find the right words, not to mention her secretarial skills. Stung by what he believed to be shortsightedness on the part of the committee members, he wanted to write a powerful dissenting opinion.

The Baker Board, formed in response to the series of fatal crashes, suffered during the Air Corps' attempt to deliver mail, and charged with the investigation of the role of aviation in the United States, would determine the fate of the Army Air Corps. Commissioned by the War Department the Baker committee included civilian members Dr. Karl Taylor Compton, president of MIT; industrialist Edgar S. Gorrell; and George William Lewis, director of research for the National Advisory Committee for Aeronautics. Military brass, including Major General Hugh A. Drum, Deputy Chief of Staff of the War Department; and Major General Benjamin D. Foulois, Chief of the Army Air Corps; represented the armed forces. The only pilots on the board were General Foulois, Clarence Chamberlain, and Jimmy.

After twenty-five days of testimony from 105 witnesses, the committee issued its findings. All members, except Jimmy, concurred that "the fear that has been cultivated in this country by various zealots that American aviation is inferior to that of the rest of the world is, as a whole, unfounded."

Jimmy had witnessed the development of aviation in Europe and Asia. The Japanese had already meticulously built and maintained an air force superior to the United States Army Air Corps. Commercial airlines like Royal Dutch Airlines flourished in Europe. Germany's aviation, thinly veiled as commercial, could easily be converted to military use. Try as he might, he couldn't get the other members to listen.

Five hundred and thirty-six Air Corps officers filed letters in support of a separate Air Force, with a separate budget, answerable to its own commanders. The Commission ignored the letters. Their only concession: the creation of the General Headquarters Air Force, subservient to the Army General Staff.

Members of the Board either ignored or misunderstood the potential of the airplane as a weapon. Jim's frustration hit a boiling point as he reviewed the findings:

"The limitations of the airplane show that the idea that aviation, acting alone, can control the sea lanes, or defend the coast, or produce decisive results are all visionary, as is the idea that a very large and independent air force is necessary to defend our country against air attack."

Had everyone forgotten Billy Mitchell's sinking of the German battleship *Ostfriesland*? That attack decisively demonstrated the superiority of air power. Jimmy picked up his pen and started to write:

"I believe in aviation—both civil and military. I believe that the future security of our Nation is dependent upon an adequate air force. This is true at the present time and will become increasingly important as the science of aviation advances and the airplane lends itself more and more to the art of warfare.

"I am convinced that the required air force can be more rapidly organized, equipped and trained if it is completely separated from the Army and developed as an entirely separate arm. If complete separation is not the desire of the committee, I recommend an air force as part of the Army but with a separate budget, a separate promotion list and removed from the control of the General Staff. These are my sincere convictions. Failing either, I feel that the Air Corps should be developed under the General Staff as recommended above."

The press printed the findings, and Jimmy, disgusted with the shortsightedness of the committee members, quickly spoke out against them. When asked his thoughts by a reporter, Jimmy answered,

"The country will someday pay for the stupidities of those who were in the majority on this commission. They know as much about the future of aviation as they do about the sign writings of the Aztecs."

CHAPTER 12

THE COMING WAR

"The superior man, when resting in
safety, does not forget that danger
may come. When in a state of security, he does not forget the possibility
of ruin. When all is orderly, he does
not forget that disorder may come.
Thus his person is not endangered,
and his States and all their clans
are preserved."

— Confucius

ALTHOUGH vocally opposed to closed-circuit racing, Jimmy
still participated in racing point-to-point against the clock, especially if it promoted commercial aviation.

Billy Mitchell's prediction that "commercial air passengers
would be as familiar a sight as train passengers and that distances
between the West Coast and East Coast would be figured in terms
not of miles but of hours" was on the brink of becoming a reality.
In December 1933, Eddie Rickenbacker set a coast-to-coast record
in an Eastern Airlines' DC-2 of twelve-hours, three minutes. Rising
to the challenge, American Airlines asked Jimmy to fly a single-
engine, eight-passenger Consolidated Vultee from Burbank to
Floyd Bennett Field in New York.

Knowing that 100 mph tail winds aided Rickenbacker in his
flight and hoping to benefit from the same, Jimmy contacted
Irving Krick, meteorologist and faculty member from California

Institute of Technology, for advice on timing for the flight. Based on his studies of air masses and their movement, and confident that he could predict weather for months in advance, Krick advised Jimmy to "plan on the night of January 14, 1934. You'll have typical California overcast at takeoff time, but once on top, you'll have clear skies and tail winds all the way to New York."

Trusting Krick's weather report, Jimmy, Joe and Robert Adamson, Shell's publicist, arrived at Burbank Airport in a thick overcast. Joe quickly settled back into her seat as Jimmy taxied into position, revved the engine and climbed into the thick fog that clung to the skies over Southern California.

Bob Adamson, sitting across the isle, looked out the window, then back at Joe.

"Looks pretty thick out there," he said.

"Irving promises an absolutely perfect flight to New York with tail winds all the way," Joe said, looking out the window. The night sky, blanketed in white clouds, pressed close against the cabin. She didn't know much about predicting weather, but she hoped Krick did.

Jimmy leveled off at 15,000 feet, but the fog persisted. Joe wrapped her coat tighter, pulling it up around her neck and fastening the buttons. She slipped her hands into the pockets, shivering slightly. The plane bumped along, tossed in the turbulent air.

Giving up on any thought of sleep, Joe made her way up to the cockpit.

"How's it going?" she asked.

"This weather isn't clearing up." Jimmy answered. "We're over Arizona, and it's still pea soup out there."

Joe watched the sea of white clouds blow against the windshield.

"I'm a little concerned about ice. It has already knocked out the radio." He added, looking out at the wing. The fiery exhaust burned blue out the side of the windshield, but did little to keep the ice off the wings. "It's cold up here."

Joe hunched a little further into her coat. It wasn't her nature to complain, but Jim was right, it was cold up here. They flew along in silence, each lost in thought.

"I'm heading south to see if I can find warmer weather." Jimmy said.

Fighting the bucking of the plane, Joe made her way slowly back to her seat and tightened the safety strap. A slight headache pressing between her eyes reminded her that the air was thin, and she needed to conserve oxygen.

Joe felt the shift as Jimmy banked the plane right and headed south. The icy fog stayed with them. The wings became heavy, coated with ice, and the plane lost speed. She hoped they wouldn't stall.

"Hold on. I'm going to try to knock some of this ice off." Jimmy's voice crackled over the headset.

Joe leaned her head against the window, allowing the stream of cold air from the cockpit ventilator to blow against her face. The headache spread from between her eyes to a band circling her forehead.

She clutched the handrails with frozen fingers as the Vultee bucked the winds. Closing her eyes, she willed the pain to recede.

Joe's eyes flew open as a splash of icy water made its way through the vent, hitting her full in the face. With frozen fingers, she wiped away the moisture. Although still surrounded in fog, Joe hoped the splash of water promised less ice.

"I'm going up to 16,500 feet," Jimmy said through the headphones. "Put on your oxygen."

Joe pulled on her mask and settled her head against the back of the seat. The oxygen helped her headache. Her heavy eyelids drifted closed and she began to relax.

"Are you okay?" Jimmy's voice buzzed in her ears.

"A little dizzy," she answered.

"How's Bob?"

Joe looked across the isle. Bob was slumped in his seat.

"I think he's passed out." Joe answered.

"Can you hold on?" he asked, dropping back into the fog and the oxygen rich air.

"I ...can...hold...on...if...you...can," she answered.

"Good...Girl! You're...promoted...to...radio...man." Jim's voice sounded farther away.

They flew most of the night in the thick clouds. Occasionally they climbed to higher altitude to keep more ice from forming, and then dove back into the white mist. Jimmy held his compass on course, but the winds had shifted strongly to the northwest, blowing the Vultee south.

Finally, as daylight broke, the worst of the cloud cover cleared and the ice melted. Jimmy peered out the window at the landscape.

"We're over Richmond." Jimmy said, waking Joe from a restless sleep.

"How far off course?" she asked.

"Two-hundred fifty miles," Jim answered. "We might still make it if I push hard."

Joe felt the power increase. Without the ice from the night before, the 750-horsepower Wright Cyclone burst to life. Jimmy banked left and the plane soared north toward New York.

Eleven hours and fifty-nine minutes after taking off in Burbank, the Consolidated Vultee landed at Floyd Bennett Field. Although the first to break twelve hours, Jimmy did not receive the official record. Breaking a record required a five-minute improvement—Jim's time was only four minutes faster that Eddie Rickenbacker's flight a month before. He was, however, recognized as the first to fly a transport plane with passengers from one coast to the other, nonstop in less than half a day.

Joe could see through Jimmy's mantle of good humor and knew he was disappointed with his time and performance.

"The old man is slipping; I should have arrived two hours ago!" a grinning Jimmy told the press.

"If I hadn't gotten lost, I would have been here an hour and a half ago!" grin in place, he told another.

"Mrs. Doolittle, how was the flight?" a reporter yelled from the pack.

"It was an uncomfortable flight," she answered with a smile. "I could hardly sleep."

"Joe, did you wear a parachute?"

"Whatever for?" she asked.

The crowd of reporters laughed.

★ ★ ★ ★

In March 1935, Hitler, in direct defiance of the Treaty of Versailles, announced the existence of the Luftwaffe. A year later, in March 1936, German troops marched into and occupied the Rhineland, the demilitarized zone protecting France and Belgium. Jimmy paid close attention to the developments in Europe, and, when asked in late summer of 1937 to return to Europe on Shell business, he jumped at the opportunity.

Germany had changed dramatically since his first visit in 1930. At that timethe German people had seemed dejected and disappointed. By 1933, the spirit of the country had improved, and the people seemed optimistic that Hitler would restore their national strength and pride. But now, in 1937, bands of uniformed children marched through the streets of Berlin, their voices raised in Nazi war songs. The mood of the country was different and Jimmy felt vaguely uncomfortable.

Jimmy's reunion with Ernst Udet, however, went well. He was relieved to find his old friend unchanged, still the fun loving, good-humored pilot who, like Jimmy, enjoyed pushing an airplane to the edge of its limits.

Ernst never ceased to amaze Jimmy. A brilliant conversationalist, fluent in German and English, he also recited poetry and possessed a beautiful singing voice. A talented artist, his hand-drawn caricatures covered the walls of his apartment.

Ernst's professional career also reflected his multi-faceted personality—a World War I flying ace, actor and stunt man in the German film industry, multiple attempts in business, and currently head of the Luftwaffe Technical Development.

Jim spent much of his free time in Berlin with Ernst, frequently ending up in the German's apartment, where they shared first-rate French champagne and swapped stories of their more recent exploits.

One evening, well into their second bottle of champagne, Ernst, who was an excellent marksman, suggested a little contest.

"Let's have some pistol practice." Ernst said, swaying slightly from the excess of champagne.

"Where?" Jimmy asked.

"Right here." Ernst retrieved a ten-inch, sand-filled steel box from the hall closet and placed it on a stack of technical papers sitting on the mantle.

After attaching a paper target, Ernst leveled a small, powerful air-pistol and squeezed the trigger. The pellet burst from the muzzle and slammed dead center into the target.

"Bravo!" Jimmy cheered.

Accepting the pistol, Jimmy walked to the back wall. Carefully he aimed, squeezed the trigger, and placed a pellet right next to Ernst's in the bull's eye.

Taking turns, the two men shot round after round, hitting the target each time.

They opened a third bottle of champagne.

"This isn't much competition." Ernst said, making his way unsteadily to the bedroom. A few minutes later, he returned carrying a full-sized .455 service revolver.

"Here, Jim," he said, handing over the revolver.

Jimmy weaved slightly, aimed and shot low. The papers propping up the target flew in every direction.

"Blast it, Jimmy! Those are reports I need to read!" Ernst said, retrieving the pistol.

Staggering to the back of the room, Ernst leveled the pistol, swayed and shot a three-inch hole in the apartment wall. The two men, stunned at first, dissolved into laugher when the neighbor's eye appeared in the opening.

"I think we'd better put that away," Jimmy said.

Afraid that a police report would be filed, Jimmy looked nervously at the hole. Ernst, unfazed by the incident, leveled the gun again.

"No, really," Jimmy said, slumping onto the couch, "I think we've done enough damage for the night."

Ernst reluctantly returned the gun to his room. A few minutes later, he appeared in the doorway, a lock of dark hair pulled across his eye and a small black comb propped on his upper lip.

"Heil!" he shouted, giving Jimmy a stiff-armed salute. "Heil Hitler!'"

Jimmy laughed, but looked nervously around the room. He shared Ernst's dislike of Hitler and disrespect of Goering, but he was reluctant to encourage criticism of the Furher. What if the neighbors decided to report them? Hitler might resent one of his senior officers mocking him.

As head of Luftwaffe Technical Developments, Ernst's free time was limited to evening hours, so he assigned Jimmy a military aide, gave him use of his personal plane, and encouraged Jimmy to visit aircraft manufacturers.

Disturbed by what he saw, Jimmy walked through the modern plant where the aircraft rolled off the production line at an alarming rate. He realized that German engineers had based some of their concepts on the Curtiss-Wright Hawk. Jimmy thought about the two Hawks that he helped sell to Udet.

He visited the Mercedes-Benz factory where they produced engines for the Messerschmitt Me-109 and Me-110. Unrestricted access to German aircraft design and manufacturing processes reinforced two disturbing thoughts: the Germans were in the process of reconstructing a first-rate Air Force, and the Americans lagged even further behind than he first suspected.

Jimmy returned from Europe concerned about the new climate in Germany and the comparative complacency and military weaknesses of England and France. Haunted by the questions raised by Hitler and his mass production of airplanes, Jimmy renewed his efforts to push the development of 100-octane fuel, and to build up the American Army Air Corps.

★ ★ ★ ★

Joe sat at her writing desk, pen in hand, and surveyed the frozen February landscape. Snow blanketed the lawn and clung to the branches of the trees. She sighed, and moved her pen across the page:

Many changes since we last saw you…first last July we moved," she wrote to her friend, Ethel Craig. "With the prospect of being much alone, I set out to find smaller quarters. After a long search, came upon this dear, little new house in the country...far removed from the city noise and smoke. I'm happier than I've ever been, mid-west.

She looked around the cozy little room, warm and snug, and then turned her attention back to the letter.

In August poor Mary was taken ill...had two operations and finally, just before New Year's, was able to leave the hospital...still missing from here, but thank goodness, seems to be mending...I've missed her terribly.

Joe chewed on the end of her pen. She missed Mary, not so much for her help with the housework, but for the company. The two women had grown very close, and Joe knew that Mary loved the boys almost as much as she did.

The boys too have fled...John is at Culver and young Jim at Purdue...Jim is here at the moment, but is, as usual, much away...

She gazed out the window and thought about Ethel in Los Angeles. How she longed for the warmth of Southern California and the company of her family. Her mother hadn't written in months and Gracie rarely wrote. She and Jimmy had supported her mother for the past ten years, but Gracie took care of her. Guilt picked away at contentment. She wondered what Gracie was doing. A sudden breeze picked up, blowing a swirl of snow against the window and knocking Joe out of her reverie.

We have had, comparatively, a mild winter with a wide variety of weather, however...from spring-like days to the dead of winter and back again without the benefit of much warning...reckon I'm growing sissy-like for I long for sunnier climes...would that I could go south with the birds and remain until spring...

★ ★ ★ ★

In September 1938, a false sense of peace had permeated Europe. British Prime Minister Neville Chamberlain, after attending a conference in Munich with French Premier Edouard Daladier, Mussolini, and Hitler, declared "peace in our time."

By January 1939, Roosevelt recognized the ominous changes in Europe and noted that "military aviation today is increasing at an unprecedented and alarming rate. Increased range, increased speed, increased capacity of airplanes abroad, have changed our requirements for defensive aviation." A week later, in a message to Congress, Roosevelt acknowledged the weakness of American aviation, declaring that the Army Air Corps was "so utterly inadequate" that it "must be immediately strengthened."

Roosevelt spoke the truth. Congress had invested little money in the military since World War I, and not much of that on the Army Air Corps. The United States Army ranked eighteenth in the world, far behind Germany and Japan.

In March of 1939, Hitler sent his troops into the Sudetenland, and within days of his invasion declared, "Czechoslovakia has ceased to exist." A shocked Prime Minister Chamberlain complained that Hitler had not kept his word.

Jimmy returned to Germany in midsummer 1939. Standing with his old friend Ernst Udet at an air show in Frankfurt, he was shocked and dismayed by the changes in both his friend and in Germany.

The only American present, Jimmy surveyed the crowd. The Germans returned his curiosity with hostile stares and open aggression. The air show itself displayed Germany's ostensible military superiority. Instead of small, agile planes performing aerobatic routines, bombers and fighters blackened the sky, blocking the sun and leaving Jimmy with an ominous feeling of foreboding. He looked up at the blanket of aircraft and wondered what new designs currently covered German sketchpads.

German pilots no longer shared openly with Jimmy and spoke to him with a curt, inconsiderate impudence that bordered on rudeness.

Jimmy observed the transformation in Ernst. Gone were the ready smile and the happy-go-lucky air of joviality. Instead, Udet, now Director General of the German Air Ministry, seemed ill at ease in the company of his American friend.

Jimmy found many changes in the people, too. The German spirit, crushed by World War I, showed signs of recovery. The optimism that had lifted the spirit of German citizens two years before, had been replaced with military posturing and aggression. Soldiers, boys really, marched in formation through city streets, their jackboots echoing off buildings, down allies, and across empty parks.

The air show over, Udet walked Jimmy to his car.

"I'm off to Munich for a little holiday," Ernst said. "Would you care to join me for a few days?"

For a second, catching a glimpse of his old friend Ernst, Jimmy wanted to go.

"I'd better not," Jimmy answered.

He couldn't bring himself to take advantage of an old friendship. He knew that anything Ernst said, he would feel compelled to report back to Washington. He'd expect no less of Udet. Besides, he thought, it might be political suicide for Ernst to be seen with an American officer. War, Jimmy believed, was inevitable. Regardless of Ernst's personal feelings against Hitler and Goering, he and Jimmy would fight on opposite sides.

The car drew up to the hotel, and Jimmy clasped hands with Udet. Momentarily, he mourned the passing of a great friendship, then released Ernst's hand and climbed out of the car.

A few days later, Jimmy stopped at the American Embassy in London.

"I'd like to see Major Scanlon," Jimmy said, referring to Major Martin "Mike" Scanlon, the air attaché.

Sitting in front of Mike's desk, Jimmy outlined his concerns.

"Germany has built up a fleet of fighters and bombers," Jimmy said. "It's obvious from the display of military strength that Hitler is planning aggression against his neighbors."

"Jimmy, there's nothing I can do about it," Mike replied, shrugging his shoulders.

"There's nothing you can do? Or nothing you *will* do?" Jimmy asked, his face florid with anger.

"Jimmy, you know Hap Arnold." Mike said. "Go back and tell him what you saw."

Jimmy returned to the United States anxious to report his findings to General Arnold. His first stop was Washington, D.C.

"We will be unable to remain aloof from whatever happens in Europe," Jimmy said as he walked through the door of General Henry H. "Hap" Arnold's office.

Hap looked up from his desk. "What's on your mind, Jimmy?" he asked.

"I've just returned from Germany, and what I saw there has me worried." Jimmy said as he sat across from Hap. "Planes that were on the drawing boards two years ago are flying now. Uniformed troops march through the streets of Frankfurt wearing jackboots and sporting swastikas. There is an edge to the country of imminent war."

Hap listened intently to Jimmy's opinion. Both men knew the weakness of the Army Air Corps. Production of aircraft increased after Roosevelt's January speech to Congress and the infusion of $300 million, but retooling took time. Americans were still recovering from the depression, and reluctant to involve themselves in another world war.

"Your report confirms what Charles Lindbergh said last year," Hap said. Although Lindbergh advocated isolationism, he supported the construction of high-speed, high-altitude aircraft.

"Lindbergh believes we can stay out of the conflict." Hap said.

"I'm totally convinced that war is inevitable, and that we will become involved in the hostilities." Jimmy said. "I'm so sure of it, in fact, that I'm willing to resign from Shell and serve full-time or part-time, in uniform or out, in any way you think I can be useful."

"That would be a sizable cut in pay." Hap said smiling. "But your flying background and years in the aviation industry would be invaluable if America became involved in the war."

"Not if, but when."

"Jimmy, I can't reactivate you immediately because of your rank. But I can recall you at the start of the fiscal year. So next July, expect to be back in uniform. Until then, keep the pressure on."

Two weeks after this meeting, on September 1st, 1939, 1400 Luftwaffe planes bombed and strafed the cities and towns of

Poland. Hitler's invasion had begun in earnest. On September 3rd, Britain declared war on Germany. France reluctantly followed suit and Europe erupted into World War II.

Within a week, Roosevelt declared a State of National Emergency. Although many Americans, like Lindbergh, supported an isolationist policy, others recognized the inevitability of U. S. involvement in the war.

Jimmy felt some vindication for pushing 100-octane fuel but no satisfaction in being right in his objection to the findings of the Baker Board. The U.S. Army Air Corps ranked sixth in the world, not nearly good enough for successful embroilment in the war in Europe.

Jimmy was anxious to do what he could while waiting to be called back into active service. In January 1940, he was named President of the prestigious Institute of Aeronautical Sciences, an organization whose members represented the whole spectrum of aeronautical interests from airline executives to aircraft component manufacturers. As President, he visited engineering schools throughout the country, encouraging students to study aeronautical engineering. Restless, he spent more and more time on the road, traveling frequently to New York City, where trouble of a new kind waited.

★ ★ ★ ★

Joe sat alone, deep in the shadows of her bedroom. Darkness crept across the sky, punctured by bright stars and illuminated by the dim yellow glow of street lamps on the country lane leading to their house. White sheers alternately billowed in the breeze then hung limply at the windows.

Swallowed up by the high back chair, she clutched a sheet of pink stationery in one hand and a brandy in the other. Heavy perfume drifted up from the paper as flowery tendrils of ink wove threats across the page, "I'll write your wife." The phrase echoed in her thoughts.

Surely there should be some comfort in the knowledge that the woman knew him so poorly as to think he would fall for blackmail.

And how like Jimmy to confront the dilemma head on. There could be hundreds of excuses offered by hundreds of husbands caught in similar situations. But Jimmy would not offer them, nor would Joe accept them.

She took a sip of brandy; it burned its way down her throat to her heart.

He had stood before her, letter extended, regret etched on his face. He was sorry, deeply sorry. He would never stray again.

The woman was a New York model, Jimmy told her. The affair was just a fling, lasting only a few weeks. Not so long, she thought, but long enough.

"Do you want a divorce?" Joe had asked, her voice little more than a whisper.

"No," he said shaking his head.

Ubiquitous opportunities for indiscretions existed, especially for someone in the public eye, as Jimmy had been for the last fifteen years. This Joe knew, but it didn't help.

"Leave me be," she said, more an order than a request. He had walked away, closing the door behind him, leaving her in solitude.

The soft ticking of the mantle clock drew her eyes. This room reflected their life together:sage green rug over hardwood floor, white heirloom bedspread on a double bed,pictures of Jimmy and the boys. The hope chest at the foot of the bed stuffed with memorabilia from over two decades together.

She looked back at the note, spidery handwriting unraveling a web of deceit. They would never discuss it again. Any decision made tonight would be final. Another sip of brandy burned, bringing fresh tears. She looked back at the street. Eventually, the streetlights extinguished and the breaking dawn stained the sky.

Joe rose slowly from her chair. Her body, unusually stiff, deadened. She sat down at her writing desk, and picked up a sheet of cream stationery—Mrs. James H. Doolittle embossed across the top.

She ran a hand through her short white hair and down her stiff neck, and then lifted her pen.

"He never bought *me* a mink coat;" she wrote. "I don't know how *you* could possibly expect one."

★ ★ ★ ★

On May 10, 1940, Germany invaded the Low Countries and Neville Chamberlain stepped down as Britain's Prime Minister. Winston Churchill was selected to replace Chamberlain. Roosevelt, speaking to Congress declared, "These are ominous days. Days whose swift and shocking developments force every neutral nation to look at its defenses." France fell in June.

Jimmy, still waiting for orders to return to uniform, stood in the door, watching as Joe moved around the kitchen. A pork roast, rotating on the rotisserie, filled the air with the sweet smell of apricots. With quick efficient movements, Joe basted the meat with a marinade made of strained apricots, honey, lemon juice, soy sauce, garlic, onion, ginger ale, ginger, and pepper. As a bride, she knew nothing about cooking, but she had become an expert. Jimmy marveled at her ability to master anything to which she set her mind.

The house was quiet. She handed him two plates. He took them into the dining room and set them on the table.

"I've been called back to active duty," Jimmy said, when he returned to the kitchen. "This is from Ira Eaker." He removed Ira's letter from his back pocket.

"He wants to know if I'm interested in reporting for active duty on July 1st. I'll be stationed at the Allison plant to straighten out production problems with the Allison engine.

"Is that in Indianapolis?" Joe asked.

"Yes, but that's just one option."

"What are the others?"

"I could go directly to Washington and serve on Hap Arnold's staff."

Joe basted the roast a last time before removing it from the spit. Sprinkling it with grated coconut, she carried the platter to the table. Rarely did they have the house to themselves. Usually, friends crowded around the table.

"What will you do?" she asked once they served themselves.

"I'll tell him that I will accept any job that will take advantage of my particular experience, associations and abilities."

Placing a slice of pork roast on her plate, she passed the platter to Jimmy.

"It might be best for me to headquarter in Washington and work out of there, taking on the Indianapolis job as a first detail then returning to Washington when and if the production problems there are straightened out."

"How long will you be in Indianapolis?" she asked.

"Hopefully only a few months. But I'll stay for as long as it takes. When I'm finished and assigned to Washington, I'd like you to join me."

★ ★ ★ ★

France had surrendered to Germany on June 22, 1940. Britain stood alone against the Nazis.

Finally, on July 1, 1940, Shell granted Jimmy an indefinite leave of absence and he returned to active duty. As assistant supervisor of the Central Army Air Corps Procurement Center, Jimmy straddled two lifestyles: military and civilian. In Indianapolis, he found numerous problems with the Allison Plant, and he met with resistance from both quarters. Many career military personnel considered him Arnold's "Golden Boy," while aircraft industry personnel were reluctant to cooperate with competitors.

Allison, a division of General Motors, built liquid-cooled engines for airplanes. Jimmy studied plant operations and isolated two problems: an attitude favoring quantity over quality, and dirt. He started working on the solutions. With the help of O.E. Hunt, chief engineer for General Motors, they shut down the Allison plant for two weeks and reorganized production.

In the meantime, Jimmy requested and received a P-40 with an Allison engine for his personal use. His job, which required frequent trips between Indianapolis, Dayton and Washington, benefited from his exclusive use of the plane, and the hours he spent flying gave him first-hand knowledge of the capabilities of, and problems with, the Allison engine.

P-40 pilots had trouble in bad weather and were prohibited from taking off under instrument conditions. Jimmy discovered that these restrictions included him.

A young second lieutenant, an operations duty officer, refused to sign Jimmy's instrument clearance.

"I'm sorry, Sir," the young man said holding his own. "But this weather is below minimum for fighter aircraft."

"Son, I have extensive experience in weather flying and I have important business in Dayton." Jimmy said.

"I'm sorry, Sir. I know who you are and what you've accomplished, but the regulations are clear. No pursuit plane is allowed clearance in this weather."

Jimmy felt respect for the lad, but he also felt angry and frustrated. He left the airport and drove back to his office at Allison. Within minutes, he had Hap on the phone.

"Hap, I've been grounded in Indianapolis by a second lieutenant. Some rule about weather restrictions for fighter planes. Anything you can do about it?"

He heard Hap chuckle on the other end of the phone. "Jimmy, what do you need?"

"How about a special dispensation to go when and where I want to, regardless of regulations."

"Consider it done."

"And Hap, if you think about it, weather restrictions for fighters is somewhat self-defeating." Jim continued. "I'd like to install some special navigational equipment in the fighters. I think it might help solve the current problems. That and some additional instrument training for fighter pilots to cope with bad weather."

"Just let me know what you need." Hap said, and then hung up the phone.

Roosevelt's goal of 50,000 planes a year required cooperation between the automotive and aircraft industries. Reluctance on the part of both industries forced Arnold to intervene. He sent Jimmy to Detroit in November 1940 to facilitate a "shotgun marriage."

In August 1941, Hap sent Jimmy to war-torn England as a military observer. Jimmy noted that spare parts for planes and engines were in critically short supply. He was impressed with the British optimism, and the way women filled factory jobs. He also noted British efforts to place manufacturing factories underground.

Jimmy returned from England even more convinced that the United States would soon become involved in the war. In less than four months, his fears became reality.

On December 7, 1941, the Japanese bombed Pearl Harbor. One hundred eighty-nine Japanese planes dropped clusters of torpedo bombs on the Pacific Fleet. Eight American battleships, three destroyers and three light cruisers were hit. Two thousand four hundred and three sailors, soldiers and civilians died. One thousand one hundred and seventy-eight were injured. Like it or not, America had entered World War II.

PART 3

A WING AND A PRAYER

"Friendship has a real meaning to the Doolittles. It would be difficult to estimate the number of people who have been helped by their thoughtfulness. If a friend is sick, in trouble, down on his luck, the Doolittles are the first to offer help. They share their home, and their lives with their friends, and, somehow or other, it's their courage they share too."

—*Liberty Magazine,* July 25, 1942

CHAPTER 13

★ ★ ★ ★

AMERICA STRIKES BACK

"Doolittle, an arresting example
of thoughtful engineer and swashbuckling adventurer, was the only
conceivable airman who could have
headed up the preposterously complex and breathtakingly dangerous
first raid on Tokyo."

—Bob Considine, "The 10
Most Colorful Men I've
Met," *The American Weekly*

WHEN the first rush of adrenalin wore off, America's spirit hit
a new low. Japanese forces defeated the United States in one battle
after another. Blackout drills on both coasts unnerved many people. Their homeland had suffered a devastating attack. Could it
possibly happen again?

Two weeks after the attack on Pearl Harbor, President Franklin
D. Roosevelt called a meeting at the White House to discuss an
American attack on Japan. The attendees included: General George
C. Marshall, Army chief of staff; General Henry H. "Hap" Arnold,
chief of staff of the Army Air Forces; Admiral Ernest J. King, chief
of naval operations; Henry Hopkins, Roosevelt's special advisor;
Admiral Harold R. Stark; Secretary of War Henry Stimson; and
Secretary of the Navy Frank Knox. Roosevelt's goal was to take the
war to the Land of the Rising Sun by bombing Japan.

On January 10, 1941, Captain Francis S. Low, a submariner and operations officer on King's staff, met with the Admiral in his second office on the *Vixen,* a former German yacht.

"What's on your mind, Captain?" King asked when Low arrived that evening.

"Sir, I've got an idea for bombing Japan. I flew down to Norfolk today to check on the *Hornet,* our new carrier, and saw something that started me thinking."

King sat back in his chair and focused on Low.

"Today as we were taking off, I saw the outline of a carrier deck painted on the airfield where pilots are trained in carrier takeoffs and landings."

"I don't see what you're getting at, Low," King interrupted.

"Our radius of action for our carrier planes is about 300 miles. I thought if the Army has some twin-engine bombers with a range greater than our fighters, it seems to me a few of them could be loaded on a carrier and used to bomb Japan."

King was silent for a full minute before he spoke.

"You may have something there, Low. Talk to Duncan about it in the morning. And don't tell anyone else about this."

Early on the morning of January 11, 1941, Low met with Captain Donald B. "Wu" Duncan, King's air operations officer. Duncan listened carefully as Low explained his idea.

"As I see it, Low said, "there are two big questions: Can an Army medium land-based bomber land aboard a carrier? And can a land-based bomber loaded down with bombs, gas and a crew take off from a carrier deck?"

"The answer to your first question is a definite negative. A carrier deck is too short to land an Army bomber safely."

"And my second question?"

"I'll have to get back to you on that."

Five days later, Duncan completed a 30-page handwritten analysis in which he cautioned that the mission would require absolute secrecy and that few, if any, records should be kept. The vital element, he concluded, would be surprise.

On January 17th, Duncan and Low approached General Arnold. Intrigued by the idea, Hap Arnold called Jimmy.

23. *During the first blind flight a hood was pulled over the cockpit of the NY-2 ensuring that Jimmy could not see anything except the instruments. Lt. Ben Kelsey, holding his hands over his head or resting them on the wings, flew in the front seat as a safety precaution.*

24. *The Doolittles threw a dinner party after the first blind flight. Joe had everyone sign a damask tablecloth and embroidered the names in black DMC silk thread. She continued to have dinner guests sign the table cloth, which became a virtual Who's Who in aviation and is now at the Smithsonian Air and Space Museum in Washington, D.C.*

25. *Jimmy retired from the Army Air Corps and accepted a position with Shell Petroleum Company.*

26. *John, Joe and Jim, Jr. in their home in St. Louis.*

27. John, Jimmy, and Jim, Jr.

28. Jimmy believed racing would help to develop faster planes and better fuel as well as keep Shell's name before the public.

29. Jimmy won the 1932 Thompson Trophy in the Gee Bee.

30. Jimmy took Joe on a trip around the world in 1933. This picture was taken in Peking. General Linson E. Dzau of the Chinese Air Force; Joe; Mrs. Jack Jouette, wife of the former commander of the Chinese aviation school at Hangchow; film producer Mark L. Moody; Jimmy.

31. Joe frequently traveled with Jimmy for Shell.

33. Jimmy standing in front of a B-25—the type of plane he flew in the raid on Tokyo.

32. General Henry H. "Hap" Arnold asked Jimmy what plane could take off from a 500-foot runway fully loaded with bombs. He selected Jimmy to lead the Tokyo Raid.

34. Crew #1 (left to right) Lt. Henry A. Potter (navigator); Lt. Col. James H. Doolittle (pilot); S/Sgt. Fred A. Braemer (bombardier); Lt. Richard E. Cole (co-pilot); S/Sgt Paul J. Leonard (engineer-gunner).

35. Doolittle's B-25 taking off from the USS Hornet.

36. Jimmy sits by the wreckage of his B-25 on a Chinese hillside. Dejected, he believed the mission was a failure. This photograph was taken by Paul Leonard.

37. *Jimmy was promoted to brigadier general after the raid, skipping the rank of colonel. It was rare for anyone to skip a rank, even in war time.*

38. *President Roosevelt pins the Medal of Honor on Doolittle. "I'll spend the rest of my life trying to earn it," Jimmy told Hap Arnold. (left to right) General Henry H. "Hap" Arnold, Joe Doolittle, Jimmy Doolittle, General George C. Marshal, and President Franklin D. Roosevelt (seated)*

39. Joe interviewed Bob Hope for her weekly radio program Broadway Matinee. *Bob and Delores Hope were good friends of the Doolittles.*

40. Joe also interviewed Eleanor Roosevelt for her Broadway Matinee *radio program. She and the First Lady shared an interest in many of the same causes.*

41. Joe attended many USO functions. Her pet project was helping soldiers readjust at the convalescent facility in Pawling, New York.

42. Joe regularly attended War Bond Rallies and fundraisers for the Red Cross.

43. Joe toured factories where she paid special attention to the women whose husbands and sons were in harm's way.

44. Joe launches the new aircraft carrier USS Shangri-La. *Rear Admiral Felix X. Gygax, the Navy Yard Commandant, is seen holding a microphone close to the champagne bottle as it smashes into the new carrier's bow.*

45. Jimmy rose from Major to Lieutenant General during the war years. He was awarded his fourth star in 1985.

46. *Lieutenant General Carl "Tooey" Spaatz; General George Patton; General James H. "Jimmy" Doolittle; Maj. General Hoyt S. Vandenberg; Maj. General O.P. Weyland.*

48. *Bob Hope and Francis Langford visited the troops with USO shows.*

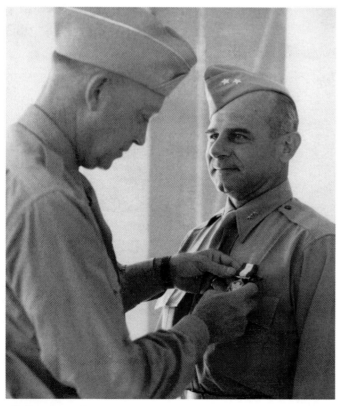

47. *Jimmy received his first Distinguished Service Medal from General Dwight D. Eisenhower in North Africa in 1943.*

"Jim, what airplane do we have that will take off in less than 500 feet, with a two thousand pound bomb load, and fly 2,000 miles?"

"General, give me a little time and I'll give you an answer."

Jimmy pondered the question for twenty-four hours. He narrowed the choices to the B-18, B-23 and the B-25, providing that they could be fitted with extra gas tanks.

The next day he reported back to Hap.

"Either the B-23 or the B-25," Jimmy said.

"One thing I forgot to tell you," Arnold said. "The plane must take off from a narrow area not over 75 feet wide."

"Then the B-25's your plane. The B-23's wingspan would make it a close call," Jimmy said. "Now can you tell me why you asked the question?"

"The idea is to load medium range bombers onto the deck of an aircraft carrier, and take them within striking distance of Japan. Army pilots will take off, bomb military targets in the Japanese homeland, and fly to safety in China." Arnold said. "Your choice of the B-25 confirms Duncan's calculations."

Jimmy immediately warmed to the idea.

"Jim, I need someone to take over this job…"

"And I know where you can get that somebody," Jim said, before Hap could finish the sentence.

"Okay, Jim. It's your baby. You'll have first priority on anything you need to get the job done. Get in touch with me directly if anyone gets in your way."

Duncan took over planning for the Navy's part of the operation dubbed Special Aviation Project Number 1, an operation that would eventually be called the Tokyo Raid.

Meanwhile, Jimmy oversaw the design and installation of additional gas tanks. In Maryland, Edgewood Arsenal manufactured special incendiary cluster bombs.

Only a few key individuals knew about the proposed operation. Mission success depended on total secrecy. If word leaked out, Japan, with her numerically superior Air Force and Navy, would be lying in wait.

On January 28, 1942, Hap Arnold met with President Roosevelt to discuss ideas for bombing Japan from China and Russia. He did not discuss a carrier-based mission. Only five men knew of the plans for the Tokyo Raid: King, Arnold, Duncan, Low and Doolittle. Secrecy was imperative.

The search for pilots and planes narrowed down to the 17th Bombardment Group commanded by Lt. Col. William C. Mills, and its associated 89th Reconnaissance Squadron, under Major John A. "Jack" Hilger. The units were sent to Eglin Field in Florida.

Squadron commanders Captains Edward J. "Ski" York, Al Rutherford and Karl Baumeister whittled the list to twenty-four crews. Every man had volunteered for the secret mission.

On March 3rd, Jimmy called the men together.

Jimmy looked around the room at the assembly of airmen. A ripple of excitement spread through the troops. Each airman waited anxiously to meet the new commander and discover what the topsecret mission entailed.

The room went dead silent as Jimmy walked up to the podium. Every man in the room had heard of Jimmy Doolittle and his accomplishments in aviation.

"Men, the mission we face is extremely dangerous." Jimmy said, as he looked around the room, making eye contact with as many men as possible. "I want only volunteers. Anyone can drop out for whatever reason and nothing will ever be said about it."

No one moved. Jimmy restrained a smile.

"Sir," a young pilot from the center of the room raised his hand.

"Yes," Jimmy answered.

"Can you give us any more information?"

"No. You might guess why we're doing certain things, but the entire operation is top secret, and I don't want you discussing your guesses, even among yourselves. There's no way to tell who else might be listening."

Jim stopped talking and looked around the room, again making eye contact.

"I can't stress enough the need for secrecy. Any violation could mean the lives of hundreds of people would be at risk. Be careful of rumors. And if anyone gets particularly nosy about why we're at Eglin or what we're doing, give me his name and the FBI will take it from there."

"This mission will require teamwork in getting your planes in shape. Pilots, your job is to learn how to take your B-25's off in the shortest possible distance with heavy loads. I want every man to understand the jobs of each crew member and be able to fill them in an emergency."

Again, he looked at the men assembled before him. No one spoke. Each man focused on Doolittle, the mood sober.

"This is Lieutenant Henry Miller from the U.S. Navy. He will assist with your training."

Hank Miller stepped forward, acknowledging Jimmy's introduction.

"We have about three weeks, maybe less, to get ready."

Jimmy watched the men as they filed out of the briefing room and past his office door. He knew it wasn't easy for a pilot to practice minimum-speed takeoffs. They were taught to have plenty of airspeed before lifting off. Now they would be required to yank their B-25's off the ground at near stalling speed, a maneuver that went against their natural instincts and required courage. He also knew they would succeed.

Jimmy walked out to the flight line, climbed into his own B-25 and awaited instructions from Hank Miller. He was determined to go on the mission along with his men. But at 45, if he couldn't pass the course, or wasn't as good as the younger pilots, he would give up the first seat and go along as a co-pilot.

The early weeks of training flew by, and in mid-March, less than a week before the planes were moved to California, Jim stood in the front of Arnold's desk.

"General," Jimmy said, "it occurred to me that I'm the only guy in this project who knows more about it than anyone else. You asked me to modify the planes and train the crews. This is being done. They're the finest bunch of boys I've ever worked with. I'd like your authorization to lead this mission myself."

Hap's smile disappeared.

"I'm sorry, Jim. I need you right here on my staff. I can't afford to let you go on every mission you might help to plan."

"General, these are boys we're sending on this mission. They deserve to have their leader with them," Jimmy continued, attacking the problem from every angle until Hap finally relented.

"All right, Jim," Hap put his right hand out, signaling stop. "It's all right with me, provided it's all right with Miff Harmon."

Brigadier General Millard F. Harmon, Jr., Hap's Chief of Staff, sat in his office down the hall from Arnold. Jimmy smelled a rat.

"Thank you, Sir." Jimmy said, saluting. Then, without another word, Jimmy turned and literally ran down the corridor to Miff's office. He knocked and, without waiting for an answer, opened the door.

"Miff," Jimmy said catching his breath. "I've just been to see Hap about that project I've been working on, and said I wanted to lead the mission. Hap said it was okay with him if it's okay with you."

"Well, whatever is all right with Hap is certainly all right with me." Miff said.

"Thank you, Sir," Jimmy said and closed the door. Just as he did, Jimmy heard Hap's voice on Miff's intercom.

"But Hap," Miff replied, "I just told him he could go."

Not waiting around for either general to change his mind, Jimmy rushed directly to Bolling Field, climbed into his B-25, and hightailed it back to Eglin.

★ ★ ★ ★

"TELL JIMMY TO GET ON HIS HORSE." The seven word signal arrived on March 23rd. Jimmy called his crews together.

"Men, prepare to move out." Jimmy said. "Don't tell anyone what you were doing here at Eglin—not your families, wives, anybody. The lives of your buddies and a lot of other people depend on you keeping everything you saw and did here a secret."

Excitement built. This was it!

He then dismissed all but twenty-two crews. The men dismissed would return to Columbia. The remaining twenty-two had different orders.

"You men are to take your planes to the air depot at McClellan Army Air Field, in Sacramento, California." He looked at their eager faces.

"En route," Jim continued, "You are to get some low-level navigational experience."

The men looked at each other. It was a rare treat to do some legal hedgehopping.

In the meantime, news from the Pacific was bad. Guam, Wake Island, and Hong Kong fell to the Japanese in December of 1941. On January 2, 1942, Manila fell, forcing the American troops under General Douglas MacArthur to withdraw to the Bataan peninsula. On March 1st, the Japanese defeated the U. S. Navy in the Battle of the Java Sea. They forced American and Philippine prisoners, from the defeat at Bataan, to march eighty-five miles in six days. 5,200 Americans died on the Bataan Death March. America desperately needed a victory. General Marshall looked to the Tokyo Raiders to provide that lift.

However, things were not progressing fast enough for Jimmy. Fuming over the leisurely pace and gross incompetence of the maintenance crews at McClellan, Jimmy called his men together for a briefing. He explained to Col. John M. Clark, commander of the depot, the work needed on the B-25's. He specified that NOTHING should be removed from the aircraft, and NO ONE should touch the carburetors. However, time after time, he discovered that the local mechanics ignored his orders.

"I want you men to stay with your planes and watch the work being done." Jimmy said, barely holding his temper in check. "Report, either directly to me or to Ski York, anything you don't like."

Within days, the complaints had multiplied so quickly that Jimmy called Washington.

"I need to speak to General Arnold," he said, brooking no argument or excuses.

"Hap," Jimmy said. "Things out here are going too slow. I'd appreciate it very much if you would build a fire under these people. They're treating this job as routine and that won't get it done in time."

After the phone call to Arnold, progress improved, but the civilian maintenance personnel still exhibited open resentment toward the Army crews.

The following day, Jimmy, standing with two of his pilots, heard the B-25's engine choke, once, twice, three times, as a civilian worker tried to start it. Eventually, the engine caught, followed by the bark of a loud backfire. Black smoke and flames poured out of the exhaust stacks.

Breaking away mid-sentence, Jimmy ran toward the plane.

"Shut the engine down!" he shouted. The mechanic either didn't hear, or ignored the instructions.

Fueled by anger, Jimmy climbed up into the cockpit and yelled into the man's ear.

"Shut this plane down, now!"

The shaken mechanic shut the engine off, as Jimmy continued shouting.

"What do you think you're doing?"

"I'm just following procedure," the mechanic replied. "An engine must be run up whenever carburetors are adjusted or changed."

For a fleeting moment, Jimmy literally saw red. Every one of those carburetors had been bench-checked at Eglin to run as lean as possible. He curbed his temper, but just barely. The mechanic was just following instructions. Blame, quite literally, belonged at the top. Obviously, his orders had not filtered down to the mechanics who actually did the work.

"Get out of this plane right now, and don't touch another of our B-25s unless I personally tell you to."

With that, Jimmy followed the mechanic out of the plane, and headed for Col. Clark's office.

April Fools day, 1942, broke sunny and warm. Jimmy called his men together. The planes still needed a little work, but there simply wasn't time to do anything more. He'd allow this next flight to shake out the problems.

"Your next stop is Alameda." Jimmy told the men. "I want each crew to get at least an hour's flying time before landing at the naval base."

Jimmy and Ski York met every plane as it landed at Alameda.

"How's your plane? Any malfunctions?" Jimmy asked, as the B-25 approached the flight line.

"It's fine, Sir." Lt. William Bower answered.

"Good, then taxi down to the ramp near the wharf."

One by one, Navy seamen loaded the bombers without any malfunctions onto the *USS Hornet*. As each engine shut down, Navy handlers drained the gas and hooked up the nose wheel tow bar. They towed the B-25's to the side of the *Hornet* and hoisted them aboard. Crewmembers followed their planes.

Bill Bower picked up his bag, and led his crew up the gangplank and onto the *Hornet*.

"Lieutenant William Bower reporting for duty," he said, saluting the officer of the deck.

"Good to see you, Bill," Hank Miller said, as the crew of the twelfth plane came aboard.

★ ★ ★ ★

Jimmy spotted Admiral William F. Halsey, Wu Duncan, and Miles Browning, Halsey's Chief of Staff, as he walked into the bar at the Fairmont Hotel in San Francisco. Always widely recognized, Jimmy turned heads as he crossed the room and joined the other men.

Nervous that Jimmy drew too much attention to their meeting, Halsey suggested that they retire to his room.

"Jim, what are your ideas if you're spotted before our planned takeoff?" Halsey asked.

Jim had spent long hours contemplating various scenarios.

"If we're within range of Japan, we'll go ahead and bomb our targets, fly out to sea, and wait to be picked up by your submarines."

"If we're within range of the Hawaiian Islands or Midway, we'll immediately take off and proceed to the closer of the two."

"You understand, Jim," Halsey said, "If we aren't within range of anything, I'll order the planes pushed overboard so we can clear the decks for our fighters to protect the task force."

Jimmy nodded his head, sobered by the thought.

The Navy took an extraordinary risk with this mission. The task force included sixteen ships. Loss of the two carriers, the cruisers and the destroyers, would critically jeopardize the American naval strength in the Pacific.

The afternoon of April 1st, the *Hornet* pulled into San Francisco Bay.

"You men have shore leave tonight," Jimmy told his crews as they met on the flight deck, "but remember, secrecy is of the utmost importance. One word could jeopardize the entire mission."

His announcement roused a spontaneous cheer. Jimmy watched as his boys made their way down the gangplank. They were just kids. He thought again about the dangers involved in bombing Tokyo.

This mission epitomized a calculated risk, one of many he'd taken in his lifetime, but the first in which he'd led men. If everything went as planned, they would bomb Japan, refuel in China, and deliver the planes to the 10th Air Force in Burma—with no American casualties. But if *anything* went wrong, any number of them could be killed, or, even worse, captured and imprisoned.

Jimmy, still deep in thought, walked down the gangplank and into a waiting cab.

"The Mark Hopkins," he told the driver as he settled down into the seat. The cab reeked of stale cigarette smoke, the windows smudged from a child's sticky fingers. Jimmy brushed a piece of lint from his khaki uniform pants, and checked the mirror-like shine of his brown shoes.

The cab pulled up in front of the Mark, and a bellman immediately opened the door. Paying the driver, Jimmy thanked the bellman and crossed the lobby to the bank of elevators.

"Understand you're moving out tomorrow," the elevator operator said.

The comment hit Jimmy like a punch to the gut. Certainly, the *Hornet* was sitting in the middle of San Francisco Bay with 16 Army Air Force bombers on deck, obviously ready to go somewhere. But who said tomorrow?

Jimmy felt a chill shudder up his spine. It would be very difficult to keep the mission a secret, and yet, secrecy was imperative to its success.

Still shocked by the elevator operator's casual remark, Jimmy walked down the hallway, to the room where Joe waited.

"I'll be out of the country for a while." Jimmy said, over an early breakfast the following morning.

Joe fiddled with the silverware. Jimmy, who had always shared his itinerary during civilian life, was back in uniform, and military rules applied. She wouldn't think of asking him where he was going.

She saw a trace of sadness, maybe a hint of concern, in his eyes, and reached across the small table, taking his hand in hers.

"Take care of the boys," he said, squeezing her hand.

★ ★ ★ ★

Joe smoothed out the wrinkles in his undershirt and folded it, handing it to Jimmy as he finished packing his B-4 bag later that morning. She watched him zip the last compartment, and lift the bag off the bed.

She fought hard to control the tears poised on the brink of spilling down her face. She felt it imperative to show Jimmy a brave countenance, so she smiled as naturally as she could manage, and kissed him good-bye.

He held her tight, much longer than usual.

"Godspeed," she whispered, as he turned and walked down the hall.

★ ★ ★ ★

Jim dropped his B-4 bag on the bed in Captain Mitscher's quarters. The small, but comfortable suite, situated under the flight deck, had an adjoining conference room, perfect for meetings and briefings. At first, Jimmy declined the offer of his quarters, but Capt. Mitscher insisted, and Jimmy finally acquiesced. He had to agree that the rooms would provide the privacy he needed to confer with his men.

Jimmy studied the messages delivered that morning. The first, from Hap, wished him good luck, and confirmed the requested arrangements for China. Jimmy smiled, a little relieved. He half expected Hap to rescind his permission to let Jimmy lead the raid.

A second message, from General Marshall, also wished him luck. The third, a handwritten note from Admiral King, lifted his spirits further.

"When I learned that you were to lead the Army air contingent of the *Hornet* expedition, I knew that the degree of success had been greatly increased. To you, your officers and men, I extend heartfelt wishes for success in your job and 'happy landings' and 'good hunting'."

Jimmy smiled, reading the note again, before joining his men on deck.

They watched as the first of the seven ships accompanying them sailed under the Golden Gate Bridge in bright daylight.

"Sir, if our mission is top secret, why are we leaving at a time when all of San Francisco can see the B-25's on the deck?" Nolan Herndon asked.

"Good question, son." Jimmy answered. "Your guess is as good as mine."

"Col. Doolittle," a Navy crewmember tapped Jimmy on the arm to get his attention, and then saluted.

Jimmy returned the salute.

"You have an urgent phone call. I'm to take you ashore."

Jimmy's heart sank. Certain it was Hap telling him he couldn't go on the mission, Jimmy mentally reviewed his arguments.

"General Marshall on the line, Colonel," the operator told Jimmy as he entered the room.

Jimmy's heart sank further. He'd been dreading this call for weeks. Hap was a friend, he could argue with Hap. But Marshall, well, Jimmy would never consider arguing with Marshall.

Jimmy accepted the phone.

"Doolittle." General Marshall's gruff voice rumbled over the line.

"Yes, sir."

"I just called to personally wish you the best of luck," the General said. "Our thoughts and our prayers will be with you. Good-bye. Good luck. And come home safely."

"Thank you Sir. Thank you." Jim's heart soared. Not only had he *not* been ordered off the ship, but the highest-ranked General of the United States Army had called to wish him luck.

As the task force set sail for Japan, Jimmy's crews gathered in the boardroom off the Captain's quarters. The men still hadn't been given their destination, and Jimmy decided to end the suspense.

"Our mission," he said, "is to bomb Tokyo, Yokohama, Kobe, Nagoya and Osaka. He looked around the room and saw relief on the men's faces.

"Again, I want to stress that this is a volunteer mission. Now that you know our destination, you might feel differently. If anyone wants out, there are plenty of crew members to take your place. No questions asked."

No one said a word. No one wanted out.

"Each pilot will choose primary targets and alternative targets. I will take off about three hours before the rest of you and drop incendiary bombs on Tokyo." Jimmy unrolled a map of Japan on the table.

"The balance of the planes will be divided into five flights of three bombers each. We will spread the mission over a fifty-mile front to give the illusion of a larger force and to dilute enemy air and ground fire."

He indicated the areas to be bombed on the map.

"The five flights are assigned as follows: Lieutenant Hoover, you are to cover the northern part of Tokyo. Captain Jones, you'll hit southern Tokyo. Captain York, your crews will bomb southern Tokyo and the north-central part of the Tokyo Bay area. The forth flight, led by Captain Ross Greening, will cover the southern part of Kanagawa, the city of Yokohama, and the Yokosuka Navy Yard. Hilger's flight will go around southern Tokyo, proceed to Nagoya, and break up, with one plane bombing Nagoya, one Osaka, and the third Kobe."

Every airman in the room watched the map, visualizing his course.

"You hit your targets and fly to Chuchow. Beacons will be set out to guide you. You refuel, and then you're off to Chungking, where you leave the plane for the 10th Air Force." Jimmy's finger rested on Chungking.

"Once the mission takes off, everyone is on his own. We will not fly in formation. There will be no radio communication of any kind. We want to avoid alerting the Japanese." Jimmy looked around the room.

"Any questions?"

No one raised his hand.

"This is Lieutenant Commander Stephen Jurika. Commander Jurika is the *Hornet's* intelligence officer and the former assistant naval attaché to Japan. He will be a great source of information on the location of targets."

Turning the meeting over to Jurika, Jimmy walked to the back of the room. Jurika had extensive knowledge of Japanese geography and the industrial areas. With his guidance, each crew selected primary targets and alternate targets to be hit if the weather or other conditions prohibited completion of mission primaries.

★ ★ ★ ★

As the last sliver of land receded off the stern, and the gray Pacific expanse blended into the horizon off the bow, Captain Mitscher's voice resounded over the *Hornet's* loudspeaker.

"This force is bound for Tokyo!"

Cheers sang out from every corner of the ship.

Day after day, they studied their maps. It was imperative that each pilot be able to identify his target from a low altitude. In order to avoid detection, the B-25's would be required to fly low over the Japanese landscape until they identified their target. At that point, they would pull up for proper distribution of the incendiary clusters, as well as, to avoid damage from fragments.

"Sir, what about the Temple of Heaven?" one of the crewmembers asked Jurika, referring to the Emperor's Palace.

Jim jumped to his feet.

"You are to bomb military targets only," he said. Some of the crewmembers avoided eye contact. Jimmy directed his comments to them.

"The Temple of Heaven is the home of Japan's venerated spiritual leader. It is of great spiritual and historic value to the Japanese. To bomb it will only serve to unite the people of Japan."

Jim walked up to the front of the room. "The palace is not a military target! You are also instructed to avoid hospitals, schools, and other non-military targets."

Still agitated by the idea that one of his men would willingly attack the palace, Jim continued. "Gentlemen, I was in London last year when the Luftwaffe bombed Buckingham Palace. There was very little damage to the building, but the attack served to further unite the British people."

Several days later Jimmy got word that the crews were drawing cards to see who would get the Emperor's Palace. At the next meeting Jimmy reiterated,

"It's not worth a plane factory, a shipyard, or an oil refinery, so leave the Imperial Palace alone!"

Fierce storms with gale force winds and heavy seas plagued the task force. Rain squalls and thick fog hampered visibility. Winds loosened the ropes that held down the planes, and mechanical difficulties cropped up on an hourly basis.

Jimmy made his way from one plane to the next, inspecting from the nose wheel lines to the false broomstick guns in the rear. He questioned the crews and shared their concerns over leaky hydraulic lines, fouled spark plugs and drippy gas tanks.

Gunners practiced shooting at kites from the *Hornet's* decks. Navigators took celestial shots, coordinating course and position along with the Navy navigators. Doc White gave lectures on first-aid and sanitation. The chaplain made himself available around the clock. Card games went late into the night. Even so, time weighed heavily on their hands.

News of the surrender of the American garrison on Bataan to overwhelming Japanese forces strengthened their resolve. They held daily bull sessions, discussing targets, and what they believed lay ahead.

"Colonel, what should we do if we lose an engine, or something else goes wrong, and we have to crash land in Japan?"

"Each pilot is in command of his own plane when we leave the carrier. He alone is responsible for the decision he makes for his own plane and crew. Each man must eventually decide for himself what he will do when the chips are down. Personally," Jimmy said, "I know exactly what I'm going to do."

Silence gripped the room, and then the same chap asked.

"Sir, what will you do?"

"I don't intend to be taken prisoner," Jimmy said. "I'm forty-five years old and have lived a full life. If my plane is crippled beyond any possibility of fighting or escape, I'm going to have my crew bail out and then I'm going to dive my B-25 into the best military target I can find."

He looked into the eager faces of his men, and continued, "You fellows are all younger and have a long life ahead of you. I don't expect any of the rest of you to do what I intend to do."

On April 13th, Admiral Halsey, on the *Enterprise,* rendezvoused with the *Hornet.* The combined task force totaled sixteen ships.

Rough seas tossed the ships around like toy boats in a bathtub. The task force pressed forward at maximum speed, making it impossible for the eight destroyers to keep up. On April 16th, the *Hornet* and *Enterprise,* risking serious handicap if attacked, left the destroyers behind.

On the 17th, the Enterprise launched a fighter to scout bomber patrols. Navy crews spotted the B-25's on the flight deck for take off. Jimmy's plane stood only 467 feet from the forward edge of the deck. The sixteenth airplane's tail extended over the stern. Two white lines, painted on the runway, marked the course, one for the left wheel and the other for the nose wheel. Lined up, the B-25's would miss the island on the right by six feet.

Captain Mitscher called Jimmy to the bridge.

"Jim, we're in the enemy's backyard now," he said. "Anything could happen from here on in. I think its time for that little ceremony we talked about."

"I think you're right," Jimmy answered.

Airmen and sailors gathered on the flight deck.

"Secretary of the Navy, Frank Knox asked me to return these to Japan," Captain Mitscher said, holding up three Japanese medals awarded to former Navy enlisted men. He passed the medals to Jimmy.

Walking to the first bomb, Jimmy attached the medals to the casing.

"Here, send this one, too!" Lieutenant Jurika said, adding a Japanese medal he'd received in 1940.

The troops gathered around the bombs.

"You'll get a BANG out of this!" one of the men wrote on a bomb.

Another added, "I don't want to set the world on fire, just Tokyo!"

Cheers went up around the deck.

"You men get your equipment packed," Jimmy said before the group broke up. "Make final inspections of your planes and meet me at 1500 hours in the briefing room."

"It looks like we might take off tomorrow instead of the 19th," Jimmy said when all the crews had assembled in the briefing room. "If all goes well, I'll take off so as to arrive over Tokyo at dusk. The rest of you will take off two or three hours later and can use my fires as a homing beacon."

"Gunners, remember to punch holes in the five-gallon gas cans when they're empty. And be sure to drop them all at once. We don't want a trail leading back to the fleet."

"I want to remind you once more to stay away from the Emperor's Palace. Any questions?"

No one spoke, so Jimmy continued.

"Get rid of all film, identification, orders, letters, diaries and anything that might link you to the *Hornet*, your units in the States or the places we trained. The Navy will mail anything you leave behind back to your homes."

Jimmy allowed a minute to pass in silence.

"You can still drop out if you need or want to. Again, no questions asked."

No one moved. Jim looked around the room at the boys. They were like sons to him and he wished each and every one of them well. He believed they were ready.

"One more thing, boys," he said before they left the room. "When we get to Chungking, I'm going to give you all a party."

The men stood and cheered—each hoped he'd be there to celebrate.

The throbbing of the *Hornet's* massive engines receded as Jimmy climbed up through the belly of his plane and into the cockpit later that evening. A tempestuous sky wrapped the night in heavy arms of fog, and the wind hurled fat raindrops against the windshield.

The countdown, which officially started with the loading of bombs, topping of gas tanks, and last-minute engine run-ups earlier in the day, ticked away in painful slowness. Jimmy's emotions played tug-of-war. If the task force remained undetected for another twenty-four hours, he believed all sixteen crews could deliver their payload of bombs, refuel, and turn over their planes to the 10th Air Force in Burma. Each mile brought them closer to probable success.

Jimmy looked over the flight deck. Deck crews had repositioned the planes as far back as possible, but the runway still looked critically short. He opened the hatch to inspect their supplies. Survival equipment included Navy gas masks, .45 automatics, clips of ammunition, hunting knives, flash lights, emergency rations, first aid-kits, canteens, compasses, and life jackets— enough for each crew member—stored by the engineer-gunner Paul Leonard. Each man had been issued a backpack parachute at Eglin. Jimmy stored his under the pilot's seat. Doc White drilled the men on the importance of keeping cuts and abrasions clean. Infection, he cautioned, spread easily, and had potentially dire consequences.

Jimmy checked the five-man life raft and wondered if they would need it. God willing, they would deliver all the supplies with the planes in Chungking.

The wind howled, pelting the deck with saltwater spray. The B-25 strained at her ties as the *Hornet* heaved on the thirty-foot swells.

Jimmy sat quietly, thinking about the men on his crew. He couldn't have asked for a better bunch of boys for his first combat mission. Young, eager, bright—they epitomized everything that was right in America, and he felt proud to lead them.

As pilot, he knew his own crew exceeded his expectations. He trusted his co-pilot, Dick Cole, implicitly, knowing the younger man would step up and take command if anything happened. He felt the same way about each of the men on his crew. Chance had landed him on his crew, due to a vacancy left by Captain Vernon Stinzi, but Jimmy knew he couldn't have done better if he'd handpicked each man. He believed every pilot on the raid felt the same way about hismen. Needless to say, their lives depended upon how well they worked together.

Jimmy climbed down from the plane and headed below deck. The flags snapped in the gusty winds. He pulled the collar of his leather jacket up around his ears, but cold, wet rivulets found their way down his neck and across his back.

Navigating the maze of corridors, he stopped at an open doorway and watched his men play cards with the *Hornet's* crew. The natural rivalry between Army Air Corps and Navy personnel had melted away with the announcement of their intended destination.

"Hey, Boss, you want to play?" Ski York asked when he spotted Jimmy.

"No, thanks," Jimmy answered. Never one to gamble on cards, he went back to the Captain's quarters and got ready to turn in.

Dark thoughts kept him company. They sailed in dangerous waters and risked discovery at any moment. The Japanese attack on Pearl Harbor had destroyed or damaged nearly half the Pacific Fleet. Jimmy tried not to dwell on negative scenarios, but the responsibility he felt for the lives of his men and the successful outcome of their mission made it difficult. He closed his eyes and willed himself to sleep.

The *Hornet* and *Enterprise,* accompanied by the reduced task force, made headway toward the Japanese homeland during the night. Heavy seas continued to batter the ships and high winds kept everyone not required on deck inside.

The sounding of General Quarters tore Jimmy from fitful sleep. His watch read 3:00 A. M. ship time. He felt the change in course as he pulled on his uniform and joined Captain Mitscher on the bridge.

"What gives?" Jimmy asked, after being admitted.

"Big 'E's' spotted two enemy craft." Mitscher answered. "We're changing course to avoid detection."

They exchanged knowing looks. Detection at this point would send all 16 bombers to the bottom of the ocean. Jimmy waited silently, his eyes searching, his ears listening, his heart pounding double-time. Eventually the All Clear sounded and the task force resumed its westerly course.

With dawn, the seas picked up. Large swells smacked at the *Hornet*, sending sheets of salt water over the deck. Rain squalls merged with the cresting waves, drenching the deck crews as they went about their duties.

Bitter winds drove rain against the window of the *Hornet*'s bridge. Jimmy shivered as he watched the *Hornet's* crew check the lines securing the bombers. A low ceiling of grey fog threatened to engulf the task force. Patrol planes, launched from the *Enterprise*, searched for an enemy presence. All eyes on the bridge scanned the horizon.

"One of the scout planes is returning," Mitscher said.

Jimmy watched as the plane passed low over the *Enterprise's* flight deck. A container dropped from the plane. Seconds later, a sailor scooped it up and ran for the bridge.

Jimmy and Mitscher waited in silence, eyes glued to the *Enterprise's* Bridge. Within minutes, Admiral Halsey ordered the fleet to alter course. Neither Jimmy nor Mitscher voiced the question. Had the scout been spotted?

"Sir, there's a small vessel about 20,000 yards directly to the northwest," the radar operator said. A light in the distance struggled to pierce the fog.

Mitscher looked over the man's shoulder. The even cadence of a single blip lit the screen.

"Sir," the radioman interrupted, "I'm intercepting a Japanese message from close by."

Another blip marked a location 12,000 yards straight ahead. Mitscher raised his binoculars. A Japanese picket boat rode the swells. A message from Admiral Halsey flashed to the *Nashville*. Within minutes the picket boat exploded.

"It looks like you'll be on your way soon," Mitscher said.

At 0800 hours, Halsey flashed a message from the *Enterprise* to the *Hornet*:

"LAUNCH PLANES X TO DOOLITTLE AND GALLANT COMMAND GOOD LUCK AND GOD BLESS YOU."

"Good luck, Jimmy," Mitscher said, shaking Jimmy's hand.

"Thank you, Marc . . . Safe sailing to you, too."

Jimmy ran to the Captain's cabin and grabbed his bag.

"Get your gear together," he said to a group of airmen. "We've been spotted!"

Before Jimmy had reached his plane, the ear shattering bellow of a Klaxon horn split the air, followed by a booming voice.

"Now hear this! Now hear this! Army pilots, man you planes!"

While the *Hornet* plunged headlong into mountainous waves, the bomber crews scrambled, slipping and sliding, to their B-25's. Navy deck handlers swarmed the planes, helping the airmen remove the engine and gun turret covers. They unfastened the ties, pulled the chocks, and maneuvered the B-25's into takeoff position.

Hank Miller ran up to Jim's plane.

"Watch the blackboard!" Miller shouted. "I'll be standing over by the island. I'll write any last-minute instructions, plus the carrier's headings."

He turned to Hank Potter, Jimmy's navigator. "Compare your plane's compass to my headings, and set your directional gyros."

Hank, like all the other navigators, worried about the compass calibrations. Two weeks on a carrier next to metal could really mess things up. If the overcast skies persisted, his sextant would be useless.

Sergeant Paul J. Leonard stowed his bag and toolbox, and helped the Navy deck crew position Jimmy's B-25. As soon as the plane was set, Paul chocked the wheels, climbed in and pulled the hatch shut.

"All ready, Sir," Paul said.

Jimmy started the engines and let them warm up. He looked out the window and spotted the deck-launching officer with the checkered flag. Once the engines warmed up, Jimmy flashed a thumbs-up.

Deck handlers pulled the chocks. Watching the *Hornet's* bow, the launching officer waved the flag in a circular motion.

Jimmy pushed the throttles forward to the stops. Just as the ship reached the bottom of her roll and the deck began her upward pitch, the launch officer swung the flag forward and dropped to the deck.

Jimmy released the brakes, aligned the wheels with the two white lines painted on the deck, and let her go.

He knew that the eyes of every man on the *Hornet* watched him expectantly—his takeoff would set the tone of the entire mission. If he failed, he knew his boys would try anyway, but his success would give them confidence.

The deck reached its maximum pitch and the B-25 lifted into the sky with feet to spare. It was 8:20 ship time. Instead of the planned 400 to 500 miles, the Raiders faced 824 statute miles to the targets in Tokyo.

Jimmy signaled for Dick to raise the landing gear. As the plane gained altitude, he leveled off and swung around, flying over the carrier so Hank could check his compass and set his directional gyroscope.

Jimmy settled back into his seat. The take off went well. He was certain his boys would have no trouble getting off the carrier.

Flying low, about 200 feet off the water, Jimmy focused his attention on the raid.

"I think that's Travis on our left," Paul reported thirty minutes into the flight.

Jimmy looked out the window. Sure enough, Travis Hoover's B-25 moved into loose formation.

An hour later, with Dick Cole at the controls, Jimmy spotted a Japanese ship under camouflage netting. He hoped the low ceiling concealed their plane. They wanted to visit Tokyo without advanced warning.

Jimmy checked the fuel consumption against the estimates. He knew the crews of all sixteen planes worried about the gas. The mechanics at McClellan concerned him, almost as much as the added miles. If the mechanics had adjusted any of the carburetors, it could spell disaster for the crews.

Thick fog still clung in layers over the ocean. Jimmy scanned the horizon. Travis held his position to the left. Jimmy peered through the windshield. A mass loomed straight ahead in the mist.

"What do you think that is?" Jimmy spoke into the interphone.

"I'm not sure, Boss." Dick answered.

The mass began to take shape. A large Japanese multi-motored land plane appeared to float at about 3,000 feet. It headed directly toward the task force. Still skimming the water at 200 feet, the B-25 escaped detection.

They hit landfall just above Inubo Shima, eighty miles north of Tokyo. Gradually the weather improved, allowing them visual contact with the island of Honshu. The Japanese people had been assured that their islands were sacred and protected from foreign invasion. They stopped their labors in the fields to wave to the planes flying overhead.

Airfields dotted the picturesque countryside and small planes, mostly bi-winged trainers, circled lazily in the sky.

"Enemy fighters at three o'clock," Dick called out over the interphone.

Paul identified them from the turret. Nine Japanese Zeroes, grouped in three flights of three, directly to their right. The crew collectively held their breath until the Zeroes had passed.

"There's the factory," Jimmy said as he pulled up to 1200 feet. "Fred, open the bomb doors, and release when ready."

Fred Braemer opened the bomb bay, and, using a makeshift bombsight, lined up the factory. As soon as he had the target in sight, he toggled off all four incendiaries in rapid succession.

The factory exploded in flames. The percussion from the explosion shook the plane. As soon as possible, Jimmy dropped back down to rooftop level, skirting the western edge of the city.

As they sped toward the coast, Jimmy spotted an aircraft factory. A dozen completed planes sat like ducks on the flight line.

"Do you want me to strafe that field, Boss?" Paul asked, almost reading Jimmy's mind.

Jimmy looked longingly at the line of planes. He'd like nothing more than to destroy them. But word of the attack on Tokyo would be out and any American downed in Japan would face certain torture and death.

"Better not, Paul," he answered with one last wistful look at the field.

"Five enemy fighters approaching from the rear," Paul called out.

Jimmy spotted two hills jutting up from the countryside at 11 o'clock. He kept the bomber at low altitude, and pulled around the first hill, hugging close in the top curve of an S-turn. The fighters followed suit, breaking formation to hug the side of the hill. Quickly changing direction, Jim swung the B-25 around the second hill, completing the S-turn. Unaware of his maneuver, the five fighters continued on their way in the opposite direction.

Staying low, he ducked between hills until they reached the China Sea. Once over the water, he skimmed the surface.

Hank Potter called out the coordinates, heading set to Yakushima.

The weather deteriorated further. Waterspouts developed over the rough seas, and thick clouds massed, forming a ceiling at around 600 feet.

Banking west they encountered a headwind. Jimmy checked the fuel gauges.

"If this headwind continues, we'll run out of gas in about 135 miles," Hank informed the rest of the crew.

Jimmy looked out over the water. Sharks swam just below. Three Japanese Navy vessels and numerous fishing boats dotted the surface. He found the idea of ditching in the China Sea less than appealing.

But luck or divine intervention prevailed. The B-25 picked up a tailwind of 25 knots. Jimmy breathed a sigh of relief and said a silent prayer of thanks.

"Any luck raising Chuchow?" he asked Dick.

"No, sir. There's no response."

Gray clouds gathered and settled in for the night. The lack of visibility made skimming dangerous. Mindful of the fuel shortage, Jimmy pulled up to 6,000 feet, relying on instruments.

"Still no contact with Chuchow?" he asked.

"No, Boss, not a peep."

Occasionally, faint lights punctured the haze, pulling them off course, but Hank watched the coordinates, posting them at regular intervals.

Everyone on board knew hisodds of landing safely in Chuchow evaporated in radio silence. Nervously, each pilot and navigator checked the gauges. Their critically low fuel dictated their course.

Paul removed the film from the cameras in the rear of the fuselage and tucked the rolls into his shirt.

Jimmy looked out at the inky black sky, then down at the fuel gauge. The needle rested on empty. Time was up.

CHAPTER 14

I AM AN AMERICAN

"Lieutenant General James H. Doolittle is less well known than any other top-ranking officer. Through the years, stories of Doolittle's flying feats have created a picture of a sort of one-man flying circus. But the real Jimmy, far from being the grandstander that most people imagine him to be, is a self-effacing team man all the way. Everybody under him worships him, and would go through hell if he ordered it."

—Arthur Bartlett, *Los Angeles Times,* May 14, 1944

"BRAEMER, you jump first. Followed by Potter, Leonard and Cole. I'll drop you in as straight a line as possible." Jimmy said. "Try to space yourselves and hopefully we'll be able to find each other."

Jimmy watched as Dick dropped from the escape hatch and disappeared into the night. He took one last look around, shut off both gas cocks, and moved to the lower hatch. With palpable tenderness, he saluted the B-25, and then jumped into the void. The darkness engulfed him. Doolittle and his crew had no way of knowing whether they had jumped over Chinese-held, friendly territory, or territory already occupied by the Japanese.

Jimmy worried about his ankles. They had never fully recovered from his fall in Chile. A broken bone or two would slow his escape.

Air rushed past him, catching in the opening 'chute, jerking him hard before cradling him in silence.

Anticipating the landing, Jimmy bent his knees. He hit the ground, and kept going. His feet struck the liquid surface of a rice paddy. His bottom followed.

Submerged to his neck in water and "night soil," Jimmy struggled to his feet and unclipped his parachute. Thoroughly chilled, he sloshed through the rice paddy, his feet sinking into the mud. A small farmhouse, not more than a hundred yards away, stood adjacent to the rice paddy. Jimmy waded toward it.

Finally, he reached the farmhouse and banged on the door.

"*Lushu hoo megwa fugi*," he said, depending on the phrase Lt. Commander Stephen Jurika had taught all the men on the raid. "I am an American."

Shivering from head to toe, he pounded again. The lights went out, and the bolt slid shut on the other side of the door. Jimmy wrapped his arms around his wet body for warmth. Obviously, the inhabitants of the farmhouse weren't interested in helping an American.

Jimmy tried one last time before wandering on. His wet trousers clung to his legs. An icy cold rain began to fall. He stumbled across the uneven ground, eventually coming upon a dirt road.

With mud squishing out of his boots, and wet skin rubbing blisters against his hard leather boots, he trudged on.

About a half mile down the road, he spotted a large wooden box suspended between two sawhorses. Teeth chattering and cruelly cold wind whistling in his ears, he climbed up onto the sawhorses, pushed aside the cover, and dropped into the box.

Jimmy's feet touched someone.

"*Lushu hoo megwa fugi*," he said, before realizing that the resident couldn't care less.

Jimmy reached down and lightly brushed his hands over the face. A long, thin beard sprouted from a man's chin. His skin felt cold, even to Jimmy's frozen fingers.

The wind pummeled the open box. Jimmy hadn't stopped shivering. At least the coffin offered a little shelter from the elements.

"Care for a little company?" he asked, as he settled down next to the old Chinese man, and pulled the cover back into place.

But the relentless wind seeped through the wood, penetrating his wet clothing and reaching into his bones.

Jimmy climbed out of the coffin and made his way back to the road. The wind wailed with greater intensity, hurling raindrops in every direction. Eventually, Jimmy came upon an old, broken-down water mill. Relieved to find a relatively dry shelter, Jimmy curled up in a corner, away from the draft seeping under the door.

He tried to settle himself against the wall, but he couldn't get comfortable. He wondered about his crew. Were they safe? Warm and dry? Protected by friendly Chinese? Prisoners of the Japanese? What about the 15 other crews? Had any landed safely? Unable to quiet his thoughts, or warm his body, Jimmy tried to exercise to build up some body heat. His damp clothes refused to move when he did, irritating his skin.

The night dragged on, and physical comfort eluded him. His uniform, retained fragments of night soil and reeked of human feces. He rubbed his hands together, then crossed and rubbed his arms, but the friction did little to warm him.

Morning came, and, although the rain had stopped, the gray overcast still clung to the earth. Stiff and cold, Jim left the mill and found the road. He followed the muddy path in the weak morning light, until he stumbled upon an old Chinese farmer.

"*Lushu hoo megwa fugi*," Jimmy said.

The old man stared at him.

"American," Jimmy said, pointing to his chest. "I am an American."

The old farmer still stared.

Jimmy withdrew a damp pad of paper from his flight suit. He drew a picture of a train, added a question mark, and passed it to the old farmer.

The farmer nodded, smiled and motioned for Jimmy to follow.

For a mile, Jim walked in silence beside the old farmer. They stopped, not at the train depot, but the local Chinese military headquarters.

The Major eyed Jimmy from head to toe, and then held his hand out for Jimmy's gun.

"No," Jimmy said, shaking his head. "I'm an American."

Jimmy made eye contact and held it. "American. Ally of the Chinese."

The Major eyed him dubiously. Three soldiers, cradling Tommy guns, stepped closer.

"I parachuted out of an American plane last night," Jimmy explained. "I'll take you to my parachute."

Jim retraced his steps along the narrow road, past the old mill and the old Chinese man in his coffin. He walked with the Major, surrounded by about a dozen armed soldiers. Finally they arrived at the farmhouse and Jim walked to the edge of the rice paddy.

His parachute wasn't there.

The soldiers muttered between themselves. The Major looked at Jimmy, disbelief clearly stamped on his face.

"I banged on their door last night," Jim said indicating the nearby farmhouse, "Ask them, I'm sure they'll tell you."

Still skeptical, the Major led the way to the farmhouse and knocked on the door.

A farmer, his wife, and two children stood before them shaking their heads. Jimmy stood in silence as soft Chinese whispering filled the morning. Denial, he guessed, from the constant head shaking of the farmer and his family, and agreement from the soldiers.

"They say they heard no noise during the night. They say they heard no plane. They say they saw no parachute," the Major said, a menacing look on his face. "They say you lie."

A cold sweat broke out on Jimmy's forehead.

A soldier stepped forward, reaching for Jimmy's gun. Jimmy stepped backward.

"I am an American officer," he said. "My crew and I bombed Tokyo yesterday and bailed out last night."

The Major watched him with continuing disbelief. Jim wondered if his men were experiencing similar situations. He saw the
suspicion in the Major's eyes. Nothing he said convinced the man.
They stood face to face, neither backing down.

Scuffling from the farmhouse drew their attention. Two
soldiers with broad smiles carried Jimmy's parachute.

A matching smile split the Major's face as he reached out to
pump Jimmy's hand. Still smiling, he turned, and in rapid Chinese,
gave orders to his men.

Within minutes, they had secured a small meal from the
farmer's wife. A band of soldiers went off in search of Jim's crew.

Escorted back to headquarters, Jimmy received a warm meal
and a much needed bath. Unfortunately, although dry, his uniform still smelled.

The Chinese search party found the other members of Jimmy's
crew and brought them back to headquarters. By day's end, all five
men had been reunited.

Early the following morning, Jimmy and Paul Leonard climbed
the hillside to the spot where their B-25 went down. Jimmy's heart,
already heavy, sank further as he surveyed the wreckage.

The Mitchell bomber hit just below the crest of a hill and scattered debris over several acres. One engine, ripped away on impact,
nestled among rocks at the foot of the hill, marking one boundary.
A wing panel, flung a quarter mile away, marked another.

Jimmy and Paul dug through the debris, looking for anything
worth salvaging. Their efforts came a day too late. The wreckage,
picked over by scavengers, yielded nothing useable. Even Jimmy's
uniform blouse, stained across the chest with oil, had been stripped
of its brass buttons.

Jimmy sat on the ground next to the wing of his shattered
plane and dropped his head into his hands.

He had failed his first combat mission. He had lost his own
aircraft and had no idea where the others were. Because of the
silence from Chuchow, he doubted any of his planes had found
the airstrip. In all likelihood, they had all perished. Never in his
life had Jimmy felt such failure.

Only God knew where his boys were. Scattered across the Chinese countryside, he had no way of knowing if they were safe. If they had fallen into the hands of the Japanese. If they were alive. He could account only for the four men on his own crew.

Paul snapped a picture and then sat on the ground next to his boss.

"What do you think will happen when you go home, Colonel?"

"Well, I guess they'll court-martial me and send me to prison at Fort Leavenworth."

"No, sir. I'll tell you what will happen. They're going to make you a general."

Jimmy smiled weakly and shook his head.

"And," Paul continued, "They're going to give you the Congressional Medal of Honor."

Jimmy smiled again, knowing that Paul was trying to cheer him, but the smile didn't quite reach his eyes.

"Colonel, I know they're going to give you another airplane and when they do, I'd like to fly with you again as your crew chief."

Tears filled Jimmy's eyes and spilled down his cheeks.

"Thank you, Paul," Jimmy said. "If I ever have another airplane and you want to be my crew chief, I would be honored to have you."

As much as Jimmy appreciated Paul's efforts, he believed that when Washington received word of the mission's outcome, he would either be court-martialed or spend the balance of his career flying a desk.

By the time Jimmy and Paul returned to headquarters, four more crews had been rescued. Although relieved to discover the fate of 20 more men, Jimmy still worried about the 55 boys still missing. With a heavy heart, he wired Hap Arnold:

"TOKYO SUCESSFULLY BOMBED. DUE TO BAD WEATHER ON CHINA COAST BELIEVE ALL AIRPLANES WRECKED FIVE CREWS FOUND SAFE IN CHINA SO FAR."

On April 28, 1942, Jimmy received a promotion to Brigadier General, and Hap Arnold ordered him to return to Washington "by any means possible" and "in the shortest possible time" with "absolutely no publicity."

The mission, in Jimmy's eyes, failed. Little by little, news of his boys trickled in—much of it bad: Leland Faktor died bailing out; W. J. Dieter and D. E. Fitzmaurice drowned after ditching in the water: Dean E. Hallmark, Chase J. Nielsen, Robert J. Meder, William G. Farrow, George Barr, Harold A. Spatz, Robert L. Hite and Jacob DeShazer were captured by the Japanese; Edward J. "Ski" York, Nolan Herndon, Theodore H. Laban, Robert G. Emmens and David W. Pohl were interned by the Russians when they landed near Vladivostok; Russia. All sixteen of his planes had been lost.

★ ★ ★ ★

Jimmy boarded a China National Airways Corporation 21-passenger DC-3 in Chungking on May 5, 1942. Piloted by Captain Moon Chin, a native of Baltimore, Maryland, the plane took off and headed for Myitkina, Burma.

Jimmy settled into his seat. His tattered uniform, although washed, still retained the stench from the rice paddy, and he pitied the man sitting next to him in the closed airplane. As the plane lifted into the sky, Jimmy thought about the troops still in China. Every man expected to return to the United States after the mission, and Jimmy believed himself just the first to receive orders.

The raid on Japan was *not* a suicide mission. Every man believed he would successfully bomb his primary target, and then deliver his plane to Chungking. They each knew the risk, especially after being forced to take off early, but every one of them believed they would return safely.

Jim stretched his legs, leaned back in his seat, and closed his eyes. He'd had precious little sleep since bailing out over China, and the fatigue finally caught up with him. He still didn't know the fate of some of his men, and the thought of those suffering at the hands of the Japanese gave him nightmares. The psychological effect of an American attack on the Japanese homeland carried swift and brutal repercussions. Madame Chiang Kai-shek assured him that they were doing everything possible to secure the release of the two crews, but nothing had happened to free them yet.

Lulled by the drone of the engines, Jimmy's head nodded, and he surrendered himself to a brief nap.

Awakened by the change in cabin pressure as the DC-3 began her descent, Jimmy looked out the window. An isolated airfield stretched out in the middle of thick vegetation.

"Where are we?" Jimmy asked Chin when he emerged from the cockpit.

"An emergency field about an hour out," he answered. "The airport at Myitkina is under attack from Japanese fighter planes. We'll wait here until we get the all clear."

Jim followed the other passengers down the ramp. An hour later, Chin joined him.

"We're clear," Chin said. "Let's load up and go."

The flight was short. Before long, the DC-3 circled the airstrip at Myitkina. They landed without incident, but as soon as the plane stopped, refugees fleeing from the Japanese mobbed it.

Chin opened the doors, and as locals refueled the DC-3, he began loading passengers.

Jimmy watched the cabin fill with bodies. Frail old men, women clutching babies to their chests and dragging toddlers, old women with bundles strapped to their backs. One after another they boarded the plane. The DC-3 holds twenty-one passengers. Jimmy counted thirty, then forty, then fifty.

"I hope you know what you're doing," Jimmy said to Chin, as the last of sixty passengers climbed aboard.

"We're fighting a war over here. You do lots of things here you wouldn't do at home," Chin responded.

Jimmy looked over the motley collection of humanity. Most of the refugees were small of stature; many were children. He settled back into his seat, and mentally calculated the odds of a safe takeoff and flight.

The Gooney Bird revved her engines, then sped down the runway. Within minutes she lifted easily into the sky and turned toward Calcutta. The air in the cabin quickly turned stale. Babies, pressed against their mothers, whimpered but did not cry. An old man's phlegm-filled cough rattled his chest and the odor of fear and promise filled the cabin. Chin was right: in war you did things differently.

Looking out the window, Jimmy discovered the profile of Calcutta and felt the plane descend. As the DC-3 bumped her way onto the runway, wide-eyed children fell silent. A swift wave of chatter swept through the cabin as passengers pressed toward the cabin door.

After four hours in the cramped quarters of the overloaded airplane, Jimmy debarked. Stretching, he turned to thank Moon Chin. As he did, the rear baggage compartment popped open and eight more disheveled Chinese tumbled out.

His four days in Calcutta included a reunion with several more of his boys. The night before he left, they threw Jimmy a little going away party, gifting him with a chamber pot as a remembrance of the "screamers"—a malady they all shared in some degree since their arrival in China.

Two weeks after leaving Chunking, Jimmy arrived in Washington, D.C. Hap Arnold sent a staff car to meet him.

"Hap," Jimmy said, sitting across the desk from his commander. "I lost all sixteen planes. One of my men died bailing out, two drowned after ditching, and eight were captured by the Japanese. God only knows what they're going through."

Struggling to hide the depth of his emotions, Jimmy got up and walked to the window. "Four of my boys are seriously injured and five are being held as prisoners in Russia. I find it hard to consider that a successful mission."

"Jim, you're not looking at the big picture. The Japanese never thought their homeland would be attacked. The raid forced them to pull back troops to protect it," Hap said, talking to Jimmy's back.

"What's more, your boys boosted American morale when it was at the lowest point. Jim, you and your boys are American heroes."

Jimmy turned to look at Hap. He didn't feel like a hero, not with his boys still in Japanese and Russian hands.

★ ★ ★ ★

Every time the telephone rang, Joe's heart raced just a little, and she'd think, "Maybe it's Jimmy." This time was no different, but when she heard Hap's voice, her heart stopped for just a second, fearing bad news.

But Hap had no news at all, really—just a request for her to return to Washington. She'd heard news reports about the bombing of Tokyo and suspected that Jimmy had been involved, but wasn't sure. Hap didn't sound upset, so she assumed everything was all right.

She'd been in California with her family since early April, while Jimmy trained in Florida. Following her father's death, just two weeks after Jimmy set sail on the *Hornet*, Joe had no desire to return to an empty apartment.

"Of course, Hap," she said. "I'll come directly."

Bags needed packing, laundry needed doing, and perhaps she and Gracie could share one last dinner before she left.

"Today?" she asked Hap. "This afternoon? Well, of course I can be ready." She looked at her watch and mentally shrugged. Living with Jimmy kept her agile. Luckily, Gracie didn't live far from the airport.

She had no idea why Hap Arnold wanted her in Washington, D.C., and she didn't ask. But she suspected it had something to do with the raid on Tokyo.

Joe packed her bags in record time, and stood in the foyer hugging her little sister goodbye.

"Take care of yourself," Joe said. Gracie had withered away to a mere waif since her battle with tuberculosis, and Joe worried about her.

With one last hug, Joe toted her bag to the curb. The cab driver hoisted it into the trunk.

She settled into her seat on the commercial flight and used the opportunity to catch up with some of her letter writing.

Afternoon sunlight gave way to dusk, followed by the deep shadows of night. Joe shifted in her seat, trying to get comfortable. The man sitting in the aisle seat beside her, snored lightly in his sleep. She didn't want to wake him. She resigned herself to a certain level of discomfort. They weren't too far from Pittsburgh. She could use the facilities there before catching her flight to D.C.

The plane touched down in Pittsburgh, and Joe gathered her belongings. Her clothes had "sitting wrinkles" and a layer of invisible grime coated her face and arms.

She checked her watch and sighed with anticipated relief. She had time to use the facilities and perform a quick sponge bath before catching her connection to Washington.

Joe waited for most of the passengers to clear before leaving her seat. She stepped out of the plane into the fresh air. The cool morning breeze felt wonderful after spending the night cooped up in the small plane.

She gripped the metal handrail, picked up her briefcase with the other hand, and climbed down the steps onto the tarmac.

"Mrs. Doolittle?"

"Yes?" Joe turned at the sound of her name. A young lieutenant waited on the tarmac.

"General Arnold sent his plane to take you to Washington," he said, retrieving her bags from the baggage compartment.

"How nice," she said, hiding her discomfort, "but first do you mind if I make a quick stop…"

"We've got to hurry, Ma'am," he said, steering her by the elbow toward Hap's plane.

With a deep breath, Joe climbed into the plane, trying not to focus on the growing pressure in her bladder.

With priority clearance, the plane moved to the head of the line and took off within minutes of loading. Like most military planes, female passengers had not been taken into consideration when installing facilities.

Joe attempted to smooth the wrinkles from her skirt and jacket. Her hat sagged on her head, and her white hair hung limp and lifeless around her face.

Flying with Jimmy had taught her control, but her situation had become desperate. Any minute, she feared, her eyes would turn yellow. Afraid to either laugh or cough, she tried to focus on anything but moving water.

Joe pulled her hat off and ran her hands through her hair. Her face and neck felt sticky. She longed for a warm washcloth, and to use the toothbrush she carried in her purse.

The Potomac River meandered across the landscape below the plane. Joe averted her eyes. Beads of moisture built up on the outside of the plane and ran in rivulets down the window. She turned away. Everywhere she looked, she saw water. All she could think about was relieving herself.

Finally, the plane touched down in Washington, D.C. Joe braced herself, suspending her body slightly on her hands to absorb any bouncing.

Carefully, she stood, smoothing the army of wrinkles from her skirt with sweaty hands. She ran her tongue over the film on her teeth. Her mouth felt dry. She blew into her cupped hand and cringed. Maybe she'd have an extra minute before meeting Hap.

A staff car, engine running, waited next to the plane. Before Joe reached the bottom step, her bags had already been loaded into the trunk and the passenger door held open.

"I need to make a quick stop," Joe said, trying to keep the panic out of her voice.

"Ma'am, we've got to hurry."

"I've got to hurry, too! No matter where we're going, it can't be as important as where I need to go!"

"Mrs. Doolittle, I'm sorry, but we're due at the White House in ten minutes."

★ ★ ★ ★

Jimmy stood on the street outside his apartment waiting for the staff car. Within minutes of the phone call, General Arnold's car pulled up.

Surprised to see General Marshall sitting next to Hap in the back seat, Jimmy snapped to attention and saluted. He climbed into the front seat and the trio rode in silence for a few minutes.

"Can you tell me where we're headed, Hap?" Jimmy asked turning to look over the back of the seat.

"Jim, we're going to the White House." Hap said.

"Well, I'm not a very smart fellow and I don't want to embarrass anyone." Jimmy said after brief period of silence. "What are we going to do there?"

"The President is going to give you the Medal of Honor." General Marshall answered.

A cloud of emotion darkened Jimmy's face and mood.

"General, that award should be reserved for those who risk their lives trying to save someone else. Every man on our mission took the same risk I did. I don't think I'm entitled to the Medal of Honor."

Hap, his face flushed red with anger, bit back an angry retort.

"I happen to think you do," Marshall said.

An awkward silence filled the car. Marshall, the highest ranking officer in the Army, scowled in the back seat. Hap Arnold glowered beside him and Jimmy brooded in the front.

Jimmy felt strongly that the Medal of Honor should not be given for individual feats like shooting down a number of enemy planes or bombing enemy targets. Anything less than its true intention—saving the lives of others in combat—cheapened the honor.

★ ★ ★ ★

Jimmy turned when the door opened.

"Hello, Doolittle," Joe said her eyes suddenly glassy with unshed tears. "How are you?"

Jim couldn't remember ever seeing a more beautiful sight. He wanted to call her from the apartment, but he had been ordered not to contact anyone.

"Hello, Duchess," he replied, crossing the room in long strides and embracing her.

Hap and Marshall exchanged smiles.

"General Marshall," Joe said, extending her hand. "It's nice to see you again."

"It's good to see you, Joe," Marshall said taking her hand.

"Now you see why I wanted you to come to Washington," Hap said hugging Joe.

"I'm not quite sure why we're at the White House."

"The President is giving Jimmy the Congressional Medal of Honor." Marshall answered.

Joe looked over at Jimmy. His scowl had returned.

"May I ask one favor, General?" Joe turned back to General Marshall. "I left Los Angeles at 4:15 yesterday afternoon. May I please, just have five minutes in a White House bathroom?"

"Of course."

But just then a door opened to the Oval Office.

"The President will see you now," a White House aide said.

Joe took a deep breath, said a little prayer, and followed the men into the room. Franklin Roosevelt, backlit by an open window, sat behind his desk. His eyes, heavily smudged with shadows of fatigue, lit up when Jimmy entered.

"Jimmy, I'm proud of you," he said, shaking Jimmy's hand. "All of America is proud of you, and as their President, it is my privilege to present you with the Medal of Honor."

"Thank you, Sir."

"This raid on Japan had the precise favorable effect on American morale that I hoped for."

Joe smiled as a presidential aide handed General Marshall the citation. Marshall, hunched slightly forward, read the words printed on the scrolled page:

For conspicuous leadership above and beyond the call of duty, involving personal valor and intrepidity at an extreme hazard to life. With the apparent certainty of being forced to land in enemy territory or to perish at sea, General Doolittle personally led a squadron of Army bombers, manned by volunteer crews, in a highly destructive raid on the Japanese mainland.

★ ★ ★ ★

When Marshall finished reading, he rolled the citation and handed it to Joe.

Jimmy stepped forward.

Joe held the citation tightly with both hands, twisting it slightly as she watched the President pin the Medal of Honor on Jim's blouse. She was so proud of him. She wished her parents had lived long enough to see Jimmy receive the highest honor in the country.

"Thank you, Mr. President," Jimmy said, as he turned and followed the aide out of the Oval Office.

"Now if you'll excuse me for a minute," Joe said almost running down the hall.

"Congratulations, Jim," Hap said when they reached the front steps of the White House.

Jimmy touched the medal pinned to his chest.

"I'll accept this on behalf of all the boys who were on the raid because they shared the same risk I did," he said, looking directly into Hap's eyes. "And spend the rest of my life trying to earn it."

CHAPTER 15

★ ★ ★ ★

"DEAREST JOE;"

"The era of World War II was a high
point in the history of our country.
It was a time of great patriotism,
duty and courage, but it was also a
time of great sacrifice for many at
home and for those in the military
service. It produced great men and
outstanding leaders who would
bring our country to the pinnacle
of glory and honor. It would forge
men of character into roles of
world leadership that would bring
peace to a world which had nearly
been destroyed by tyranny."

—John P. Doolittle

J O E found focusing on other people the best way to get through
difficult times. She lived, not only by the Golden Rule, but by the
self-set goal of giving someone a "lift" every day. She kept a list of
"shut-ins"— friends and acquaintances who suffered illness, lost
loved ones or were lonely—and wrote them daily. She wrote 25
to 50 notes and letters per day.

With Jimmy on his way to North Africa, young Jim in the
South Pacific, and John at West Point, Joe needed more than let-
ter writing to keep herself occupied. She volunteered her time to
War Bond drives and the Red Cross. She gave pep-talks to sol-

diers' wives and girlfriends. She wrote a newspaper column offering advice on surviving on the home front. She traveled from one coast to the other, giving speeches, visiting factories, and lending a hand wherever she could. She even accepted a spot on *Broadway Matinee*, a weekly radio program.

But, as busy as she kept herself, she couldn't forget that her boys were in harm's way. The thread connecting them was their letters to one another, like the one John wrote to his father:

> *Dear Dad,*
>
> *Am a little late thanking you for the check. Thanks…It covered the dorm bill and left enough to cover the one due the 1st…At present I'm sitting pretty…Won't be needing reimbursement for a month or so.*
>
> *Was glad to get an opportunity to get down to Dayton and see the Bubble [Jim, Jr.] …It's been almost a year since I gazed on his fair puss. Really did the old heart good to see him. Certainly wish that you and the Duchess [Mom] [had been there] to make the gathering complete.*
>
> *Was very pleased to meet the new sister [Jim, Jr.'s new wife, Elva], and might I add that I'm more than proud to have her as such. She's o.k. by this lad.*
>
> *Would appreciate any dope concerning your present status. Have heard rumors, but would like any official dope that can be let out.*
>
> *Haven't had any news from Mom of late. Sent my last note to California. Assume that she's still in those parts. Really hope that she's enjoying her visit.*
>
> *Spent several minutes in a motor-driven turret, and got a big kick out of it. Saw a P-47, and was very impressed. It's really a smooth looking job. It looks plenty potent.*
>
> *Keep the old "snozzle" clean. See you.*
>
> *John*

Six B-17's lined the runway, waiting to deliver General Dwight D. "Ike" Eisenhower, his staff, generals, and his British counterpart to the North African Invasion command post, situated deep within the dark, stale tunnels under the Rock of Gibraltar. Against the advice of both Marshall and Eisenhower, Roosevelt ordered Operation Torch, the joint American-British effort to drive the Germans and Italians out of North Africa.

General George Patton commanded the ground troops, and Jimmy, reluctantly selected by Eisenhower, organized and commanded the newly-formed Twelfth Air Force.

Jimmy climbed aboard the sixth B-17, and settled into his seat. He shared the plane with General Lemnitzer, temporary Chief of Staff for the invasion; Colonel T.J. Davis, Ike's adjutant general; Major Joe Phillips, former editor of *Newsweek* and Public Relations Officer for the Allied Force Headquarters; Freeman Matthews, Political Advisor to Ike; and W.H. B. Mack from the British Foreign Office.

The pilot, Lieutenant John C. Summers, fired up the engines on the Flying Fortress and waited his turn to taxi up to the runway.

Lieutenant Thomas F. Lohr, copilot, turned to look at the passengers occupying crew positions on the aircraft. Jimmy felt a surge of sympathy for the boy. The flight was so heavy with brass and their baggage, the gunner and most of the regular crewmembers were forced to stay behind.

As the fifth plane took its place, Summers signaled the ground crew to remove the chocks and began to taxi toward the line of B-17's. Approaching his position, Summers applied pressure to the brakes. The Fortress continued to roll.

"We've lost hydraulic pressure," Summers said to Lohr. "Hit the wobble pump."

Summers switched the hydraulic selector to normal, while Lohr reached down with his right hand and grabbed the hand pump.

Beads of sweat gathered on Summers's forehead. Five fully loaded B-17s, carrying the American and British top command, sat on the runway directly in front of his plane. The fuel from one plane would make a spectacular bonfire; six would compete with the sun.

"Pump! Pump!" Summers yelled, as he hit the brakes hard.

The left brake caught, and the Fortress, barely missing the last B-17, spun around, slid sideways and came to rest in the mud.

Stranded, Jimmy and the other passengers of the sixth plane stood on the runway and watched as the North African Command Staff taxied and then lifted into the morning sky.

Twenty-four hours later, the sixth B-17 took off, and headed southwest over the Atlantic. The route paralleled the coast of France and swung around Portugal to the British air base at Gibraltar. Flying without escort, and with minimal fire power, the crew followed a course presumably well out of range of the German fighters.

Jimmy sat in the radio bay and contemplated the impending invasion of North Africa. American resources, stretched thin between the Pacific and European Theaters, experienced severe shortages of essential equipment and trained crews. Pressure on the automotive and aviation industries by the Roosevelt Administration, resulted in significant increases in the number of American airplanes, but not enough to compensate for the lack of military spending after World War I.

The 12th Air Force, hastily formed to accompany Patton's ground forces, pilfered crews and equipment from Ira Eaker's 8th Air Force. All together, fourteen units of fighters, bombers and transports had been diverted, leaving Eaker with only half his previous strength.

North Africa lacked a couple of essentials as well—suitable airports and decent weather.

But Jimmy's paramount concern involved the lack of time allocated to training ground and air troops. Would the steep learning curve be responsible for an increase in American and British casualties?

"Junkers approaching from eleven o'clock!" Summers's voice jerked Jimmy from his thoughts.

Jimmy spotted the German Ju-88's. They made a reconnaissance pass, two on either side of the Fortress. He watched them swing around and line up for an off-angle, head-on pass.

Summers held a steady course, and then kicked the rudder, putting the B-17 into a skid.

Bursts of machine gun fire shot tracers at the German fighters, as Lemnitzer manned the gun in the radio bay.

Summers threw the throttles full forward and skimmed just above the water.

The Ju-88's lined up for a second pass. Summers, attempting to minimize the target, headed straight for the line of fighters. Lemintzer loosed a barrage of fire as the Junkers approached the Fortress.

Glass shattered and rained down into the cockpit. Summers struggled to maintain control of the plane. Lohr slumped against the controls. Blood seeped through the sleeve of his jacket and ran down his arm. Jimmy hurried forward to steady him.

Lemintzer abandoned the gun and helped lower Lohr into a seat in the radio compartment. Jimmy removed his scarf and tied it around Lohr's arm, putting pressure on the wound.

"General Doolittle," Summers called.

Jimmy turned at the sound of his name. Summers nodded toward the vacant copilot's seat and Jimmy moved forward to take it.

"What would you like me to do, Son?" Jimmy asked. He saw bravery laced with fear in the pilot's eyes. He rested his hand on Summers's shoulder.

"It's your plane, Son, and you're doing a good job."

Jimmy took the right seat and checked the engine. The number three propeller had been hit and spun wildly, running away. If the propeller came loose it would slice through the fuselage. Jimmy pulled the throttle, prop andmixture back. He then feathered the prop by turning the blades parallel to the fuselage, minimizing resistance.

Summers fought to keep the plane steady on three engines, skimming as close to the water's surface as possible.

The Ju-88's lined up for a third pass. The crippled Fortress lumbered along, a sitting duck for the German fighters. Lemnitzer returned to the radio compartment and took up his gun. Tracers streaked across the open water, as he emptied round after round into the approaching German planes.

Suddenly, the four fighters pulled away, heading for shore. Smoke poured from one that lagged noticeably behind the others. Jimmy allowed himself a slight smile. With any luck, she wouldn't make it back to base.

Jimmy looked over at the young pilot, perspiration tinted pink from the small cuts dotting his forehead and cheeks.

"Good job, Son," Jimmy said.

A smile adhered itself to Summers's face and remained stuck there as they landed at Gibraltar two hours later.

The invasion of North Africa commenced on Sunday, November 8, 1942. Reports of fewer casualties than expected delighted President Roosevelt. Americans at home embraced the North African campaign as proof that the United States could mount a successful offensive.

A number of problems plagued the invasion as it moved forward. First, a dreadful lack of radio communication made it virtually impossible to speak with pilots once they'd taken off.

Secondly, the United States' fledgling Office of Strategic Services (OSS), new to the intelligence game, lacked the operatives and experience to provide necessary information on the North African operation. Jimmy relied on British intelligence, much of which was out of date and inaccurate.

★ ★ ★ ★

Joe sat in the fading light, Jimmy's letter open in her lap. The invasion of North Africa had definitely lifted the spirits on the home front. By taking the offensive, Americans felt their contributions made a difference.

More and more women joined the work force, earning the respect of their male coworkers. The Roosevelt administration instituted a system of rationing in the summer of 1942. Local communities got together and participated in drives to collect rubber and aluminum. Housewives planted victory gardens in their backyards, and used corn syrup and saccharin to sweeten cakes and cookies.

Joe believed Americans at home would do whatever it took to aid in an Allied victory. Like everyone else, she missed her boys. It was only through letters that Jimmy could contact Joe. She read and reread them, imagining what his life was like halfway around the world.

November 23, 1942

Dearest Joe;
Haven't had a letter since I was a little boy. (But then no one else has either.)
Wrote a personal report to Hap Arnold as of November 19th giving a resume of our activities. Think it would be interesting to you if compatible with his policy to let you see it.
Jack [Allard] is fine and is having the time of his life. All the rest of the gang here that you know are well and happy.
Tooey Spaatz and Pinky Craig were through here to look over our set up and apparently were favorably impressed.
Read in the paper day before last that I had been promoted. Haven't received official word yet so don't know what kind of a general I am. Am still wearing one star and will continue to until definite word comes thru [sic].
Am far more interested in promotions for Hoyt Vandenberg, my Chief of Staff, and Tommy Blackburn and Claude Duncan. Their names have been in for some time and I haven't heard a word on them. All are doing outstanding jobs.
How are your boys getting on? Don't know where Jim is now but presume he is having some part in the South Pacific action.
Have run into several people who have boys at West Point and all tell about John having to bomb Tokyo. Seems that the little fellow has his problems.
Have a million things to tell you as soon as censorship is lifted. In the meantime can say: "I love you."
As ever,
Jim

An unnatural silence settled over the airfield at Youkes-les-Bains, Algeria. Skeletons of airplanes sat near on the tarmac, victims of German bombs. A jeep, carrying Jimmy, Jack Allard and Colonel Tommy Blackburn, skidded to a stop next to the pitted runway.

"As soon as it began, General, your crew chief taxied your B-26 down to the far end of the field," a grimy mechanic told Jimmy.

The jeep took off.

"What happened here?" Jimmy asked the assortment of ground crew members standing around his plane.

"When those dive bombers came, General, your crew chief climbed into the plane and started shooting. He got at least one of the bastards, too, and then ran out of ammo."

"I hope he got out of the plane and into a slit trench then," Jimmy said.

"Yeah, he did. He played it by the book." The men exchanged looks.

"Paul," Jimmy called as he approached his B-26. Spent .50 caliber casings littered the ground around his plane.

"General," one of the men called to Jimmy.

But Jimmy kept going. He climbed aboard.

"Paul?" he called, more softly this time.

Jimmy stepped into the gun turret. Additional spent casings lay on the floor.

The sour taste of fear filled Jimmy's mouth. Paul had stayed with the plane, while Jimmy and Jack attended a meeting at the command post a mile away. A direct hit on the ammunition factory, on the only road connecting the airport to the town, slowed their return. Jimmy knew his crew chief well enough to realize that Paul would never leave the plane unattended.

Jimmy climbed down from the B-26 and surveyed the airstrip. Bomb-craters pocked the face of the field. The crater next to his Marauder crumbled in upon itself. Saliva dried in Jimmy's mouth, and his tongue felt thick. Drawn to the partially-filled hole, Jimmy walked slowly to the crater's edge. At first his mind refused to function. He pictured the events. Paul, after moving the plane, climbed into the top turret and returned fire until his ammunition ran out. Then, seeking protection, he jumped into the slit trench. But a second bomb, probably meant for the plane, hit the old crater. Tears filled Jimmy's eyes. Paul had asked to fly with him. He'd sat on that hillside in China and tried every way he could to cheer Jimmy at the lowest moment in his life, then asked to be his crew chief.

Jimmy reached down to touch Paul's hand. Paul's watch still clung to the severed wrist, the only thing left of his friend.

"He was a good friend of mine," Jimmy told Jack, when he climbed out of the crater.

Jimmy walked back to his B-26. Inch by inch, he inspected the plane, much the way Charles Todd had taught him in flight school thirty-plus years before. Satisfied, he climbed into the cockpit and started the engines. Slowly, very slowly, he taxied to the runway.

"Think she's all right?" Jack asked, worried more about Jimmy than the plane.

"She's all right." Jimmy snapped.

"Seems OK." Jack said.

"She's okay."

★ ★ ★ ★

The fledgling 12th Air Force suffered growing pains as she fought her way through North Africa. In January 1943, Roosevelt joined Prime Minister Winston Churchill in a top-secret meeting in Casablanca. Believing that combined efforts between Allied forces would be more effective, American and British Chiefs of Staff decided to bring all Allied Air Forces under one command. General Carl A. "Tooey" Spaatz made the announcement. Air Chief Marshall, Sir Arthur Tedder, became the overall chief of all air units. The restructuring combined the Eastern and 12th Air Forces, forming the Northwest African Air Force (NAAF), directly under General Spaatz. The reorganization relieved Jimmy of his command of the technically defunct 12th and placed him in charge of the Strategic Division of NAAF.

Jimmy's fingers struck the keys of the typewriter, each stroke releasing a bit of tension. He felt strongly that the reorganization was a demotion:

Headquarters Twelfth Air Force
A.P.O. 650, U. S. Army

Dear Joe;

I have, as you have probably heard, for bad news travels fast, lost and am losing the major part of my command. The Air Support Command was the first part to go. I am still nominally Commanding General of the Twelfth Air Force but no longer have operational control over the tactical forces and will soon lose control of the strategic forces. The present plan is for me to continue to exercise administrative control of the American air effort, provided it is permitted to retain its identity, and be charged with personnel, training, supply, etc., turning over the A-2 and A-3 functions to the new command. Alternatively I may be given command of the combined striking force which is substantially the Twelfth Air Force Bomber Command with two R.A.F. Wellington squadrons added to it.

My destruction came in three steps. First Tooey Spaatz was called down from London to coordinate the two air agencies; the Eastern Air Command and the Twelfth Air Force. This coordination was necessary because the eastward movement of the Twelfth Air Force was far more rapid than had been originally intended and they were soon operating in the same area with the E.A.C. The second step was the establishment of the Allied Air Force with Tooey commanding both the Twelfth and the E.A.C. but with each one retaining its identity. The third step was the combining of all air in North West Africa under one single command and the absorption of the E.A.C. and Twelfth in this new unified command. Details of the plan and conversion are presently being worked out and formal notification will be given in the next few days.

I feel no resentment over the change only a very keen disappointment that I have failed my gang. I had the administrative, technical and even the tactical side in hand. The latter through competent staff and command personnel. On advertising and politics I was weak. I have found many times in the past that one can't simply do a job and rest on results. There are "angles" and in a job as big as mine was here, where conflicting desires between services and nations exist, there are more angles than a diamond has facets.

In retrospect I see many mistakes. Places of weakness where immediate ruthless remedial action should have been taken. Accomplishments should have been pointed out—advertised. Above all I should have fought for my job—thrown what little weight I had around in an effort to direct policy and overcome adverse politics. Politics! I have always sneered at the word "politics". Whenever anyone has failed he has never said "I couldn't cut her." Always "politics booted me out." Now I at least appreciate the power of politics, realize that it must be molded in one's favor and understand that in some instances, nothing can be done about it by the individual involved.

I have advised Tooey that I will be glad to accept any job that he feels will take advantage of my training, experience and ability and am now, much smarter, ready, willing and anxious to start over again.

As ever,
Jim
J.H. Doolittle

Joe opened the windows and allowed the cold, crisp March air to breeze through the stale apartment. She had spent the last few weeks on the road, encouraging the purchase of war bonds, and looked forward to a few days' rest. A stack of mail waited on the dining room table. She sorted through it, stopping at Jimmy's latest letter:

20-2-'43

Dearest Joe;
If you haven't sent any mem-index cards yet give them to Jack Allard as I plan to glom on to his. You will see him presently.
I've been given command of the North West African Strategic Air Force. It represents a considerable part of my previous command together with some R.A.F. units. A bit of a come down but I can take it. New A.P.O. # will be 520 instead of 650. Am really relieving Joe Cannon who will have the replacement and training center.
Have been on a half dozen missions recently and thoroughly enjoyed them. Got a bang out of watching our fine American boys in action. They are tops. On one occasion with flak bursting on all sides—we were taking violent evasive action—one burst went off right in front of the bombardier in the nose of the plane. (a B26) I was in the co-pilot's seat and watched him throw up his hands and fall back. Thought he was hit but it was only a close miss and he promptly glued his eye to the bomb sight

and as we were near the target calmly said, "Hold her steady now, sir." Every inclination was to call for further evasive action but he had a job to do so requested straight level flight. It was the most intensive and accurate flak I or any of the rest of the gang had ever seen. We lost two ships to enemy fighters and one was badly shot up with flak on this mission. The latter got home and with only one badly wounded crew member.

On another occasion we were attacked from below by five fighters. One boy said, "Shall I cut down on them?" Another said, "Don't shoot yet; you will scare them away. Wait until they get closer." No worry about what the fighter might do to him, only wanted to be sure that they got close enough so he could knock them off. They must have had a premonition.

Haven't heard from the boys, directly, since I've been away and its been a long time since you have passed on any news. How is John making out at the Academy? Has Jim got his own plane yet or is he still a co-pilot? As a matter of fact he should be getting along to the flight leader stage soon.

Bruce Johnson is a Major now and is doing a great job as Headquarters Commandant.

Jack has his show organized so well that he has worked himself about out of a job and is looking for more work to do.

Loads of love and lets hear from you.

Love,

Jim

Jimmy threw himself into his new assignment. He still believed that strategic bombing could significantly alter the course of the war, and planned missions to take full advantage of those capabilities.

Northwest African Strategic Air Force
4-4-'43

Dearest Joe;

Mail fell on Northwest Africa! Got three long letters from you in as many days. Saw Clare yesterday, for the first time. He got in the day before. He also advised that Jack was still boiling. He, Jack, apparently has had his ears batted down pretty good. He hasn't my simple philosophy.

"If you don't like it and it can be corrected, fix it. If it is not possible to change the undesirable condition, then accept it and don't get your bowels in an uproar." Hard to swallow sometimes, but sound.

Luckiest thing in the world that John was whipped by the Syracuse boy. Sometimes in life we have to learn how to lose and the sooner the better. I don't mean that a chap should lose often but no matter how well he plans or how hard he works he can't attain perfection on the earth. If he really does his best he will win most of the time. Every boy should learn how to win graciously and lose courageously. Your John was getting the big head a little as indicated by his gripe, earlier in the month, about not being selected for the first team right off. Please tell him these things for men and also tell him that every time, in the last 46 years, that his old man even started to be satisfied with himself he got his ears batted down, for his own good—although it was pretty hard to see it that way at the time.

Hap's telegram was swell. I've let both him and General Marshall, who had confidence in me, down here, but am doing better now and am going to vindicate their confidence in me yet. Hap needs people to help him. His commanding generals should make his lot easier not take up his time helping them.Am doing my best and working the old shell twenty four hours a day. One problem originally was that I argued with my superiors and, according to Army standards, wasn't severe enough with my subordinates. Have improved quite a bit. Now avoid inviting attention to the stupidity of my superiors but haven't yet mastered the art of bawling out my subordinates to cover up my own stupidity.

Jim seems rather ambitious—wanting enough Jap scalps to make a rug! Don't know from his letter if he had had a chance to fly a fighter in combat or is just hopping them around camp. He spoke of being a "pea shooter" pilot in one of his letters to you.

You must be pretty sassy with a $500.00 bond. 'Twas nice of Mr. Frazer and Shell. I'm glad you are wrestling with the money people and not me. I've no interest in their $100,000.00 either, except to pass it on to some wartime charity. Have to make the transfer direct or you find yourself paying income tax on the amount after you've given it away.

If Ted [Lawson] can make an honest penny then more power to him. He needs it and has suffered a real loss. We haven't lost anything and don't need it. Of course that doesn't say we never will, but I'll gamble on that. As regards "Allowing General Doolittle's character to be portrayed on the screen." It seems to me that that is a problem for me to settle and my feeling is that it should be tied in with the Air Force and with Lowell Thomas. If we can do real good for the Air Force without doing harm to me then okay. You know Lowell and I have an agreement on the books that neither of us gets anything. The proceeds, if any, go to an Air Force charity. I think the picture should be tied to the book and be on the same basis as far as Lowell and I are concerned. The only case in which I'd have any interest in making money on my name would be if I were so incapacitated as to be unable to make a living otherwise.

Sorry Howard isn't happy. I'd like to have him with me but will have to wait until I get my old command back or another one. My present work is almost 100% strategic and tactical and Howard's training doesn't fit him for that type of organization. You know I command only the heavy bombers, medium bombers and escort fighters now. I could have used him and George too when I had the whole show including Air Transport, Troop Carriers, etc.

Just heard a roar and went to the window. It was my heavies coming home. Guess I'm soft—the tears came to my eyes as I saw them lumbering along on the last leg of their trip home. Think we made history today so remember the date. Imagine you will see the dope in the morning papers. Had intended to go along but got tied up in a conference and couldn't make it.

Think you might as well let George dispose of the car. Unless I do something terribly stupid I'll not be sent home for a long time. Of course one never knows but I think the rumors of my coming home are as far-fetched as the reports that I've been wounded. There is a bare chance that I'll be recalled for a short conference after the Tunisian battle is won but the chances are that Tooey will be sent over if anyone is. Regarding my wounds. The only wounds I've received have been to my feelings and they are healed up now.

Loads of love,

Jim

P.S. Flash report from the field that today's mission was a win and all my big babies home safely.

On April 18, 1943—the first anniversary of the Tokyo Raid—Roosevelt announced that Dean Hallmark, William Farrow and Harold Spatz had been executed by the Japanese.

"It is with a feeling of deepest horror, which I know will be shared by all civilized peoples that I have to announce the barbarous execution by the Japanese government of some of the members of this country's armed forces." Roosevelt said in an address to the American people. "In violation of every rule of military procedure and of every concept of human decency, the Japanese have executed several of your brave comrades who took part in the first Tokyo raid. These men died heroes."

Devastated by the execution of three of his boys, Jimmy focused on finishing the war in Europe.

The North African Campaign ended with an Allied victory on May 13, 1943. The Northwest African Air Forces made three significant contributions to this victory: They established complete air superiority over the African mainland; successfully interdicted the Axis supply lines; and gave air support to American ground troops.

Jimmy was particularly pleased by a letter he received from General Eisenhower:

President Roosevelt has asked that I convey his thanks for the superb job you have done in the Tunisian campaign. I am profoundly grateful to you and all portions of your command for having carried out their assigned tasks so magnificently as to earn this commendation from the President.

Jimmy's joy from Ike's letter was interrupted when he spotted the headlines from the nationally syndicated muck-raking columnist Drew Pearson. "Headlines for Doolittle, but No Planes; He's Restless and Unhappy."

Jimmy paced his quarters, attempting to gain control of his temper. Drew Pearson's article lay spread out on his desk. Targeted by the press in the past, he resigned himself to the fact that he paid a penalty for being in the public eye. But this time they'd gone too far. He stopped pacing and picked up the article:

While Jimmy Doolittle has been getting the headlines here, things haven't gone so well with him in North Africa. This is no fault of Jimmy's, just Army politics. Actually, it began long before the raid on Tokyo, when Doolittle, a flier in the last war, wanted to get in again. Jimmy held only temporary rank in the first war and was a Major in the Reserve Corps before this war started. So despite the fact that he had won the Schneider Trophy, the Bendix, Thompson and Mackay trophies, also had set the world's speed record, Army bureaucrats at first wanted to reinstate him as a Captain. They were overruled, however, and he came in as a Colonel, later climbing swiftly up the promotion ladder with the raid on Tokyo. In North Africa, however, Doolittle has chafed at inactivity. Here he was given a "strategic" command, not a "tactical" command. A "strategic" command means bombing fixed objects; a "tactical" command gets into active battle with the enemy. Doolittle found that there wasn't much strategic bombing to be done in North Africa. Also he found that his bombers gradually melted away. He could get few replacements. Finally he was left with only a baker's dozen. Restless, chafing, he finally staged his bombing of Palermo, which electrified the world. Jimmy will never complain and probably will deny this, but he still is not too happy. An active racing pilot all his life, he wants to be in the thick of things. But Regular Army Air Force commanders, always favoring Regular Army, don't give him planes.

He never understood why journalists, who would never physically mistreat someone, would willfully harm them with false statements. Drew Pearson never even bothered to check his facts. He wrote a story filled with lies and misrepresentations in order to make a headline. Jimmy had worked hard to earn Eisenhower's confidence. Months of trying to prove himself to Ike could be destroyed in one article.

Sorry about the Drew Pearson column. Can only say it's 100% not so," he wrote to Joe. *"The unfortunate part is that my superiors will feel that I instigated it, directly or indirectly. That is also not so. I have the best and most interesting job in the Air Force now. Strategic bombing is the Air Force. It represents Air Power. Tactical bombing is support of the*

Army. Naturally I'd like to retrieve the Twelfth Air Force (now operationally non-existent) but that is a matter of pride only.

Joe recently had her own run-in with the press. Walter Winchell wrote that Joe, decked out in silver fox, had been spotted ice-skating with a gentleman in Central Park.

Jimmy sympathized with her. Joe hadn't been in New York at the time, couldn't ice skate, and didn't own a sliver fox. As for the gentleman in question, she'd never even met him.

When he finished his letter to Joe, Jimmy wrote Tooey Spaatz:

Am sorry the attached article by Drew Pearson was printed. It is wholly incorrect. Am afraid my superiors will feel that I, directly or indirectly, instigated it. This is also incorrect. I have the best job in the Air Force. Strategic bombing is the Air Force. It represents Air Power.

As a matter of personal pride, I should like someday, if it is ever unraveled, to resume command of the Twelfth Air Force. In the meantime, I am thoroughly happy and can think of no one I would care to trade places with.

Within a very short time Jimmy heard back from Tooey:

I would not trade you for anyone else to be in command of the Northwest African Strategic Air Force.

The tiny island of Pantelleria sat in the Mediterranean Sea between Tunisia and Sicily. With only one harbor and no beaches, the island offered shelter for over 200 Italian gun emplacements and an opportunity for Jimmy to prove that, properly applied, air power could break an enemy's will to resist.

Believing he had a chance to prove Billy Mitchell's assertions regarding the usefulness of strategic air missions, Jimmy ordered his bombers to attack Pantelleria around the clock with everything they had. Four groups of B-17's, two groups of B-25's, three groups of B-26's, one P-40 squadron, plus three wings of Wellingtons and South African and British units, pummeled the island.

His "heavies" targeted supply dumps and munitions storage. Medium bombers aimed at smaller targets, and fighters strafed anything that moved.

Fatigue bit at Jimmy's heals, but he continued to push himself. Knowing that his men were equally tired, he approached the co-pilot assigned to a B-26.

"Would you like the day off, son?"

"Yes, sir." The lad answered, knowing that Doolittle would reject any other response.

"Then head on in and get some rest. I'll take your place." Jimmy climbed into the cockpit and settled into the right seat.

It was his policy to hop flights and evaluate, first hand, what his boys faced on missions. He had flown with every one of his bomber groups either as co-pilot or observer. They expected him.

Anti-aircraft flak exploded around the B-26, but she held a steady course to target.

Descending over the target, Jimmy watched as the bombardier dropped his load. The explosion shook the plane, even as she pulled up.

For several days, around the clock, Jimmy's forces pounded the island. But as the deadline drew near for the land troops to storm ashore, intelligence filtered back that Jimmy's boys had failed to secure the island.

With heavy heart, Jimmy offered air support for the boys storming the harbor. He'd been certain that they could make a difference, and his heart ached with the anticipated loss of American lives.

Ordering one last mission before the ground invasion, Jimmy waited for their report.

"There's a huge white cross painted on the runway, sir," the pilot reported.

"And a white flag flying on the hill overlooking the harbor," the copilot added.

Jimmy felt a flush of pride. They had done it! Forced the Italians to surrender without a single soldier setting foot on the island. The surrender at Pantelleria represented a victory for America, and a definite victory for Air Power.

★ ★ ★ ★

Jimmy stood in the back of the room and watched Colonel Leroy Rainey brief his men. The combined American and British forces had fought their way through Italy, and now faced a moral dilemma. The marshaling yards at San Lorenzo and Littorio provided supplies to keep Mussolini's military fighting, and brought in German troops to reinforce the Italians. Air strikes on the yards, Jimmy believed, would shorten the duration of the Italian campaign.

"Gentlemen, about a year ago a guy named Tojo stuck his neck out," Rainey said to the assembled crews. "And, about four months later a man named Doolittle slapped him down with the first air raid on Tokyo. Today we are flying the first air raid on Rome, and General Doolittle will be leading us."

Jimmy, dressed in a flight suit, walked to the front of the room.

"We face a dilemma here," he said, as he stood in front of the troops. "The great hub of the Italian railway system is centered in two marshaling yards. San Lorenzo," he used a pointer to indicate the location on a map, "and Littorio are not far from the center of Rome. However, priceless art treasures and architecture are a part of the city, as well, and must NOT be damaged."

"We also know that Rome is the heart of world Catholicism. Any of you who need to excuse yourselves from the mission on religious grounds, are encouraged to do so."

He passed out target maps to the crews. Four areas on the target maps were boldly outlined in white. White block letters labeled them as "Vatican City," "St. Maria Maggiore," "St. John Lateran," and "St. Paolo Basilica."

"These areas MUST ON NO ACCOUNT BE DAMAGED," Jimmy continued. "There can be no mistakes. Do you all understand?"

He looked around the room. Every man's eyes were on the map hanging behind Jimmy. No one in that room wanted to contribute to the loss of world treasures, and no one wanted to face the wrath of an angry world if mistakes occurred.

"Colonel Rainey will lead the mission, I'll be his co-pilot. We'll use 500 aircraft." Jimmy said. "Secondary targets are outlined on your target maps." He passed the flimsies around the room. Then, very calmly, without a hint of braggadocio, stated, "But we'll hit the primary targets."

Jimmy flew with the last group in "Tail End Charlie," an especially dangerous position because each plane followed a common lane to avoid the shrine areas. Tail End Charlie gave flak batteries a steady aiming point.

Smoke from the bombs of preceding groups blotted out targets and obscured the entire city, including the Vatican. Using the most up-to-date equipment available, the bombardiers aimed carefully, and dropped their loads.

Overall the mission succeeded. The marshaling yards suffered major damage, and most of the sensitive targets in Rome escaped injury.

The basilica at San Lorenzo, however, suffered damage from percussion. The British and American press ran with the story, criticizing the mission with volumes of negative print.

On July 25, 1943, six days after the assault, Mussolini stepped down.

★ ★ ★ ★

Joe continued to find solace in her work. *Broadway Matinee* provided her the opportunity to meet and interview a series of interesting people. Most recently she had interviewed Eleanor Roosevelt. She found that touring factories, with their increasing number of women employees, proved particularly rewarding. Her work for the Red Cross and drives for war bonds kept her crisscrossing the country. The constant activity helped to keep her mind occupied and her hands busy, but she thrived on letters from her family.

Jimmy's letters from the front contained info about individual friends, but lacked specific war news. They were, however, filled with advice for his wife and sons. "Tell John that if I had had the advantage of learning thru the Plebe or an associated system, I'd have avoided a great deal of the official difficulty that I have experienced from time to time."

He also wanted pictures. "Thanks for the pictures of you and John. Had already seen them in the paper. Will send one back as you suggest. Want—when available—recent individual photos of you, Jim and John."

She smiled at his concern for her. "Hear from all sides of the excellent work you are doing. Am proud of you but don't overdo. It will be a long haul yet."

★ ★ ★ ★

The value of strategic air strikes finally registered with the Chiefs of Staff. The 12th Air Force was divided into two separate forces. The 12th Air Force would continue with tactical missions supporting the Army. The new 15th Air Force, created on November 1, 1943, would make strategic strikes on industrial targets in Germany. Jimmy, long-time proponent of strategic air operations, was named commander. Focused on communication centers, railroad marshaling yards, airfields, and factories, the Fifteenth would attack German positions in the Balkans, in preparation for the invasion of Southern France.

On November 22, 1943, President Roosevelt and Prime Minister Winston Churchill met in Cairo, prompting another reorganization of American and British Air Forces. Much to Ira's disappointment, he was named Commander-in-Chief of the Mediterranean Allied Air Forces. Major General Nathan F. Twining replaced Jimmy as commander of the 15th, and Jimmy was given the Mighty Eighth Air Force, based in England. Two months later he was promoted to Lieutenant General.

CHAPTER 16

THE MIGHTY EIGHTH

"Doolittle's personality, his eager-
ness, and his loyalty to his men did
things for that command that no
planning could ever do. Here was
a flyer's flyer come to lead them,
and the men told me many times
afterward that they'd follow Jimmy
Doolittle through hell. He pulls
men up out of their troubles and
never lets them down. He merits
respect; he doesn't command it."

—Merrill "Red" Mueller,
Liberty Magazine

JIMMY took command of the Eighth on January 5, 1944. His mission—to destroy the Luftwaffe and the German aircraft industry—
gave him an opportunity to implement strategic missions. Jimmy
wrote Joe on January 14th:

*As you can well imagine I've been up to my ears in work. Guess you
know all the dope. Ira [Eaker] has gone to a larger job, replacing a four
star RAF officer and taking on the overall air responsibility in the
Mediterranean. Tooey is here and has taken on part of Ira's job and I
have been given a part.*

*Hated to leave my little flock down below but the assignment of this
command was a great compliment and indicated confidence on the part*

of Hap and Tooey. It is the biggest, most difficult, and most interesting job I've ever had and it goes without saying that I'll do my best.

However, Jimmy felt empathy for Ira. Ira had built the Eighth Air Force from scratch, and would not be around to command the final victory. And victory, Jimmy knew, would follow on the heels of General Arnold's New Year's message: "Destroy the enemy Air Force wherever you find them, in the air, on the ground and in the factory."

Joe chuckled as she read Jimmy's letter from February 20, 1944:

Had an odd experience the other night. Just before quitting time a chap called up and asked if I was General Doolittle.

I stated that I was and he advised me in turn that he was Captain Doolittle. There is a Captain Doolittle on my staff. I had not yet seen the boy but had planned to look him up. Thinking that he had beaten me to the punch I asked what I could do for him.

He said, "I would like to see you."

I said, "That is fine. I should like to see you. Come around any time. Just give me a buzz ahead of time so I will be sure and be here."

Was about to hang up when he said, "Say Dad, Mom sent some stuff for you."

It was the first realization I had that it was your little man talking. I had not expected him over for a couple of months yet. We had a good visit. He spent two nights and a day here with me and then reported to the Ninth for duty.

Thought I was doing him a favor in flying him all around this part of the country the one day we had together. I had forgotten that he had been two full days flying the North Atlantic and was, temporarily at least, tired of flying as a passenger in an airplane. He looks well, a bit on the fat side, and his attitude is very good. He was to have notified me as soon as he received permanent station orders, advising duty and location. Haven't heard from him but expect to soon.

★ ★ ★ ★

She missed young Jim, but found comfort in knowing he could visit with his father. Maybe they would keep an eye on each other. She saw John at West Point on long weekends, holidays, whenever their schedules permitted. But, her own schedule kept her on the road most of the time. She had added a new project — counseling young soldiers returned from the war. That left little time to sit around and brood. Still, she experienced a certain comfort in knowing her Jims had each other.

2-29-'44

Dearest Joe;
Had a weekend in town with young Jim. Invited him to supper. We meditated for a few hours and then sent down for supper. The dining room was closed, but after exerting considerable 'influence' we were successful in getting a dish of the only kind of sandwiches available in the place—SPAM. The first time I took the kid out I gave him an airplane ride after he had been sitting for two days in an airplane. The next time I invited him to dinner and fed him Spam. Doubt if I will be able to get another appointment with him.
Regardless of how the kid felt, I thoroughly enjoyed the evening in his company. His attitude is excellent and I am sure that he is going to do a fine job over here. He has been given, as I understand it, a staff job in the Operations Section of a Bomber Wing. Don't think he particularly likes this but is accepting it well and feels that he can do a job if he is able to get in a few missions and learn what the score is around here.

The "Big Week" began on February 19th with the bombings of Berlin and Leipzig. For the next seven days, the Eighth Air Force, in concert with the Fifteenth Air Force, dropped nearly ten thousand tons of bombs, destroying or damaging seventy percent of Germany's aircraft industry.

By the end of the week, the Air Force losses totaled 226 bombers and 28 fighters—roughly six percent of the total aircraft involved in the mission. Jimmy found the numbers unacceptable. In human terms, 2,600 men were dead, missing or wounded.

Unhappy with the stats, he set out to tip future odds in America's favor.

Jimmy believed the battle of Pantelleria had demonstrated the ability of the Air Force to break the will of the enemy to wage war. He made a number of controversial decisions based on that belief.

Major General William E. Kepner, commander of the Eighth Fighter Command, saluted Jimmy before shaking his hand.

"Good to see you, Bill," Jimmy said, settling into a chair.

Troubled by the "don't leave the bombers" escort policy, Jimmy looked for a way to broach the subject. The opening presented itself when he spied a sign on Kepner's wall: "THE FIRST DUTY OF THE EIGHTH AIR FORCE FIGHTERS IS TO BRING THE BOMBERS BACK ALIVE." "Who dreamed that up?" Jimmy asked, pointing to the sign.

"That was here when we arrived."

"Well," Jimmy said, "that statement is no longer in effect."

"Sir?"

"We'll never win this war by playing sheepdog. Guarding and barking won't get rid of the wolves."

"No, Sir," Bill said, the trace of a smile forming on his lips.

"Have a few of your fighters fly close cover to take care of the attackers who bust through. But instruct the majority to peel off, and chase all the Germans they spot."

Bill's smile widened.

"Chase them up and down the sky. Chase them into the ground," Jimmy said. "Chase them all the way to their airfields and bang those too."

"You mean you're authorizing me to take the offensive?"

"I'm directing you to."

"Thank God, we can now operate like fighters ought to."

"And Bill," Jimmy said, getting up to leave. "Take that sign down and replace it with one that reads—'THE FIRST DUTY OF THE EIGHTH AIR FORCE FIGHTERS IS TO DESTROY GERMAN FIGHTERS!'"

Jimmy understood Kepner's reaction. Fighter pilots, by nature, are an aggressive bunch. It galled them to simply fly escort for the bombers. The new directive allowed the pilots and planes to do what they were designed to do—engage in offensive tactics against the Germans.

As he walked out the door, he heard Kepner rip the sign from the wall.

The bomber pilots did not share Kepner's enthusiasm for the new directive. They counted on fighter protection and, in fact, during the early days of the new policy, more bombers were lost. But, U.S. fighters shot German planes out of the sky and destroyed them on the ground. Eventually, fewer enemy planes were available to attack the bombers. Coupled with the directive to stay in tight formation—"Don't throttle away from your cripples"—rather than bomb and get out, losses of Allied bombers dropped from six percent to six tenths of a percent.

Jimmy's practice of flying with his crews ended with his briefing and access to Ultra, the code-breaking system that allowed the United States to listen in on German military communications. However, he continued to keep close tabs on his men. Early on, he realized that just when the crews started functioning as efficient teams, they were relieved of duty and returned to the states. He found that it took a crew a minimum of ten missions to understand the job, then another five to become really good. That left only ten missions at peak performance. Based on his observations, Jimmy made a second controversial decision. He increased the number of combat missions flown by his crews. By increasing the number to 30, he increased productivity by 50 percent. At 35, he increased it by 100 percent. Knowing his decision would be unpopular, but believing it would make a significant contribution to the war effort, he ordered the crews to fly a minimum of 30 missions, instead of 25. The directive had an almost immediate impact on the number of planes lost. Casualties dropped significantly, while accuracy of bombing improved dramatically.

Bad weather over targets caused operational problems for all the Air Forces in Europe. To combat the problem, Jimmy initiated a scouting force of P-51's. The brainchild of Colonel Budd J. Peaslee, the 348th Bomb Group sent a fighter with one wing man ahead of the bombers, to report on weather conditions at the target. The scouts essentially eliminated the need to recall bombers due to lack of visibility over the target. Manned by pilots who had signed up for a second tour—generally bomber pilots on their first assignment—the scouts made on-the-spot decisions concerning the feasibility of missions.

While Jimmy searched for solutions to problems in Europe, Joe continued to make appearances to bolster American moral. In February 1944, she took the train to Virginia to participate in a christening ceremony for the U.S. Navy. 75,000 spectators gathered near the dock at the Norfolk Navy Yard in Portsmouth, Virginia to watch the launching of the *USS Shangri-La*, the Navy's newest, ultra-modern, 27,500-ton aircraft carrier. Joe stood on the crowded platform clutching a bottle of champagne. Governor Colgate W. Darden, Jr. stood next to her.

"The hours may come, as the onrolling thunder of aerial battle rolls across Tokyo, when we shall be able to say," the governor's voice rose above the cheers, "the planes that struck the mortal blow came from the *Shangri-La*."

Honored to be asked to sponsor the ship, Joe smiled at the Navy's choice of names. President Roosevelt had announced shortly after the Tokyo Raid that Jimmy's boys had taken off from a new secret base in Shangri-La—a place as fictional as its namesake in James Hilton's novel *Lost Horizon*.

When the speeches ended, Joe stepped forward. Lifting the bottle high in the air, she smashed it against the bow of the ship. The crowd roared its approval, and the band struck up rousing rendition of *Stars and Strips*. The cold mist of champagne caught in the breeze and was blown over the platform.

"God speed, Shangri-La," Joe whispered under her breath, "and bring all your boys safely home."

Shortly after the christening of the Shangri-La, the Eighth Air Force, in conjunction with the Army and Navy, prepared for one of the major offensives of World War II.

Operation Overlord, the code name for the Invasion of Normandy, was scheduled for early June. A window of four days provided the optimal conditions; a late-rising moon for the paratroopers, and low tide shortly after dawn.

For several weeks prior to D-Day, Jimmy ordered his crews to "soften up" the planned landing area. The Eighth carried out missions, bombing gun, radar and transportation targets, while simultaneously carrying out decoy missions. They hit 52 airfields, 45 marshaling yards, and 14 bridges.

As the date grew near, General Eisenhower agonized over the decision to begin the invasion. On June 3rd, Captain J. M. Stagg, Senior Meteorologist for the Supreme Headquarters Allied Expeditionary Force, predicted marked deterioration in the weather, calling for overcast and stormy skies with high winds and low visibility.

On June 4th, Stagg amended his predictions, calling for slight improvement in the weather. Eisenhower gave the order and Operation Overlord moved forward.

The first wave of 1,361 B-17's departed at 0615 on the morning of June 6th. They dropped 1,015 tons of bombs, striking targets in the Cherbourg Peninsula minutes before allied troops hit the beaches. But the weather did not hold. Subsequent flights, afraid of hitting their own troops, turned back.

Jimmy, in a P-38 Lightning, ducked through a hole in the clouds and turned toward the invasion beaches. Ships and boats dotted the water as far as the eye could see. For two and a half hours, he flew over the beaches. He watched as Americans, under heavy fire, stormed Omaha Beach, and, with fewer casualties, Utah Beach. He saw the Canadians battle for Juno and the British take Gold and Sword.

By nightfall, 175,000 American, Canadian and British troops had secured a toe-hold on Normandy's beaches. Over 4,900 of those troops were killed, wounded, or missing in action—2,200 of them, Americans on Omaha.

Of all the losses from the Invasion of Normandy, those caused by friendly fire bothered Jimmy the most. On two occasions, the Eighth had dropped bombs on Allied troops, killing more than 100 soldiers and injuring an additional 500. When news of these tragedies reached SHAEF headquarters, Jimmy was summoned to General Eisenhower's chief of staff, Brigadier

General Walter Bedell "Beetle" Smith's office and blamed for the tragic and costly mistake.

"I'm responsible, because I accepted the mission," Jimmy told Smith. "But 2,500 bombers cannot drop thousands of bombs accurately, especially when the target area is covered with smoke from previous bombs."

Smith's smile turned frosty. "You were directed to carry out a mission and you failed."

"My men are not trained for bombing in close support of ground troops. They were trained for high altitude bombing."

"Jimmy, I'm not looking for excuses."

"Damn it, Beetle, we shouldn't even have been there!"

"That will be all," Smith said, indicating the door. "I'll make my report to Ike, recommending you be replaced."

Jimmy felt horrible about the incident. He steadfastly maintained that his men had insufficient training for bombing in close support of ground troops. He had repeatedly resisted tactical assignments. The Eighth was a strategic Air Force and should be used as such. He waited for the axe to fall. Ike's letter helped ease his burden:

I know how badly you and your command have felt because of the accidental bombing of some of our own troops…Naturally, all of us have shared your acute distress that this should have happened. Nevertheless, it is quite important that you do not give the incident an exaggerated place either in your mind or in your future planning.

All the reports show that the great mass of the bombs from your tremendous force fell squarely on the assigned target, and I want you and your command to know that the advantages resulting from the bombardment were of inestimable value. I am perfectly certain, also, that when the ground forces again have to call on you for help you will not only be as ready as ever to cooperate, but will in the meantime have worked out some method so as to eliminate unfortunate results from the occasional gross error on the part of a single pilot or a single group.

The work of the 8th Air Force over many months in this theater has been far too valuable to allow the morale of the organization to be dampened by this incident.

Jimmy faced this dilemma the way he faced many others in his life. He set out with his troops to find a solution. They experimented with air marker bomb lines and electronic bomb line indicators. Eventually they developed an instrument system, and mounted it on a jeep. A radio beam indicated that the bombers had passed over the last of the Allied troops and could safely bomb. Although not perfect, it helped. The Eighth continued to fly tactical missions, although Jimmy believed their efforts should be focused on offensive strikes.

"We need to keep pressure on the Germans," he stressed, "to keep bombing their factories and airfields." Already noticeably fewer German aircraft filled the skies. Very few airplanes were seen during the Invasion of Normandy. But, Jimmy surmised that the Germans were conserving their planes and building new aircraft for one last super strike. He vowed the Eighth would be ready.

10 October 1944

Dearest Joe;
Colder weather, shorter days, another season and soon another year gone. How time flies—and this in spite of the constant desire to get the job done and return to the loved ones at home. Sometimes tired, particularly when things go wrong. Rested, refreshed and exhilarated when things are going smoothly. Responsibility to superiors and subordinates. Opportunity to utilize to advantage our attributes and ability. It is difficult but necessary to exercise command in such a way as to assure the respect and loyalty of subordinates and the confidence of superiors; to strive to avoid engendering antagonism and annoyance and establish approbation, admiration and even affection. The last objective is rarely achieved, particularly among our contemporaries.

I sometimes think that when this is all over I'd like to run a peanut stand. Would want it on a quiet street where there wouldn't be too many customers to interfere with meditations. Actually after about a week's rest I imagine I'd be restless and looking for work and responsibility again.

Jack Dempsey was out to supper last nite. Thoroughly enjoyed him. He mentioned having enforced a bout in which John participated. Spoke highly of the lad's pugilistic attainments and possibilities.

Haven't seen Jim since he moved away but have sent the box to him. Also sent along a silver dog tag chain which I had on hand. Couldn't think what to get the lad. He has glommed on to watches, pens, lighters, etc. on his various trips here so is pretty well fixed. Was glad to give them to him as I was developing a surplus.

Hope you had a chance to see our grandson. Am anxiously awaiting a report on him. Am sure of only one thing and that is that he is a most unusual baby.

Had a visit and supper with Georgie Patton, whom I admire tremendously, last week. He is well and is doing a swell job.

Am going to the Rhodes dinner at Orel College, Oxford tonight. Don't know what it's all about and am not quite sure I remember how I got roped into it.

Love,
Jim

Much of Joe's correspondence came from wives and mothers of soldiers fighting in the European theater. She wrote letters of condolence to many family members of boys killed in the war. With every letter, she thought of young Jim and Jimmy.

Joe continued to write her "shut-ins" and friends. She was proud of the fact that she answered every letter, sometimes writing two to three hundred letters a week.

October 19, 1944

Dear Joe,
Thank you so much for your kind letter of October 1st. It helped a lot to ease the heartache.

I did not believe that a thing like this could happen to Dale. He had more than a thousand hours of flying and was a wonderful acrobatic pilot. He had a spirit that I did not believe could be stilled by an enemy bullet. He was able to bring his ship home badly shot up on previous occasions and he had made many trips to Germany protecting bombers.

Since mid-May he had been flying his P-38 on dive bombing, skip bombing and strafing missions, and since the invasion started he had been working exclusively in support of the Ground Forces.

He was killed on June 30ᵗʰ at Charly, France about forty-five miles East of Paris while on a skip bombing mission to knock out a railway distributing center. They were flying under a low cloud cover and other pilots in the group wrote me that Dale's ship caught fire from enemy flak and that he was evidently too low to use his parachute successfully.

We do not feel bitter about our loss. In fact, we, like you, are proud and happy that we had a fine son who was willing and able to go to the aid of his country in the darkest hours of our history, and we feel grateful to kind Providence for the twenty happy years we had him with us.

I have thought so many times of you and your splendid sons and fine courageous husband who has made, and is continuing to make a colossal contribution to American's War Effort; a contribution that will be recorded magnificently in the history of our country.

Being a parent who has had to remain at home and wait for one's loved one to return, I have some small understanding of the enormous amount of courage and fortitude with which you have been so nobly endowed. You are a good soldier Joe, and Jimmy and those boys are so very proud of you and so are the rest of us Americans.

I hope and pray that the war will soon be over and that you will again have your fine family gathered around the hearth.

Thanking you again for your sympathetic words, and with kindest personal regards, I am

Gratefully yours,

Tex

The smooth, sentimental strains of Tommy Dorsey poured from the phonograph. The USO (United Service Organization) hall bustled with activity as local volunteers mingled with young servicemen preparing to deploy.

A bright-cheeked young man in a brand-new Army Air Force uniform flushed with pleasure when the USO hostess introduced him to Joe.

"I'm so proud," the youth said, eyeing her white hair, "to meet the mother of the man who bombed Tokyo."

The hostess gasped, anxious to correct the mistake. But Joe, shook her head and signaled silence with her finger.

"It's my pleasure," she said. Smiling, she watched as he made his way across the room.

"I didn't want to embarrass the boy," she said to the frowning hostess. "Besides, Doolittle would have swelled up like a pouter pigeon."

Joe's list of activities and contributions grew with each passing month. However, when what appeared to be breast cancer landed her at the Army Air Force Convalescent Training Center in Pawling, New York. After undergoing a radical mastectomy, she gathered courage by turning her focus outward. She added another service to her country, one that touched her deeply and gave her direct contact with soldiers returning home from the front.

Pawling, New York—November 13, 1944

Dear Ethel,

Just how the gray haired dame keeps friends when she is seemingly so negligent—I don't know. When she does her weekly letters to the scattered little flock there seems little or no time for other personal correspondence. I have received, enjoyed and appreciated your notes from time to time. Belated but sincere thanks!

At the moment I'm at the Army Air Force Convalescent Training Center. It is a two fold proposition. I'm to do a job—I hope—for the Medical Corps and get a rest on the side. It's a beautiful place—and I have a room in the Officer's Mess building—which is situated on the edge of a beautiful lake.

Have no desk and I'm finding my knee substituting doesn't help the already vile scrawl.

Grace, poor dear, has had a wretched struggle. I seldom hear directly, but friends report that she is a bit better. Do hope she can fully recover and soon.

Isn't it wonderful having a grandson? I, of course, haven't seen him, but am hopeful of doing so soon. Despite all of our efforts to get the big news overseas in a hurry, young Jim read in "Stars and Stripes" that he had become a father. Says grandpa is playing the role well.

Mail is taking much longer to come through lately. I gather that Jim, Sr. is tired, but doesn't want to return until it's over. He's been gone twenty-six months now.

I saw John Saturday after the Army—Notre Dame Game. He's looking fine.

You'd better say an extra prayer for me. I stole the hotel stationery before leaving New York. Had remembered to address envelopes, but exhausted my stationary supply on the train in route to New York City. Had no chance to replenish the depleted supply.

My work continues to be interesting, stimulating and my salvation.

Much love and again many thanks. A personal hope that our lines of march will cross soon, meantime, all good wishes.

Always,

Joe

"Dear Jimmy," Joe wrote, after hearing that he had been invested with the insignia of an honorary knight by King George VI. "Congratulations on being knighted 'Knight Commander of the Order of the Bath'. Sir James sounds very distinguished."

"It will, however, take more than the King of England to make a Lady out of me."

As Joe regained her strength, she stayed busy stateside. She continued to cross the country on a regular basis, visiting factories and attending rallies. Every week, she found a quiet place and wrote a column directed at the wives and sweethearts of men serving in the theaters of war. Joe believed American women were making a significant contribution to the war effort. It was, she believed, her job to support them. She lifted the copy of her latest column from the stack on her desk:

Recently I returned from a trip that took me from coast to coast and back again. In spite of the many signs I saw posted, warning against careless talk, there was an amazing amount of it in public places. I'm appealing to you to help stop the dangerous chatter.

First, when your husband receives his orders, don't ask where or when he is going. Military orders are military secrets and should remain so.

Almost two years ago my husband returned to active duty. To date I've found my first line of defense a full-time job in our home...that is, when we've been able to maintain a home. When he's away there have been many places for me to work. As a matter of fact, there is no day long enough for me to do the things I would like to do. Choose your particular place and work...work hard!

Guard yourself against the feeling of depression...it will try to overtake you. When it does, change your stance. Change horses in the middle of the stream if you have to. There again it will depend on you as an individual. Choose the thing that offers you the most.

If it's possible, write him...tell him you miss him...but don't fill your letters with petty grievances and woe. Write interestingly and amusingly. If you have a joke on yourself, repeat it.

If you have courage, strengthen it...if you have none, develop it. We'll need it all through this conflict and afterward. Develop a sense of humor and see that it helps you carry on. Tolerance, too, is essential...eliminate petty greed and jealously...start today. Think nationally rather than selfishly...let's join together...do our bit and help our men win this war!

Satisfied with her message, she placed the column back on the desk and turned her attentions to her list of "shut-ins".

20 December 1944

Dearest Joe;

Am just in receipt of your letters from November 17, 20 and 23, written from Pawling. Had heard from you just before you went and have had two letters since you left. Hadn't heard before what you were doing there and was very pleased to learn that you had a chance to visit with the kids and to get some rest. I know you needed the rest and I am sure that having you on hand as pal and mother confessor was exactly what a lot of these recuperating youngsters needed.

Never have heard whether you got to the Army-Navy game, whether John got there, whether Randy got there, and if you did, how you all enjoyed it. The last letter from John, received a few days ago, advised that he was hoping to go. Presume your letter on this subject is in the mail and later letters have played leapfrog over it. Also haven't heard whether you received some scented water that I shipped over, and if you did, whether it was to your taste and met your requirements. Told you in my last letter that I had received your package via Tony.

Apparently my introducing the most beautiful WAC in the ETO (who naturally was an Eighth Air Force girl) at the Army-Navy game here was widely publicized at home. A large percentage of letters received recently contain a clipping and a subtle interrogation.

Tuned in on the Charlie McCarthy program at nine last night and later listened to the Dinah Shore program with Jimmy Durante as a guest star. Don't know whether I was especially susceptible to music and tom-foolery, but they struck me as being two of the best programs I have ever heard. A piano-clarinet duo with Jimmy Durante and Omberto, accompanied by the customary Durante patter, was particularly good.

Enjoyed Louise Eaton's lovely letter which you enclosed. She is a splendid person. (Saw Herb in South France a short while ago. He is fine and is doing a magnificent job for Ira, who places great confidence in him.) I have been quite perturbed over something that Louise also noted. In speaking of my voice over the radio she said, "so serious, so impersonal." Am giving my Christmas message to the Eighth Air Force this year in a talking movie. Saw the preview of it a few minutes ago. It is a movie of me sitting at the desk, reading a two-minute message which constitutes my Christmas greeting to the Command. Was rather surprised in reviewing it to see that it was impersonal and quite without warmth. Am letting it go anyhow as I haven't time to do another, and am not sure that I could do better. I have watched other people here change and have felt the change in myself as well. From a fairly gregarious individual—one when upon occasion and proper stimulation made an effort, and to a degree succeeded, in being the life of the party—I have become what a friend of mine here calls "a non-convivial introvert." This, I think, is due in part to a deficiency in hearing—part to a failing memory—and most important, due to occasional mental fatigue and the resultant inability to think of more that one thing at a time, and that usually being the job immediately on hand. Knowing that this tendency inclines to grow rather than correct itself, I have been forcing myself to do a certain amount of public speaking, to meet people, and to get around more. Am leaving in a few moments (and have surreptitiously been wondering all day how I could get out of it) to have tea with the diplomatic crowd in town and later to a British-American dinner at which I have the job of introducing the Secretary of State for Air, Sir Archibald Sinclair.

Told you in my last letter that I hoped to get together with young Jim during the Christmas holidays, but now doubt whether that ambition will be realized.

Rather envy John at his being able to be with you over the Christmas holidays. Sorry that Jim and I can't be with you also. You have, however, our best wishes and our love for this year, next year and forever.

As ever,

Jim

Joe sat on the edge of her bed and looked out over the lake. She longed to see Jimmy and the boys. She stayed busy, the last two years a testament to her frenzy of activity, but she missed her boys. She unfolded Jimmy's letter of January 20, 1945 and reread it:

Now about my coming home. Tooey has asked me if I wanted to go home for a visit. Barney asked. Barney said that Hap wanted to know. I do not feel that it is expedient that I come home at this time, even for a short vacation. I may come home this spring for a short visit, provided there is a sufficiently important reason. Frankly, I think that Hap is interested in looking me over in order to assist him in making up his mind, first as to whether I am holding up well enough to continue in my present job, and second, in order that he may make a decision as to what is the best use that might be made of my services after the war. I think he wants to find out whether I have mellowed enough to get along with people, particularly in high places. I feel that I have, although the mellowing process is not yet completed. I still have the unfortunate habit of expressing whatever is on my mind, which in many cases, even though it happens to be so, had better not be expressed. This old habit of talking when I should be listening is being gradually corrected. Before sounding off now, I endeavor to analyze the situation and determine what the effect of a statement will be and then whether that effect is desirable. I still slip occasionally, but constant effort is producing results.

In connection with the above, it is probably desirable that you consider, in the selection of the many jobs available to you, first the contribution you can make to the immediate war effort, and second, what effect they will have on our post war plans. It is essential, no matter what we go into, that we continue to constitute the same effective team that we have in the past. In other words, the flag is sometimes too heavy for one individual, and therefore we have to take turns carrying it; or alternatively, if we work as a team instead of individually, we can carry twice as many flags.

Am very pleased that you are going to take on the job with the kids. They are grand youngsters. We return over 4,000 crew members monthly. A small percent need help and they need help badly. Personally, I feel that every commander has three solemn primary obligations: … It is his obligation to so employ the force under his command as to assure that it makes the greatest possible contribution of which it is capable or can be made capable to the winning of a prompt and conclusive victory. The second obligation, no less important, is to see that this is accomplished with the smallest possible sacrifice in men; and the third is to assure that those who return after their participation in the war are useful citizens, with their physical, mental and spiritual capabilities enhanced rather than impaired as a result of their war experience. This last is very difficult because, unfortunately, war tends to change our sense of values, particularly the value of human life. The law of expediency, rather than the Golden Rule, becomes the order of the day. I will continue to do everything possible here to assure the accomplishment of my three solemn obligations. In spite of that, some boys will return who need help and I can think of no one who can give that help as generously, as practically and as kindly as yourself. In connection with this, I am enclosing a letter recently received from one of my old group commanders in North Africa. I am very proud of this letter and am sending it because it may be of help to you and give you some ideas for your new job. In any case, file it away as I wouldn't want to lose it.

Spent a couple of days on the Continent this week. Planned to drop in and see Jim but again didn't get an opportunity. Wrote him today suggesting another get together.

Love,

Jim

Joe received a deep satisfaction from her work at Pawling Convalescent Training Center. She understood loss. Her recent mastectomy gave her a deeper appreciation of grief, an under-standing she communicated to boys who had lost limbs, their eyesight or even their will to live.

The center kept her busy — busy enough to take on a part-time secretary. But more than anything, she felt her involvement filled a need—and she took comfort in being needed.

★ ★ ★ ★

By February, the Eighth Air Force and the British Bomber Command demonstrated that they owned the skies by flying all over Germany, hitting targets never hit before.

On May 7, 1945, Colonel General Alfred Jodl signed documents of unconditional surrender. Churchill declared May 8th V-E Day. The war in Europe ended.

Jimmy made plans to transfer his Eighth Air Force to Kadena Air Base in Okinawa. However, misquotes in the press landed him in hot water with MacArthur before he even left England.

"DOOLITTLE TELLS OF PLANS TO WIN OTHER HALF OF THE WAR" read the headline in a London paper. Jimmy again forced to make peace with the brass—this time overcoming the preconceptions of General Douglas MacArthur—much like the way he had had to win over Eisenhower.

An Army Air Force news release in Washington on May 26th added fuel to the already explosive situation:

Japanese war industries can expect an even greater volume of air attack than was accomplished against Hitler's fortress Europe. General Doolittle is now prepared to help finish the job he started on Japan on April 18, 1942 when he hit Tokyo with carrier-based bombers with plenty of fighter coverage.

★ ★ ★ ★

Once again, Jimmy set out to sell himself to a commanding officer. But first, he and George Patton received orders to tour the United States to bolster morale and raise needed funds for the completion of the war against the Empire of Japan.

Thousands flocked to the field at Los Angeles Municipal Airport. Their cheers almost drowned out the thunder of motors as the Army planes carrying Jimmy Doolittle and George Patton landed.

Joe, standing next to Beatrice Patton, barely controlled her excitement. Jimmy had been gone almost three years, and even though they'd spent the past week together, she didn't think she'd ever tire of seeing him.

She smiled as Georgie Patton, resplendent in cavalry breeches, ribbon-adorned tunic, gleaming boots, and steel helmet, stepped from the plane. He wore his ivory-handled revolver in a holster on his side. He and Jimmy provided quite a contrast. Dressed in his khakis, only the three stars on his shoulders differentiated Jimmy from the colonels, majors, captains, lieutenants, sergeants, corporals, and privates that followed him out of the plane.

"Welcome, welcome!' Mayor Bowron greeted both generals, shaking their hands.

A bevy of journalists and photographers closed in.

"Come on, Jimmy," George said, reaching back and dragging Jimmy up beside him.

Forty-nine olive drab staff cars and jeeps lined up by the terminal. Ushered by the mayor, Jimmy, George, and the accompanying servicemen hopped aboard their vehicles.

The parade of automobiles filed down Imperial Highway, turning first onto Sepulveda Boulevard then onto La Tijera Boulevard. They passed the great war plants that turned out supplies, and passed the North American plant that built the B-25's Jimmy used on the Tokyo Raid. They turned onto Slauson Avenue, passing rows of houses and blocks of stores, then they drove up Broadway.

All along the route, spectators waved flags and threw flowers. Red, white, and blue banners hung on buildings welcoming the soldiers home. The procession stopped at the corner of Broadway and Pico, the forming ground for the official parade. George Patton, in the front car, led thirty-two cars carrying members of the ground forces. Jimmy rode in the 34th car, followed by 15 members from the Air Forces.

"Hi, George!" the crowds yelled. "Hi, Jimmy!"

The two men waived in return.

One and a half million people lined the parade route. Business came to a standstill as stores closed their doors, and workers poured out onto the streets to welcome the conquering armies.

Regrouping with marching bands, the parade wove its way up Broadway and through the streets of downtown Los Angeles, stopping at the steps of City Hall.

A blanket of 29 Liberators, gleaming silver in the sky, flew over the parade route, while a Lockheed "Shooting Star" flung itself about in breath-taking abandon.

As Jimmy and George stepped from the cars onto the broad white steps of City Hall, a thousand flags fluttered in the breeze and flowers flew through the air, landing at their feet. A seventeen-gun salute rang out from Fort Moore. Men, women and children made the air quiver with their cheers. Both Jimmy and George waved and smiled broadly. Patton, clutching a bouquet of flowers, threw kisses to the crowd.

Joe, dressed in a simple black dress, took her place on the stage. When Jimmy came up the City Hall steps, and moved to his place behind the microphone, the assembled crowd jumped to their feet in a standing ovation. Joe rose with them, applauding heartily and smiling brilliantly. Her hands rose to wipe tears from her eyes.

"I see by the papers that I'm going away again," Jimmy said. His face lit up with an impish grin, his signature twinkle in his eyes. "To the Pacific."

"Out there, we'll need supplies and ships to deliver them. We'll need two teams, one in the field and one at home. If you come through here, we'll come through there."

The crowd rose again as one, and their applause shook the walls of the City Hall.

After the ceremony, they attended a reception in the Embassy Room at the Ambassador Hotel.

"Just think—my husband and my young son both came home on my birthday," Joe said to Beatrice Patton. "I think I'm the happiest and proudest woman in the world."

At 6:00 P.M. over one hundred thousand spectators filed into the Coliseum. Judy Garland sang *God Bless America.* Joe sat beside Jimmy as a parade of stars honored the returning heroes.

Jack Benny led the cast of stars in a salute. Jimmy Durante, Frances Langford, Danny Thomas, Carmen Miranda, The Charioteers, Lena Horne, Ella Logan, and Bette Davis performed for the crowd. Miss Davis even read one of Patton's poems.

"It's good to be home—I'm lucky to be home," Jimmy said, when his turn came. "A lot of our boys didn't get home."

Jimmy looked out over the crowd that filled the Coliseum.

"The ground where they lie is hallowed ground. We salute them and pay homage to them. Many others are coming home, and some may go out to the Pacific to finish a job only half done—a tough job."

Cheers rang out from the spectators.

"If General Patton and I have achieved any success in fighting the war," Jimmy said, lightening the mood, "these two lovely ladies are responsible for that success because of their constant support, understanding and affection."

The crowd rose as one in a standing ovation when Joe and Beatrice stood up. Patton, taking his place at the microphone, leaned toward Jimmy.

The hot mike picked up Patton's casual comment and blasted throughout the Coliseum. "You son of a bitch, I wish I'd said that!"

"God damn it—it's no fun to send men you love out and say 'go get killed'." Patton boomed into the microphone. "Their sacrifices must not be in vain. You must play your part, not only with money, but with labor and sweat.

"You cannot—will not—be unfaithful to the men who have died."

Patton sat down and, when the enthusiastic applause finally quieted, the tribute continued.

Joe smiled as Humphrey Bogart presented a mock pre-Tokyo briefing. When he finished, forty-two searchlights blazed into the night sky, and a single B-25 streaked across the open stadium at 700 feet, symbolizing the raid three years before. Three B-29's—the current planes used to attack Japan—followed the Mitchell.

As the search lights dimmed, Edward G. Robinson stepped to the podium. Impersonating Patton, Robinson briefed the audience on a tank mission. Lights flooded the stadium as five 30-ton tanks fired cannons and machine guns—land mines exploded and rockets burst in a reenactment of Patton's many battles in Europe. The crowd went wild.

As the mock battle drew to a close, the lights dimmed again, and then blacked out. In the darkness, first one match was struck, followed by 105,000 others—in memory of the heroes who could not return. Margaret O'Brien, her voice strong and true, led the crowd in the Lord's Prayer. And as the matches flickered out, buglers stationed around the Coliseum played *Taps*.

Joe wiped tears from her eyes, tears for the mothers who would never hold their sons again, tears for the widows who would go on alone. As she stood for the *Star Spangled Banner*, she raised her own voice in song, in thanks for her blessings. And as she sang, she held tight to Jimmy's hand.

"Mrs. Doolittle," a reporter called as she left the stadium. "What are your plans while Jimmy is in the Pacific?"

"I can't even think beyond the present moment," Joe said, still holding Jimmy's hand. "I don't want to. This is enough. But no matter what comes, I'm not afraid."

Less than a month later, Jimmy left for Okinawa and Joe again found herself alone. Without complaint, she threw herself back into her own war efforts. Letters again connected the four Doolittles.

9 July 1945 #1

Dearest Joe;
Now I am in London and homesick. Made separation easier for me (and probably harder for you) by putting it out of mind, the last day in Washington, and concentrating on the trip, remembering not to forget

anything, etc. But loneliness has caught me here and I want my sweet-heart—Plump.

Pat is probably having his chuckle. # 1 engine on the B-29 swallowed a valve just as we were landing and my crew, mechanics, and the Wright service man have been working on it ever since. We had an extra cylinder and piston but not a fuel injection nozzle. Hope that the B-17, which is following us has one aboard or we are sunk and will have to go on on the B-17—which, by the way, is what Pat wanted me to do in the first place.

Have all my chores done and had hoped to push on tonight but can't as the B-29 is out of commission and the B-17 not here yet.

Norm Bottomly just called. He got back from America today and has invited me out to dinner tonight. Am very fond of Norm, and Mrs. (Lady) Bottomly, although a little on the austere side, is also charming.

Just talked to Walter Hill who is due any moment now. Haven't seen him yet and am anxious to have a talk, concerning my future, with him.

Think I mentioned earlier in the letter that I'd been successful in getting everyone I wanted from the old Eighth Air Force H.Q. but I didn't get some of them quite as soon as I'd like to have 'em. They have to complete redeployment here, however, and a fair compromise was affected.

Dropped over to the house where we used to live on the Thames but the Frosts were out. Tom is going over again tonight and I may drop in tomorrow. Want to leave them with a good taste in their mouths.

Had supper with Ed Sorenson last nite. He is fine and put in a plug to go [to] the Pacific. If I were to take everyone who wants to go along the New Eighth Air Force would be bigger than the old.

Loads of love,
Jim

Joe wondered how long Jimmy would remain in Okinawa. It seemed like years had passed since their family reunion a month ago. She continued working tirelessly for the boys at Pawling, but her thoughts were with Jimmy, and the war with Japan.

19 July 1945 #2

Dearest Joe;

Have been here three days now and like it. (That doesn't mean that I don't like home better.) It does mean that tho we are in tents and the living a bit more rugged than at A.P.O. 634. It is still interesting and we are all busy enough to be happy.

Was two days late due to the motor trouble which I told you about in #1. Had more trouble at Khuugafur (outside Calcutta). A vagrant zephyr blew a steel barrel into one of the B-29 props. This held it up a couple of days so I proceeded in the B-17.

Spent a day with George Kenney who is as full of pep as ever and who sends his best.

Arrived here on the 17th. Had hoped to make it on the 15th but could never make up the two days lost in the U.K.

By the way, this pen was given to me by Walter Hill. It is one of those synthetic ones which has a small ball bearing for a point and writes with a chemical (not ink) and lasts for a year or two without refill. Quite a gadget. It's a bit heavy and doesn't feel as good in the hand as the Parker 51 but has the very great advantage of never having to be filled. As a matter of fact, I haven't found how to take it to pieces yet. Understand it has to be sent home to the factory for "refill."

(20 July 1945) It rained last nite. Blew also so everything in the tent, including me, got wet. You can see that this tablet and your letter were soaked but the synthetic "ink" apparently doesn't run.

We had been warned of the "blow" so put down additional tent stakes and checked hold down ropes. Only one tent blew down but the wind was so high that the rain was blowing nearly horizontal instead of vertical. It also shifted direction rapidly so with these "ventilated" tents it practically came in one side and went out the other—except for a considerable percentage which stopped off en route. At first I barricaded myself with a pillow and went deeply to sleep. The wind changed 90* and I awakened soaked—sheets and mattress as well. I'd apparently been rained on for quite a while before waking up. Got up, put on a light raincoat—the little black one—around my feet and legs, which were wettest and went back to sleep. The only trouble was that the raincoat was wet also so I had to soak that water up before I could get dry. All in all had a good, cool but moist night's sleep.

Today is still drizzling but the wind and storm have passed on. Have to drive my Jeep in low-low and four wheel drive due to the deep slick mud. (Some difference between a muddy Jeep self-driven and a Cadillac with chauffeur.) The Caddy would be no good here today!

All in all I'm happy to be here—feel that I'm doing a job—with this rapidly growing organization. The beauty of a job like this, where things are growing, is that each day you see a substantial change and improvement and each day feel that something has been accomplished.

Haven't seen or heard from my little flock for some time now. Two weeks to be exact. Miss 'em. Doubt if you have my new A.P.O. yet so probably won't hear for another couple weeks. (Am getting this letter off in the morning with a B-29 that is going back direct so you should get it about the 25th.)

How is John coming with his flying? Did Jim get to Wright Field? What job did he get? Is he going to get a chance to go thru the Air Force Engineering School (which we went thru in '22–23) while there?

Most important; how are you and what are you doing?

Love,

Jim

On August 6, 1945 President Harry S. Truman ordered the first atomic strike against Hiroshima. At 8:15 Japanese time, Colonel Paul W. Tibbets, Commander of the 509th Bomb Group, directed weaponeer and ordnance officer William S. Parsons to arm "Little Boy." The single bomb, dropped from the Enola Gay, had the explosive power of 20,000 tons of TNT. Tibbets carried 12 cyanide capsules in the knee pocket of his flying suit. One for each member of the crew.

For the next three days, B-29's from the 20th dropped leaflets on the cities of Japan warning of a second attack, encouraging the Japanese to "petition the Emperor to end the war" and advising them to "evacuate your cities now!"

When the government of Japan failed to respond, Major Charles W. Sweeney, piloting Bock's Car, dropped "Fat Man," a second atomic bomb, on Nagasaki.

A few hours later, Sweeney landed at the American base in Okinawa and walked into Jimmy's office for a debriefing. Jimmy learned about the mission after the first bomb was dropped.

Sweeney's visit on August 9th was his first direct knowledge of the operation.

Jimmy thought long and hard about the use of such destructive weapons. In the end, he firmly believed that it saved lives. Hundreds of thousands of casualties on both sides would have resulted from a land invasion of Japan.

★ ★ ★ ★

Joe reclined on her bed in the officers' quarters at Fort Logan and listened to the news. Emperor Hirohito of Japan addressed his people, conceding victory to the Allies, and the American stations flooded the airwaves with the long-awaited announcement of the war's end. World War II was over. At long last her boys would come home.

Boisterous celebrations at the Fort Logan almost masked the knocking on her door.

"Mrs. Doolittle?"

"Yes?" Joe said as she cracked open her door. A young man she recognized from the hospital at Pawling stood in the hall.

He had crashed in the Pacific and suffered terribly from an obsession to "kill Japs."

"How are you?" she asked, offering sympathy with her eyes.

The door slammed open as the young man lunged at her.

Fighting to keep her balance, Joe stepped backward into the room. But she wasn't fast enough. Crazed, he grabbed her and threw her to the floor.

"I'm going to kill you," he raged, straddling her body, pinning her hands above her head.

"Help!" Joe screamed.

"Shut up," he cried, his sweaty hands finding her throat.

Several officers responded to her cries. Bursting into the room, they pulled the young man off her and restrained him.

"Are you all right?" a young lieutenant asked, helping Joe to her feet.

She reached up and lightly rubbed the lacing of bruises on her throat.

"I'm fine. Just a little shaken up."

"I'm sorry," the young man said, tears streaming down his face, as the officers removed him from the room.

Joe's heart went out to him—a young man whose demons could not be stilled. What, she wondered, were his chances of recovery? And how many other boys would carry the invisible demons of war?

Fort Logan, Colorado
Officer's Club—A.A.F. Convalescent Hospital
August 18, 1945

Dear Ethel,
Your letter deserved an answer long ago, but somehow the demands of the day leave little or no time for personal correspondence. Actually I don't know how I keep any friends.

Jim's brief flash through the U.S.A. seems more a dream than a reality. Our time in Los Angeles was interesting, of course, but none was allotted to seeing friends and relatives. Thank God the dreadful conflict is over. Maybe all of our men will return shortly.

I thought Gracie was looking wonderfully well. It's been ages since I've heard from her.

Have been here three weeks. Landed as a patient but am back in circulation. In addition to the usual duties, I'm sitting in on a Lecture Course, given primarily for Doctors, Nurses and Social Workers in Clinical Psychology. It's intensely interesting but sometimes over my head. The Chief is very kind, often devoting extra time to the gray haired dame.

This is a beautiful old fort—and much wonderful work is being done in reconditioning our men. Each day, I become more and more aware of the terrific problems ahead.

My last letter from Jim was dated August 1st, which I received today. Consequently I know not what to expect or whence the road ahead leads.

The climate here is wonderful. Such an improvement over that we were having in Washington. In many ways I'll hate to go back. Such a pleasure to sleep under blankets at night when one is used to having a steam bath.

When last I heard John was in the midst of basic flying training at Stewart Field and Jim, Jr. assigned to duty at Wright. Elva and adorable Junior still in San Antonio—due to the housing shortage in Dayton. They are as bad as I am about writing.

No news—do hope you've had a good rest and a wonderful summer. Thanks for your letter. Nonstop good wishes.

Always,

Joe

The surprise attack on Tokyo was viewed by the Japanese as a loss of face. Their deep humiliation had quickly turned to rage. Military personnel occupying the coastal areas of China where the American planes were believed to have gone down were ordered to "seek and find, at any cost" the American crews responsible for the bombing of the Empire of Japan. Any Chinese found to be aiding the Americans was to be executed on the spot. The bloody three-month campaign of revenge left 250,000 Chinese men, women and children dead.

Fifteen planes had gone down in Japanese-held territory. Eight American crew members from two of the planes had been captured. On August 20, 1945, the four surviving Tokyo Raiders were located and released from a Japanese war prison. After three years, four months and one week spent mostly in solitary confinement, Lt. Chase Nielsen, Lt. Robert L. "Bobby" Hite, and Cpl. Jacob "Jake" DeShazer were taken first to the Grand Hotel in Peking, then flown to Chungking. George Barr, too sick to be evacuated, would join them later.

On September 2nd, Japan surrendered, bringing to a close the "war to end all wars."

Jimmy stood on the deck of the *USS Missouri* along with all the senior flag and general officers in the Pacific and watched as the Japanese signed articles of complete surrender. Soon, he could go home.

On September 5th, Joe, still sitting in on lecture courses in Clinical Psychology at Fort Logan, received word that Chase,

Bobby, and Jake had been admitted to Walter Reed Hospital. She took the first available flight to Washington, D.C.

"Welcome home," Joe said, standing at the foot of Chase Nielsen's bed at Walter Reed Hospital. "It's a pleasure to meet you."

For the next few hours she listened to their stories. Jake DeShazer told of his decision to return to Japan as a missionary. Bobby Hite talked about his family and Chase Nielsen described his captors and their treatment.

The crew of plane number 6 included: Lt. Dean E. Hallmark (pilot); Lt. Chase J. Nielsen (navigator); Sgt. Donald E. Fitzmaurice (engineer-gunner); Lt. Robert J. Meder (co-pilot); and Sgt William J. Dieter (bombardier). They took off from the deck of the *Hornet* without incident and followed the preceding five planes to the Empire of Japan. After dropping their bombs on steel mills in Tokyo, they headed for the coast of China. Staying low, under the clouds, they flew until their fuel ran out. Forced to ditch in the water, Hallmark held the plane straight ahead as it smashed into the waves.

"It was a fast and very hard landing," Chase explained. "As the aircraft hit the water, I heard Dieter in the nose scream. I saw the water pour up over the nose and then all went black momentarily. When I came to, I was standing in water up to my waist. Dieter, having suffered a head injury and was incoherent, and Fitzmaurice had a deep hole in his forehead."

Joe watched emotion track across his face like clouds drifting in a troubled sky. Painful memories darkened his eyes, but his voice never wavered.

"We were standing on the sinking plane, trying to inflate the life raft when a huge wave washed us overboard. We called to each other, but after a few minutes, I realized that I was alone. Somehow I managed to make it to the beach and hide. The next morning I saw the bodies of Dieter and Fitzmaurice on the beach."

Joe laid a reassuring hand on his arm. His loose fitting skin draped like gauze over bone. Chase continued his story, telling of their near rescue by Chinese guerrillas, only to be betrayed by Captain Ling, the officer in charge.

Bobby Hite related a similar story. Lt. William G. Farrow was the pilot of plane number 16, the last B-25 to leave the carrier. The other crewmembers were: Lt Robert "Bobby" Hite (co-pilot); Corporal Jacob DeShazer (bombardier); Sgt Harold Spatz (engineer-gunner); and Lt. George Barr (navigator). After successfully bombing their targets in Tokyo, they flew on to Nanchung, where they were forced to bail out over Japanese-controlled territory. By the following afternoon, all five had been captured by the Japanese.

Joe fought tears as she listened to their stories of torture at the hands of the dreaded Kempei Tai, Japan's equivalent of the Nazi Gestapo. For months, the eight captured Americans were subjected to sleep deprivation, near starvation and regular beatings. As the days passed, the beatings became more violent, and Japanese interrogators found increasingly creative ways of inflicting pain. Chase remembered being strapped into a Japanese version of the infamous medieval rack; his body stretched to the edge of endurance.

"I hoped that I either passed out or died real quick," Chase told Joe. "I was sure I couldn't take this long. But I was more determined than ever that I'd die without telling them a thing."

Chase grew increasingly solemn as he recalled his captor's response.

"Well, if you insist on not telling us anything," the interrogator told Chase, "then we might as well finish the job right away."

"They placed a blindfold over my eyes and led me from the room. As we marched along the gravel path, I heard soldiers file in behind me. We went almost a thousand feet before the soldiers were ordered to stop. They led me a few feet further then halted me with my back to the firing squad."

Joe fought an increasing sense of outrage as Chase continued his story.

"As I stood there, the setting sun warm on my face, I believed that I was going to die. I thought about my family and I felt an enormous sadness that they would never know what had become of me.

"I could hear the rifle butts hit the ground, then the slight shifting noise as they were raised into position. Sweat poured down my face, but my hands were cuffed and tied behind my back, so I couldn't wipe it away.

"I stood there waiting, fighting nausea and weakness from lack of rest and food. And then the interrogator laughed. He dismissed the soldiers and told me that my execution would be delayed until morning.

"Anger replaced my fear," Chase said, his eyes bright with the memory. "My resolve to resist them strengthened."

The Japanese, Joe learned, enacted retroactive laws to punish the Doolittle Raiders. Treated as war criminals rather than prisoners of war, they were denied the rights granted by the Geneva Convention. In October, they were taken to a small courthouse. Nielsen, Hite, Meder, Spatz, DeShazer and Farrow stood before the five Japanese officers who served as judges. Barr, too weak to stand was given a chair, and Hallmark, too weak to even brush the flies away from his emaciated body, lay on a stretcher on the floor.

In a mock trial, conducted entirely in Japanese, the eight Americans were found guilty as charged and sentenced to death. On October 15, 1942, Hallmark, Farrow and Spatz were taken to Public Cemetery No. 1, tied to small wooden crosses, blindfolded and shot.

The death sentence for the other five was commuted to life imprisonment. The Japanese had no intention of ever releasing any of the Raiders, even if Japan lost the war.

Nielsen, Hite, Barr, DeShazer and Meder were returned to solitary confinement and fed almost enough to keep them alive. On December 1, 1943, Lt. Robert J. Meder died from complications of starvation and beriberi.

Each man had been changed by his experiences, but perhaps, none more profoundly than Jake DeShazer. Having spent his hours in solitary confinement studying the Bible, Jake had turned the other cheek. When he recovered, he told Joe that he planned to return to Japan as a minister of the gospel.

By the time Joe left, Chase, Bobby and Jake, weren't just Jimmy's boys; they were *her boys*, too.

While Joe was visiting the men at Walter Reed, Jimmy was winding things down in Okinawa. The past three years had left their mark and Jimmy prayed that the world would set a path toward peace. He conveyed those hopes in a letter home:

September 9. 1945

Dearest Joe;

Took a jeep trip up to the north end of the island Thursday and looked over the military government installations. They are handling over 200,000 natives. Many are still coming in from the hills and most of these are in pretty bad shape from malnutrition. Quite a few are "non-reversible" and even with the best of medical care soon succumb. Horribly infected battle casualties are still being brought in. Many of these are children and most are the handiwork of bombardment. It's distressing to realize that only two military services are constructive—the medics and the engineers. All of the rest of us are destructive.

I saw a little six year old (about the size of a four year old here) with his hand blown off by a bomb fragment and a little sock over the stump. He was all alone, an orphan, leaning against a fence post. As I met his eye I know that my glance showed guilt as well as pity. And that guilt is not only of us killers in the war, but it is on the American people at home, unless steps are taken <u>now</u> to see that we don't promptly have another war.

Those steps are:

1) A firm national policy directed toward fair dealings with all nations, and the establishment, not only of a better America, but a better world.

2) A <u>sound</u> national defense establishment, capable of rapid expansion and equipped with the most modern equipment available. It should be small but mobile, and this means prepared, equipped, and supplied bases throughout the world.

3) Universal military training as a means to rapid expansion if required.

4) A continuation of all-out scientific development so we lead the world in technology as well as tactics. This technological development will have commercial as well as military applications and will therefore assure our commercial position and place in world trade.

We want peace, and the only way we can assure peace—human nature being what it is—is to have the means of imposing our will on any misguided minority who want war.

In the meantime we should try and improve the world spiritually. Get away from the "Law of Expediency" and back to the "Golden Rule". This, however, is a long process and may well take decades, generations or centuries.

In the meantime while doing our good works I saw another little Okinawan kid with his entire right side in a plaster cast—but ambulatory—holding on to the index finger of a medical sergeant, with his good hand, and looking up to him with a look of consummate confidence in his new friend and protector. They were both just standing there. It might have appeared to the unobservant that the sergeant wasn't getting his work done, but he was. He was doing the finest job that a human can do—being kind and fair and friendly in the truest sense of the terms. He had no possibility of reward except that he knew, subconsciously perhaps, that he was making the world just a tiny bit better and war just infinitesimally a bit more remote.

We must realize that nations are just groups of individuals and if individuals will fight so will nations—more readily, as a matter of fact, if incited by mass hysteria (which can be induced by carefully arranged and controlled propaganda.)

We no longer have geographic isolation from Europe and Asia. Scientific development of the future will bring all parts of the world relatively still closer together—will shrink it still further.

Someday, I hope, we can disband our military establishment and devote ourselves wholly to truly constructive pursuits, but until that time comes, let's do everything possible to so train our children and so direct our nation as to give them both the highest possible degree of security in the world in which they find themselves.

Quite a lecture!

Love, Jim

Jimmy turned 49 years old on December 14, 1945. To celebrate he threw a party for the Tokyo Raiders in Miami, Florida—the party he had promised them on the *Hornet*. Seven men died as a direct result of the Tokyo Raid; thirteen others made the supreme sacrifice in other theatres of war. All were remembered at that first reunion.

49. Doolittle and Patton toured the United States to bolster morale after Germany surrendered. American troops were still engaged in the war with Japan.

50. *Joe and Jimmy sing with the band during a reception for Doolittle and Patton at the Ambassador Hotel in Los Angeles.*

51. *One-and-a-half million people lined the streets of Los Angeles to greet Doolittle and Patton when they visited in June 1945.*

52. *Captain James H. Doolittle—"Young Jim"*

53. *Lieutenant John Prescott Doolittle graduated from West Point.*

54. *Jimmy and Joe with their son John.*

55. *Jimmy, stationed in England during WWII, watched news clips sent from the U.S.*

56. *Joe visited the returning POWs from Japan at Walter Reed Hospital. (left to right) Lt. Robert Hite; Joe; Cpl Jacob DeShazer; Lt. Chase Nielsen. (Robert Hite Collection)*

57. *Jimmy and Joe visiting their son John and his wife Priscilla in Japan.*

58. *Jimmy enjoyed hunting and fishing. He's pictured here in 1958 on a fishing trip to Alaska.*

59. *Jimmy and Jim, Jr. in St. Louis.*

61. *U.S.O. dinner on June 9, 1976. Jimmy, Joe and Bob Hope.*

60. *Three generations of Doolittles. James H. Doolittle I, II, and III.*

62. *Joe with Tab Hunter and Natalie Wood.*

63. *Joe with her son John and granddaughters Jody and Jonna.*

64. *Jimmy with the author as a child.*

65. *Jimmy and Smokey stand in front of the "rogue's gallery" in the Santa Monica house. The display, a virtual Who's Who in history, included autographed pictures of Winston Churchill, Amelia Earhart, Slim Lindbergh, Wiley Post, Queen Elizabeth, and many others. Much of the collection is now at the Smithsonian Museum in Washington, D.C.*

66. Family reunion just a few months before Jimmy's death. Jimmy is pictured with his son John, daughter-in-law Priscilla and all five of their children, their children's spouses, and grandchildren.

67. John and Priscilla Doolittle pictured with the author and her family and James H. Doolittle III and his family.

68. Jimmy with his twin grandsons—Patrick and Peter.

69. *Joe's favorite picture was taken when Jimmy came back from England after Germany surrendered and before he left for Okinawa.*

70. *Shawna, Jimmy and Stacy. Jimmy often took his great granddaughters on walks when they visited Joe. They usually visited the cutting garden where Jimmy would allow the girls to use the scissors on his pocket knife to cut flowers for Granny.*

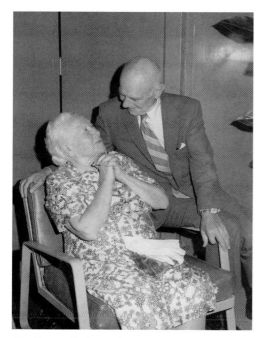

71. *Always affectionate, Jimmy and Joe in their later years.*

72. *In 1984, the Society of Experimental Test Pilots decided to give a scholarship to a deserving young engineering student in Joe's name. In addition, the group gives an annual scholarship in Jimmy's name.*

73. *Jimmy received his fourth star from President Reagan in 1985.*

74. *Jimmy at the ceremony for his fourth star sits between his son John and Barry Goldwater, a life-long friend.*

CHAPTER 17

★ ★ ★ ★

RETURN TO CIVILIAN LIFE

"Doolittle, on his side, is not an easy
'character' to digest in one gulp. He
is undeniably full of complexities
and the mental (and physical) agili-
ties that rattle conservative people.
He is aggressive, debonair, worldly;
unworshipful of brass in any calling
simply because it is brass. He has
the self-assurance of Americans who
by study and hard work and tough
scrapping win sound fame and honest fortune strictly on their own
merits. He has a resonant voice,
richly and sharply clear. He knows
his stuff—and says he knows it. He
says what he means—all of it—for
sweet clarity's sake."

—W.B. Courtney Colliers

JIMMY seriously considered staying in the service to help build
a separate Air Force. He held firm to his dissenting opinion on
the Baker Board, and he believed that the Air Force had established its rightful place in the defense community.

He testified before the Senate Military Affairs Committee
campaigning for a separate and equal Air Force under a single
Department of Defense. In the face of exaggerated claims by top

Navy brass, he calmly testified that teamwork had won the war. "Teamwork between Allied nations, teamwork between the suppliers and the users, the people at home and the people in the field, and teamwork between various services, teamwork between the Army, the Navy and the Air Force."

Industrious reporters picked up his remarks and attempted to build them into a story of conflict between the branches of military service—placing him in the center of the storm. Jimmy, discouraged by the infighting and unwilling to become embroiled in peacetime politics, decided he could do as much for the Air Force from the outside as he could from within. He requested to be relieved from active duty and on January 1, 1946, his request was granted. Allocating half of his retirement pay to the Air Force Aid Society and the other half to the Air Force Academy, Jimmy left active duty as a reservist with the rank of lieutenant general.

In mid-March 1946, he accepted an offer from Shell Oil Company with the understanding that whenever his services were requested by the United States government, including the Air Force, Shell would release him. He and Joe moved to an apartment in New York City and set up housekeeping.

Shell purchased an Army surplus B-25 which Jimmy used as a flying laboratory. Together, they flew all over the world on trips for Shell.

Joe continued her practice of writing notes and letters. On August 28, 1946 she wrote her friend Ethel from the Hotel Ritz—Place Vendome, Paris:

Dear Ethel:

You were thoughtful and kind, taking time out of your holiday period to write me. Thank you!

Your letter came just before I left New York so I hurriedly addressed an envelope to you and only at this late date am writing the letter.

I'm delighted that you could make the trip. We are indulging in an interesting one also. We've been to England, Norway, Sweden, Denmark, Holland, Belgium and here and on the morning I return to London to wait for Jim while he goes to Rome, Cairo and across North Africa.

Home is now in New York City. 1155 Park Avenue. The phone is unlisted—the numbers ATWATER 9-7654—just in case you ever come our way after October 1st.

It's been rainy and cold today and I've done my share of shivering. Doesn't seem possible that anyone could do that in August!

There are so many shortages in so many places. London and its people seem shabby. I find an empty pit stomach wise upon visiting devastated areas. One can't help but feel that all mankind should be working hard to keep the peace earned at such great cost—and to make a better place in which to live.

I do hope that you are well and happy—that you enjoyed the trip and that I'll see you soon. Until we meet again, all good wishes and my love.

Affectionately,

Joe

In 1946, Secretary of War Robert Patterson asked Jimmy to chair a board on Officer/Enlisted Men Relations. The board was promptly dubbed the G. I Gripe Board and the Doolittle Board by the press. Created in response to "public complaints about the lack of democracy in the Army, instances of incompetent leadership, the abuse of privileges, and the favorable treatment of officers compared with enlisted men during the war," the board studied the structure of ranks in the military." Jimmy promptly accepted the assignment.

Jimmy was an interesting choice for the board. Having served both as an enlisted man and as an officer, he had a unique perspective on the discipline and traditions of the regular army.

"I was uncomfortable about the invisible wall that had been erected by the regular Army between the enlisted and commissioned ranks," he wrote in his autobiography. "I have always felt that officers should do their best to earn respect from the enlisted men, not obtain it by government decree; however, I accepted the dichotomy at the time as being necessary to maintain discipline."

The son of a carpenter who followed gold to Alaska, Jimmy was not "to the manor born" like so many officers in the armed services. He'd worked hard for his accomplishments and respected hard work. As a guest in the Doolittle home, you were expected to leave your title at the front door and enter as an individual.

From the early days at Ream Field, the Doolittles entertained friends from all walks of life. They maintained that tradition throughout their lives. Visiting them was like being surrounded by an energy field of intellectual stimulation.

Closed to the press, the board listened to witnesses, read over 1,000 letters, and reviewed numerous newspaper and magazine articles, military journals and transcripts of radio programs.

"In May the unanimous report was presented to Secretary Patterson. A number of items to improve the leadership of the officer corps were recommended, including rigorous screening out of incompetents and an internal policing system to prevent abuse of privileges. The board also recommended adequate pay and allowance scales, equal accumulation of leave or furlough time, and equity of treatment of both enlisted and commissioned personnel in the administration of military justice."

The findings of the Doolittle Board irked many old-time officers who vocally viewed the decisions as the "beginning of the end of military discipline in the armed forces." An outsider when he returned to active service in 1940, he had earned his acceptance. However, once again he became the outsider.

Jimmy bounced between Shell and government assignments. He served as the first President of the Air Force Association in 1946, and campaigned vigorously for a separate Air Force. He became a member and eventually the Chairman of the National Advisory Committee for Aeronautics (later NASA). Hoyt Vandenberg, Air Force Chief of Staff, appointed him Special Assistant for Science and Technology, a high level trouble shooter for the Air Force.

His expertise continued to be in demand and he served on numerous boards and committees including the Air Force Scientific Advisory Board, the President's Foreign Intelligence Advisory Board, Smithsonian's National Space Museum's Board, and the President's Science Advisory Committee, Joint Congressional Aviation Policy Board and as an advisor to the Committee in National Security Organization. The list goes on.

President Harry Truman, after a series of tragic civilian air crashes, asked Jimmy to chair the three-man President's Airport Commission, making a complete "in-depth study of airport location and use," and insisted that the commission be "objective and realistic." The report, entitled "The Airport and Its Neighbors," submitted to the President on May 16, 1952, and immediately dubbed the "Doolittle Report," became a new source of controversy. Unwilling to bend facts or his principles for anyone, including the President, (he told Major General Robert W. Burns, advisor to President Truman, that, "if the President wants me to change that philosophy, then I'll turn in my suit and he can find another chairman."), he issued his findings, made recommendations and returned to his civilian job.

In 1955, approaching retirement age, Jimmy and Joe asked to be transferred from New York City to the West Coast. Obliging, Shell sent them to San Francisco.

PART 4

FINAL APPROACH

"The Doolittles have shared the
adventurers, the disappointments,
and the successes of Jim's colorful
career. His friends assert that Jim
Doolittle is the type of man who
could have succeeded at anything he
turned his hand to. He's a keen business executive and a thoroughgoing
scientist. But first and foremost he's
a great aviator. In Joe, his wife, he
has had a magnificent partner. Jim
himself would be the first to tell you
so. That is, if Joe didn't happen to
be around. In her presence he'd be
more apt to say: 'Oh, Mom's O.K.
You know, in spite of her being so
strict with me, I think I'll keep her,
after all.'"

—Ellen Lee Brashear and
Helen Morrin, *Liberty
Magazine*, July 25, 1942

CHAPTER 18

GRANNY AND GRAMPS

"The world would see General
James H. Doolittle as a flamboyant
Air Racer, a man of courage, a man
who volunteered for missions others
feared to lead, but I saw a man who
was the best father that a boy could
ever hope to have."

—John P. Doolittle

M Y earliest memories of my grandparents begin in their apartment across from the Mark Hopkins Hotel in San Francisco. They
are of a grandfather who loved to play almost as much as we did
and a grandmother who showered us with unconditional love.

Visits with my grandparents were wonderful times. They always
had a game table—in San Francisco it sat in a window overlooking
a small park—and it was there that my grandfather taught us to
play cards and dominos. He introduced us to Lefty and Shorty,
imaginary characters who caused a great deal of mischief. He
played with us in the park, and later during our teenage years,
Gramps walked with us on the beach in Santa Monica.

I have equally fond memories of shopping with my grandmother in downtown San Francisco. Granny did not drive, so
most of our adventures were on foot, walking up and down the
hilly streets of the city. When they moved to Southern California,
she introduced me to plays at the Schubert and concerts at the
Greek Theater. We spent long lunches at the Beverly Wilshire

with friends visiting from New York and stimulating afternoons at the World Affairs Council in Los Angeles.

Growing up, I knew that the Tokyo Raiders and their families held a special place in my grandparents' hearts. They were our extended family and their stories were part of our collective memory. Every year in mid-April, my grandparents traveled to a different city to meet with the Raiders and their wives. Sometimes we were invited to join them. The yearly reunions grew out of a promise my grandfather made on the *Hornet*.

He promised to throw a party for the boys after the raid. When the war ended, he kept that promise. On his 49th birthday, December 14, 1945, Gramps hosted a three-day bash at the McFadden-Deauville Hotel in Miami, Florida. Hotel records attest to the fact that they had a romping good time.

They gathered that first year not only to celebrate, but also to pay homage to those who couldn't make the reunion. Of the 80 men who took off that stormy night in April 1942, only 60 survived the war. The lost "boys" included: 2 who drowned when they ditched their B-25 off the coast of China; 1 who died bailing out; 13 who died in other theaters of war; and 4 who died at the hands of the Japanese. The crew of plane number 8 was detained under guard in Russia for 13 months before escaping. Of the 8 captured by the Japanese only 4 survived and returned to the United States at the end of the war. Four other Raiders were captured after subsequent missions and held as POW's by the Germans.

At that first reunion, and at every reunion thereafter, the senior officer called roll. Surviving crewmembers answered "here" for those who were missing, and a toast was offered in their honor.

At the 1959 reunion, the citizens of Tucson, Arizona presented the Raiders with 80 sterling silver goblets. Each goblet was inscribed twice: right-side-up and upside-down, so the names could be read turned-up or turned-over.

Each year, at a private ceremony, the goblets of those who have passed since the last reunion are turned over. The goblets, along with a bottle of cognac reserved for the last two Raiders, are kept at the Air Force Academy in Colorado Springs and escorted by Air Force cadets to the reunions.

The early reunions were stag affairs. However, in 1958 my grandfather invited my grandmother. Believing it would be wrong for her to attend while the other wives stayed home, she declined. But the Raiders had become very close to "Mama Joe" and wanted her there. They promptly invited all their wives.

Betty Kappeler was one of the wives at that first coed reunion.

"Frank and I had married in May of 1957, and I was three months pregnant with our first child," Betty recalled.

As a new addition to the Raider family, she wasn't quite sure what to expect, especially from the General's wife, but Joe welcomed her with open arms.

"We're so happy to meet you," Joe told Betty. "We never thought Frank would get married."

"Your grandmother was very generous and patient with all the wives," Betty told me recently. "She made us all good because she was so good."

Dawn Thatcher's first reunion was in 1960 at Colorado Springs. She felt out of place because her husband Dave had gotten out of the service after the war. She wasn't sure what she would have in common with the military wives, but my grandmother quickly put her at ease.

"She was so sweet and made us all feel so comfortable," Dawn remembered. "She was down-to-earth. Never acted like a celebrity at all. Just made me feel right at home."

Another of Dawn's memories was that my grandmother "never said an unkind word about anyone. And if the conversation turned to gossip, she changed the topic. She never participated."

My grandfather used to say, "No matter how old these fellows get, they will always be our boys." This sentiment was shared by my grandmother.

Over the years, the Raider family has grown to include "honorary Raiders" such as Tung-Sheng Liu, who risked his life helping some of the boys evade the Japanese and Carroll V. "C.V." Glines, the official Raider historian.

In 1963 at the Seattle reunion, the young, emerging author, C. V. Glines asked for the Raiders' cooperation in writing a book about the Tokyo Raid. He presented his case at the Raider business meeting. Some in the group had hoped to find a "name" author to write their story, but after Glines' presentation, my grandfather got up, walked around the table and put his arm on the author's shoulder.

"You fellas know that I have only one vote, and I vote for this fella right here." The vote was unanimous, and all agreed to cooperate with Glines.

After the meeting, Gramps reiterated to C.V. that he would cooperate with the book, but wanted to ask a question first.

"I've heard that the four POW's want to have a book written about their experiences. Can you write about the Raid and not interfere with whatever they want to do?"

"I think I can," Glines answered.

"If you agree to do that, I'll show you the difference between Doolittle's cooperation and Doolittle's *wholehearted* cooperation."

When C.V. returned home, there was a large box waiting for him from the General. It had cost $25.00 in postage to send it. When he opened it, there was an envelope inside with $25.00 in return postage to send the enclosed material back when he finished. The material Gramps sent was his *personal* file on the Raid.

After the reunion, Glines made arrangements to meet with Gramps at a hotel in Washington, D.C.

"If you meet me in the lobby at 5 o'clock and agree to drive me to my dinner engagement," Jimmy told Glines, "we'll go up to my room and you can ask me questions while I change." Gramps had a 6:00 dinner appointment at Secretary of Defense Clark Clifford's house.

Glines, lugging a large reel-to-reel tape recording machine, followed Gramps up to the room. While my grandfather ducked into the bathroom, C.V. searched for an outlet. On his hands and knees, Glines finally found an outlet in the wall under the head of the bed. As he plugged in the machine, my grandfather finished up in the bathroom and walked back into the room. Unbuttoning the top three buttons on his shirt, Gramps slipped it over his head and replaced it with a fresh shirt, also partially unbuttoned. Tucking the shirttail into his pants, he turned to C.V.

"OK, let's go. We can talk on the way."

Glines quickly unplugged the tape machine and led the way to his car. Fighting the Washington traffic at quitting time took all of C.V.'s attention. By the time they arrived at Clifford's house, most of his questions remained unasked.

"I haven't been very fair with you," my grandfather told C.V. before he got out of the car. "I tell you what. Joe and I try to take a week off every year and visit Fred Crawford on Cape Cod. You can visit us there and spend all the time you want asking questions."

When C.V. called the house to tell Gramps that he had arrived in Cape Cod, my grandparents were having lunch with the Crawfords. Fredrick Coolidge "Fred" Crawford was the founder of TRW. Gramps immediately left the table and met C.V. at the airport.

"Have you had lunch?" my grandfather asked.

"No."

"Neither have I."

They dined at the airport, and then Gramps drove C.V. back to the Crawford house on Cape Cod.

"I recall the trip to the house down narrow streets," Glines told me recently. "His depth perception was superb. I could see we missed cars on my side by fractions of an inch. I realized then how he could have been such a great low altitude acrobatic pilot."

The Raiders were so pleased with Glines's book on the Raid that the four survivors from the Japanese POW camps asked him to write their story. His book *Four Came Home* is a moving account of their starvation, torture and solitary confinement.

My grandparents attempted to keep the family part of their lives private. Even though much of their history was part of the public domain and as such open to the press, they valued their privacy and attempted to protect their children and grandchildren as much as possible.

During his lifetime, my grandfather refused to allow Hollywood to make a movie about him. He also refused to write an autobiography. He believed that "an autobiography would be too self-serving." But with prodding from my parents who believed that the details of his life should be told accurately, my grandfather agreed to have C.V. Glines co-write *I Could Never Be So Lucky*

Again. It was C.V. who first called Gramps the Master of the Calculated Risk.

My grandfather had an excellent memory, but my grandmother's was even better. Throughout their lives, with the exception of the war years, he gave her a copy of his daily itinerary. Her memory was so accurate that he would call home before a scheduled meeting, and she would remind him of details that included the last time he saw an individual, the spouse's name, the children's names and ages or any other facts that would be helpful. Frequently, when standing in a receiving line, Granny would lean over and whisper an interesting tidbit or fact that Gramps could use in his greeting.

"Jimmy, that's John Smith." Granny would whisper in his ear. "We met him and his wife Beth at an aerospace luncheon two years ago. His son Tommy is an Eagle Scout."

He always gave her credit for making him look brilliant.

Her daily correspondence was legendary. They easily received between 10 and 20 letters and notes per day and between three and five thousand Christmas cards during the holidays. My grandmother answered every letter and catalogued those cards. She sent cards or thank-you notes for every one.

Although my grandfather never officially retired until his early nineties, they did take time to travel extensively after leaving the military service. Frequently they traveled for Shell, but just as often they went for pleasure. Some trips became annual events, like their visits to Creed, Colorado with Bobby Hite's parents, fishing expeditions with his co-pilot Dick Cole and hunting trips with Bill Bower, another of the Tokyo Raiders. They toured Russia and Africa and retuned to Japan and Europe. My grandfather was on the road a good three-fourths of the time and continued that schedule into his late eighties. However, he always tried to get back to Granny on the weekends, even if it meant leaving a meeting a few minutes early to catch the last plane home.

Their lives were productive, and they were happy. However, they were not untouched by tragedy.

CHAPTER 19

UNCLE JIM

"Celebrities' children...are neither watchers nor watched, but something else, someone ambiguously in the middle. We hear about the watchers from our parents, who have trained us to be allies, and we learn about our parents from the watchers, who see us as intermediaries. Our position is an odd one, forcing us to look at our lives from opposite perspectives, occasionally both at the same time."

—Reeve Lindbergh, *The Names of the Mountains*

MY grandmother was visiting with us when my uncle Jim died. He was 38 years old, a big loveable St. Bernard who gave great hugs and had a wonderful, deep laugh.

"His heart stopped," my parents told us. I was eight and I loved him dearly.

My memory of that time is a blur of activity, of neighbors watching out for the Doolittle children, sweeping us off the street if a strange car came around, sheltering us from reporters who circled like vultures.

Ten years later, as I stood in front of a theatre in Madrid, Spain, a friend introduced me to his father.

"I knew your Uncle," the father said. "The one who killed himself."

I'm sure I conversed naturally, acted appropriately—on auto-pilot.

"How did Uncle Jimmy die?" I asked, the minute I got home.

My mother registered shock. Searching for the "right" words.

"He was sitting at his desk" "A single bullet." "No note." "No proof." "No real doubt."

There were some indications of depression just before he died. But no one knew just how deeply depressed he had been.

My grandfather's letters from the war recounted adventures shared with his oldest son. But they also expressed concern for the burden placed on one so young during time of war:

(26 December 1944)

Young Jim called yesterday and got in late last night. Had a swell visit with him. Played the Doolittle-Downey record and he got a kick out of it also. We sat around for hours and then continued to gab after going to bed. He is on "Flak Leave" for a week in the U.K. Looks fine but the responsibility of being a Flight Leader has been bothering him some. It's a bit hard for a kid to take on responsibility all at once. In peacetime one assumes obligations gradually. In war time our mistakes mean the loss of some of our buddies and it's a bit hard for some of these kids to have responsibility forced on them before they feel that they have the knowledge and experience necessary to enable them to safely assume it. Told Jimmer that he was one step from the bottom and that I was only a couple from the top and that one's obligations and responsibilities grew with each command echelon. The results of a mistake on his part affected about six planes and 36 crew members. From now on it would get tougher. That was merely one of the prices we pay for competence—more is expected of us. And so on into the night.

An "old school" mentality ran through the military. Regulars resented "mavericks" that resigned, came back as big-shots and skipped grades. Viewed as Hap's "fair-haired boy," Granddad ran into his fair share of damaged egos. His rapid rise as a reservist from Major to Lieutenant General left many career men bitter. Many officers resented the findings of the Doolittle Board which recommended restructuring the military. Some of his decisions during the war— changing the mission of the fighters from protecting the bombers to attacking the enemy, increasing the combat sorties from 25 to 35, insisting that the 12th Air Force fly strategic rather than tactical missions—caused resentment. His insistence on calling the shots as he saw them, not as some people would like them to be, made enemies. Hap Arnold, Tooey Spaatz and Ira Eaker recognized his potential and he proved himself to Marshall and Eisenhower. The men who served under him respected him. But there were those who didn't know him personally, who saw the public image of dare-devil pilot, and believed that his celebrity, not ability, had won rank.

Both my uncle and my father served under men who resented my grandfather's success.

In 1948, when my father arrived at Tachikawa Air Force Base in Japan, he immediately reported to his commanding officer. The commanding officer greeted my father by saying, "I remember you as a kid at Mitchel Field. I didn't like you then and I don't think I'm going to like you now."

My dad was only seven years old at Mitchel Field.

My uncle had suffered similar experiences. He also suffered setbacks on a personal level. His first marriage ended in divorce. His second marriage was troubled. Additionally, he had just been passed over for promotion when he died.

When anyone's parents achieve as much as Jim, Jr.'s parents had, the bar for personal acceptance is automatically set higher than normal. Even someone who had earned the Distinguished Flying Cross, received commendations for his leadership, and was loved dearly by his family and friends, could still suffer from self-doubt.

In his autobiography my grandfather wrote about his son's death:

Only when someone very near and dear to one leaves does one appreciate the stark tragedy of death. Even then, nature tends to cushion the initial shock, and the thought 'he is gone' does not carry the later realization of finality and permanence that comes only with the final indisputable understanding that 'we will never see him again'.

My grandfather threw himself back into his work. My grandmother grieved alone. Years later, I thought about my grandmother's words, of the heartache she suffered, the feelings of failure and helplessness, and her appreciation of Bob and Delores Hope, who whisked her away from the public eye and allowed her to heal in their Palm Springs estate.

"We cannot change the things that happen," she told me. "We can only choose how we deal with them."

She chose to put one foot in front of the other.

CHAPTER 20

DOOLITTLE CENTRAL

"I've been thinking we should
stake out our claim someplace in
the Monterey Bay area pretty
soon...We may not be settling
down for some years yet but ought
to be keeping our eyes open for
the right spot from now on. We
will need a home for the grandchildren as they grow up and come
to visit us and get spoiled."

—Jimmy Doolittle in a letter
to Joe, 28 July 1945

JODY was seven, I was four and Penny was fifteen months old
when my brothers were born.

"Twas twins and boys too!" my father wired my grandfather.

"No really, quit your kidding. What is the little girl's name?"
Gramps asked in a telephone conversation later that night.

A week later, while flying touch-and-go landings at McConnell
Air Force Base in Wichita, Kansas, my father received orders from
the tower.

"Break out of pattern and hold over the north beacon," the
controller said, "General Doolittle is on approach."

Gramps climbed out of the C-54 and into the waiting staff car.
The drive to our house in Wichita took less than ten minutes.

My mother, alerted by the base, had the twins side by side on the bed. She changed them both while my grandfather looked on. Bursting with pride, he kissed my mother, climbed back into the staff car, and returned to the base.

"Captain Doolittle, break out of pattern and hold over the North beacon," the controller ordered for the second time in 45 minutes. And as my father watched, the C-54 carrying his father climbed into the afternoon sky and returned to headquarters.

In 1958, my grandfather retired from Shell and accepted an offer from his friend Fred Crawford, the head of Thompson Products. Two scientists, Dean Wooldridge and Simon Ramo had teamed up with Thompson Products to form TRW. The new company was heavily involved in the emerging aerospace industry. Fred asked Gramps to sit on TRW's Board of Directors.

Because the company dealt with government contracts and money, Gramps resigned from all government boards and agencies. He never wanted a question of impropriety.

Financially comfortable, but never really "flush," my grandparents took another calculated risk and invested their savings in the new company. The fledgling company, TRW, turned out to be a wise investment, and financially secured their future.

In 1959, my grandparents left San Francisco and moved to Santa Monica where they purchased their first home. Located on Marguerita Avenue, in the first block up from Pacific Palisades Park, the house resembled a small white castle. A long, rolling green lawn swept up from the street. Furnished in an eclectic collection of treasures, their home reflected their travels. A long L-shaped hall bisected the house. Bookcases, filled with autographed books, lined the lower half of one wall and rows of 8x10 black and white autographed pictures of their friends hung on both sides. The rogues' gallery included photographs of Winston Churchill, Queen Elizabeth, Roscoe Turner, Amelia Earhart, Charles "Slim" Lindbergh, and many of his Tokyo Raiders—a veritable who's who of American and world history. It also included Bob Hope, Lawrence Tibbett, Jimmy Stewart and many others.

The basement ran the full length of the house. It was here that my grandparents displayed their various awards and trophies gathered over the years. The Thompson, Bendix, Schneider, Harmon and other mementoes graced the shelf that ran along the top of the room. Hunting trophies hung on the walls. A large polar bear rug covered the floor and various skins were draped on the furniture. Only friends and family came down to the basement. When the filmmakers of the Pearl Harbor film asked for "mementoes" to create a vanity wall in Doolittle's make-believe office, we all got a chuckle. Modest by nature, Gramps never flaunted his relationships or awards.

Granddad taught us all how to shoot in his basement. He set up a pellet range, much like the one in Ernst Udet's living room in Berlin. I shudder to think about the potential damage a misplaced pellet could have caused.

My grandfather was cordial and often autographed items in public, but occasionally fans stopped at the house, asking for a tour or "a little something" for their collection. My grandmother, always gracious, would gently refuse and turn them away.

This house, my grandmother's first permanent home since their marriage in 1917, was Doolittle Central. We often gathered there for holidays, opening gifts around the Christmas tree and hunting eggs in the rose garden.

A widowed neighbor a few blocks away was murdered in her home a few years after my grandparents moved into the house on Marguerita Avenue. After that incident, my grandfather had all the bushes cut back away from the house. Because he traveled a lot and my grandmother was frequently home alone, they purchased Smokey, a professionally trained German Shepherd, to guard their property. The back yard was surrounded by an eight-foot fence and patrolled by Smokey in the daytime. At night, the dog slept in the house. Smokey took his job seriously, and someone would have had to physically disable him to get close to my grandparents.

There are, as we all know, people in the world who get some sadistic pleasure out of watching someone or something suffer. Someone of that ilk dropped two small black kittens over the fence into Smokey's yard. My grandmother found the kittens calmly eating out of Smokey's bowl while he patiently waited his turn. The kittens instantly became members of the household.

In 1961, at sixty-five, my grandfather accepted an appointment to the Board of Directors for Mutual of Omaha. Still actively employed at 65, he spent the next 10 years traveling for Mutual. He kept an office on the seventh floor of the Mutual of Omaha building in downtown Los Angeles. He rarely used the elevator, preferring to walk the seven flights twice a day.

They sold their home in Santa Monica in 1978, and moved into a retirement community in Carmel Valley that provided medical service and dining facilities. For two years my grandparents commuted once a month to Los Angeles where Gramps maintained his office. He purchased a Volkswagen Rabbit as his little "run around" car and kept it at the Hyatt Hotel near the airport, where Mutual reserved a permanent suite for their visits to Southern California.

In 1980, Gramps gave up his seventh floor office in Los Angeles, and opened a smaller office in Monterey. My husband volunteered to drive the Rabbit up to Carmel. Stacy, our daughter, and I planned to meet him there. Not wanting his granddaughter to travel alone with his fifteen-month old great-granddaughter, Gramps offered to come along for the ride.

Stacy used this trip to discover how to unbuckle her car seat and unzip the diaper bag. Gramps, co-pilot on the trip, climbed not once, but twice into the backseat to restore order and secure the baby. He was eighty-three.

Eventually, when Stacy fell asleep, I had the opportunity to visit with my grandfather. I admired his keen ability to reach out over the generations and listen—really listen.

My father was a pilot in the Air Force and stationed in Vietnam while I was a student in high school. Although firmly behind our country, I couldn't understand how our nation became involved in a war governed by politics, rather than a real desire for victory. I confessed to my grandfather that had my father been killed in Vietnam I would have had a hard time forgiving our government.

Not only did he understand, he validated my feelings. "Americans," he said, "have always supported a conflict where we set out to win."

"Vietnam, like Korea before it, was a 'limited' war where we imposed political, economic, moral and psychological limitations on our fighting. We owed our soldiers more than this."

Both my dad and my uncle saw combat in Korea. Gramps felt strongly that, had we gone in to win in Korea, used the full force of our military and followed the supply and communications lines into China, we would not have to worry about China today.

He believed that America must carry a big stick and that the rest of the world needed to know that we were willing and able to use it. When and if we did use it, our goal must be victory, not a draw.

He explained that during World War II he ordered the fighters to attack, and the bombers to bomb in order to destroy the enemy's ability and desire to wage war. His goal was to win—as quickly and effectively as possible.

After seven hours, many of them spent entertaining a toddler, we pulled into the driveway in front of my grandparent's cottage in Carmel.

As he climbed out of the car, my grandfather winked at Stacy then turned to my grandmother.

"Joe," he said, eyes twinkling, "let's not have any more children!"

CHAPTER 21

SOUL MATES

"As we know, Jimmy has flown millions of miles and for good reasons was away from home and his dear family for ages at a time. He spent 45 years in the air. Joe Doolittle spent 45 years waiting for him to land—at military bases, at civilian air ports—and sometimes at the end of a runway that didn't exist until he landed.

"Those of us whose husbands also travel learned from her. For years, Joe was the national distributor of patience. But the Doolittles worked out a special arrangement beyond waiting. When Jimmy began setting records for passenger aircraft, Joe became his official passenger. She flew with him on more than one record flight. She didn't crave the honor. She took the job because her husband needed her. She's an amazing lady."

—Delores Hope

M Y mother called late in the afternoon on October 1, 1984. My Grandmother had suffered a stroke. I remember the urge to argue with her.

"No, Mom," I wanted to say, "You're mistaken."

But she was sure. My daughters were little, three and five. And my husband, bless him, let me go. I left that next morning and drove the entire seven hours in a state of disbelief. My grandmother, surely, wasn't really mortal—was she?

I made that trip almost every month after that. Sometimes with my family, often times alone. Granny's stroke left her paralyzed on the left side, unable to speak.

When looking for a retirement home, my grandparents had tried to plan for any eventuality. They chose Carmel Valley Manor for the beauty of its setting, the privacy of their cottage, and for the care it provided if either of them should become incapacitated.

My grandmother lived in a private room, just a short walk from the cottage they shared. My grandfather, who, until the day of her stroke, traveled extensively—quit traveling and sat by her side, holding her hand. No one ever questioned where we'd find him. We all knew he'd be with Granny.

It was important to me that my daughters remember. More often than not, they came with me. Parking at the cottage, we'd walk directly up the hill. Our frequent reunions were joyous. Granny always beamed—reaching out with her good hand— holding each of us in turn.

We would all spend time together, and then Gramps, with that impish playfulness I remembered so well, would suggest that he and the girls retreat to the cutting garden and pick flowers for the "Duchess."

One afternoon, as the sun slipped toward the horizon, I realized that Gramps and the girls had been gone longer than normal. My grandfather was ninety-one, and I began to worry that something might have happened.

I kissed my grandmother good-bye and started out around the perimeter, heading in the opposite direction from their normal walk. As I crested the hill, I spotted them, my grandfather walking without assistance and both girls using canes. They were involved in animated conversation and I could tell, from my unobserved position, that Granddad hadn't changed all that much over the years. He was still the man I remembered from my childhood.

Tears filled my eyes as I watched him play with my daughters. When I got closer and they spotted me, I learned that they had been playing school in the little chapel on the grounds, and that at 91, Jimmy Doolittle was still a naughty little boy!

Watching Granny's decline was difficult for all of us, and I struggled emotionally. My grandfather sensed my suffering, and he opened up even more. We would walk back to the cottage together after visiting Granny, and he would tell me stories of her kindness, wisdom and courage. He couldn't imagine life without her.

In the four years of her illness, my grandfather left her side only once. He traveled to Washington, D.C., to receive his fourth star from President Reagan.

I believe that sometimes, if we're fortunate, we pick the time of our death. My grandmother left us on Christmas Eve 1988. Seventy-one years, to the day, after she eloped with a scrappy Flying Cadet who promised and gave her the world.

We buried her in Arlington National Cemetery, just below the tomb of the Unknown Soldier on a clear, crisp day in December. I stood graveside, thinking that if reincarnation exists—and a soul that evolves into pure light returns to the Source—then my grandmother would not be back.

CHAPTER 22

★ ★ ★ ★

TOUCH THE FACE OF GOD

"Jimmy Doolittle had more gifts than any one man has a right to be blessed with. He had been one of America's greatest pilots for more than twenty-five years. He was bold and completely fearless. He had a great technical mind and a highly perfected education in engineering. And he was one of the most engaging human beings I ever ran across. He talked with animation, his voice was dear and keen, and it carried a sense of quick and right decision."

—Ernie Pyle in Douglas Porch's
The Path to Victory

GRAMPS didn't often speak about the war years. Growing up, the Raiders were like an extended family, but he didn't talk about the mission. When asked what he felt his greatest contribution was, Gramps said it was the first blind flight. It must have been difficult to settle on just one. Many of his projects resulted in safer, faster, and more dependable airplanes that built a safer, faster and more dependable Air Force and commercial industry.

Sometimes friends and contemporaries from his past visited and we were privileged to hear their stories. Adolph Galland, the German World War II Ace, visited several years ago. He told

Gramps that his "decision to change the mission of the fighters from 'escorting bombers' to 'search and kill the enemy' meant the end of the air war for Germany."

Gramps claimed that the hardest job he had was selling himself to Ike Eisenhower who wanted Ira Eaker, Tooey Spaatz or Walter Frank as his airman in North Africa. But, he did it.

It wasn't until my adult years that I appreciated my grandfather's public image. To me, growing up, he was just Gramps. He had a marvelous sense of humor. I remember one time when I had some pressing problem and wanted to discuss it with my grandfather.

He called me into his home office and offered me a seat on the other side of his desk.

"Gramps," I said, launching into my story.

"Just a minute," he said, holding up his hand. He then removed his hearing aide, turned it off and set it on the desk between us.

"Okay, shoot," he said with that impish twinkle in his eye.

"Gramps! I'm serious!" Well, I don't remember what my pressing problem was, but I do remember laughing. I remember laughing a lot.

When I asked my youngest daughter, Shawna, what she remembered most about Gramps, she said, "He was happy and he made us happy."

As my grandfather's health failed, my parents added a wing on their home for him. His quarters sat on the hill above the 14th Green of Pebble Beach Golf Course, and would have had a clear view, if they had cut down the forest. Over the trees, his living room and office looked out on Stillwater Cove and beyond, to the seemingly endless waters of the Pacific.

The back wall of his office and his bedroom opened to the forest, and a parade of birds performed for his enjoyment.

"Please don't let me embarrass myself," he asked my father.

So my parents protected him, inviting friends and family; shutting out those who chased celebrity, sheltering him from those who might take advantage.

Only once, when recovering from an illness in a local hospital, was he exposed. My parents went to visit and found nurses "showing off General Doolittle." They took him home.

Labor Day weekend 1993, while my brother Peter and his family visited, Gramps suffered the first of a series of strokes. My parents were cruising in the San Juan Islands when the Coast Guard reached them. They immediately returned the boat to Port Ludlow, and without taking time to stop at their house in Port Townsend, jumped into the car and drove all night to Pebble Beach.

His illness was brief. We kept the curtains in his bedroom open wide. The birds he loved so much were always in attendance and his family close by.

My cousin Jimmy sat at the end of his bed, I sat at the side, my feet propped on his mattress, my hand holding his. We told stories, remembered adventures. Every now and then, Gramps would smile, and we knew he was listening, remembering with us.

My parents managed to pull the world a little closer and surround him with love. He joined Granny on September 27, 1993 and was buried with her at Arlington National Cemetery. He was ninety-six years old.

In his autobiography Granddad wrote:

One of the privileges of age is the opportunity to sit back and ponder what you've seen and done over the years. In my nine-plus decades, I've formed some views about life and living that I have freely imposed on trusting audiences, both readers and listeners. I have concluded that we were all put on this earth for a purpose. That purpose is to make it, within our capabilities, a better place in which to live. We can do this by painting a picture, writing a poem, building a bridge, protecting the environment, combating prejudice and injustice, providing help to those in need, and in thousands of other ways. The criterion is this: if a man leaves this earth a better place than he found it, then his life has been worthwhile. (Jimmy Doolittle, *I Could Never Be So Lucky Again*).

Surely by anyone's measure, his life was worthwhile.

PART 5

MISSION ACCOMPLISHED

"Jim was a great flyer, military man, hero, and patriot—an inspiring standard for American youth. Sometimes I think that his example as a loyal and loving husband, father and grandfather is equally as important for American youth as his exciting life. He demonstrated that a devoted and loyal family provides the strength and purpose that make life successful."

—Fredrick Coolidge in Fred Crawford's *Glimpses of Jimmy Doolittle*

★ ★ ★ ★

DECORATIONS, ACHIEVEMENTS & AWARDS

DECORATIONS

Congressional Medal of Honor
Distinguished Service Medal, with Oak Leaf Cluster
Silver Star
Distinguished Flying Cross, with two Oak Leaf Clusters
Bronze Star
Air Medal, with Three Oak Leaf Clusters
Official Order of the Condor (Bolivia)
Yon-Hwei, Class III (China)
Knight Commander of the Bath (Great Britain)
Grand Officer of the Legion of Honor and Croix de Guerre, with
    Palm (France)
Grand Officer of the Crown, with Palm and Croix de Guerre,
    with Palm (Belgium)
Grand Commander (Poland)
Abdon Calderon First Class (Equador)

ACHIEVEMENTS

First cross-continental crossing in less than 24 hours, 1922
Winner, Schneider Trophy Race, 1925
First to execute outside loop, 1927
First "blind flight," 1929
Winner Bendix Trophy Race, 1931

New Transcontinental record, 1931
Winner, Thompson Trophy Race, 1932
World's Landplane Speed Record, 1932

AWARDS

Mackay Trophy, 1926
Spirit of St. Louis Award, 1929
Harmon Trophy, Ligue International des Aviateurs, 1930
Guggenheim Trophy, 1942
International Harmon Trophy, 1940, 1949
Wright Brothers Trophy, 1953
Federation Aeronautique Internationale Gold Medal, 1954
Silver Quill, 1959
International Aerospace Hall of Fame, San Diego, California, 1966
Aviation Hall of Fame, Dayton, Ohio, 1967
Thomas D. White National Defense Award, 1967
Horatio Alger Award, 1972
Conservation Hall of Fame, 1973
Wings of Man Award, Society of Experimental Test Pilots, 1973
Bishop Wright Air Industry Award, 1975
Sylvanus Thayer Award, 1983
C. C. Criss Award, 1985
Motorsports Hall of Fame Award, 1989
Grand Cross of Honour, Supreme Council of Scottish Rite, 1989
Presidential Medal of Freedom, 1989

★ ★ ★ ★

BIBLIOGRAPHY

BOOKS

Cohen, Stan, *Destination: Tokyo*, Pictorial Histories Publishing Company, ©1983

Colman, Penny, *Rosie the Riveter*, Crown Publishers, Inc., ©1995

Doolittle, James H., *I Could Never Be So Lucky Again*, Bantam Books, ©1991

Emmens, Robert G., *Guests of the Kremlin*, The Macmillan Company, ©1949

Glines, Carol V., *Jimmy Doolittle*, The Macmillan Company, ©1972

Glines, Carol V., *Doolittle's Tokyo Raiders*, D. Van Nostrand Company, Inc., ©1964

Glines, Carol V., *Master of the Calculated Risk*, Pictorial Histories Publishing Company, ©2002

Glines, Carol V., *Four Came Home*, Van Nostrand Reinhold Company, ©1966

Goodwin, Doris Kearns, *No Ordinary Time*, Simon & Schuster, ©1994

Greening, C. Ross, *Not As Briefed*, Washington State University Press, ©2001

Lawson, Ted W., *Thirty Seconds Over Tokyo*, Brassey's, Inc., ©2002

Lindbergh, Reeve, *The Names of the Mountains*, Simon & Schuster, ©1992

Pyle, Ernie, *Brave Men*, University of Nebraska Press, ©2001

Reynolds, Quentin, *The Amazing Mr. Doolittle*, Appleton-Century-Crofts, Inc., ©1953

Thomas, Lowell and Jablonski, Edward, *Doolittle*, Doubleday & Company, ©1976

Sterling, Bryan B. & Sterling, Frances N., *Wiley Post, America's Heroic Aviation Pioneer*, Carroll & Graf Publishers, ©2001

Stovall, Jack D., *Tales of the Marauders*, Wings of Courage Press, ©1994

Szurovy, Geza & Goulian, Mike, *Basic Aerobatics*, McGraw Hill, ©1994

Watkins, T.H., *The Hungry Years*, Henry Holt and Company, ©1999

Watson, C. Hoyt, *The Amazing Story of Sergeant Jacob DeShazer*, Light and Life Press, ©2002

The Artisan, Winter 1914

NEWSPAPERS

The American Weekly, 26 April 1959

The Daily News, 20 May 1942—, 4 June 1944—, 6 June 1944—, 9 June 1945—, 8 October 1945—, 19 January 1946

Entire West, 20 November 1942

Evening Outlook, 4 July 1963—, 8 December 1967

The Herald (Monterey, California), 7 July 1989

Los Angeles Examiner, 10 June 1945—, 19 April 1946

Los Angeles Herald and Express, 19 May 1942—, 17 November 1942—, 20 April 1943—, 3 June 1946—, 13 June 1947

The Los Angeles Herald Examiner, 3 December 1969

The Los Angeles Times, 12 May 1945—, 8 June 1945—, 9 June 1945—, 24 September 1945—, 5 June 1947—, 4 October 1972—, 8 May 1975—,14 December 1947—, 17 April 1982—, 18 August 1982

The Los Angeles Times, This Week Magazine, 14 May 1944

The News, 17 April 1966

The National Tribune, 24 May 1945

The Register, 22 December 1945—, 28 July 1973

San Francisco Chronicle, 13 December 1986

Spokesman Review, 15 February 1953

The Tin Can Sailor, Oct–Nov–Dec 2001

Wave Publications, January 1944—, 20 April 1944

MAGAZINES

Brashear, Ellen Lee and Morrin, Helen, "The Story of Jimmy and Joe," *Liberty,* 25 July 1942

Glines, Carroll V., "Mama Joe's Tablecloth," *Air Force Magazine,* August 1989

Glines, Carroll V., "Strike Against Japan," *Aviation Heritage,* March 1992

Hoppes, Jonna Doolittle, "Gramps," Smithsonian *Air& Space,* February/March 1994

Mazet, Horance S., "On the raid that electrified America—and foretold Japan's ultimate fate." *World War II,* March 1992

Mueller, Merrill, "General Doolittle, Flyer's Flyer," *Liberty* 1 April 1944

Oxford, Edward, "Against All Odds," *American History,* March/April 1992

Trenner, Patricia, "10 Great Pilots," *Smithsonian Air & Space—Centennial Edition,* March 2003

"Jimmy Doolittle," *Life,* January 1994

"'Blitzkrieg,' American Style: New Army Proves Its Theories," *The United States News,* 20 November 1942

INDEX

BOOKS AVAILABLE
FROM SANTA MONICA PRESS

American Hydrant
by Sean Crane
176 pages $24.95

The Book of Good Habits
Simple and Creative Ways to
Enrich Your Life
by Dirk Mathison
224 pages $9.95

The Butt Hello
and other ways my cats
drive me crazy
by Ted Meyer
96 pages $9.95

Calculated Risk
by Jonna Doolittle Hoppes
360 pages $24.95

Can a Dead Man Strike Out?
Mark S. Halfon
168 pages $11.95

Discovering the History of
Your House
and Your Neighborhood
by Betsy J. Green
288 pages $14.95

The Dog Ate My Resumé
by Zack Arnstein and Larry
Arnstein
192 pages $11.95

Dogme Uncut
Lars von Trier, Thomas Vinterberg
and the Gang That Took on
Hollywood
by Jack Stevenson
312 pages $16.95

Exotic Travel Destinations for
Families
by Jennifer M. Nichols
and Bill Nichols
360 pages $16.95

Footsteps in the Fog
Alfred Hitchcock's San Francisco
by Jeff Kraft and
Aaron Leventhal
240 pages $24.95

Free Stuff & Good Deals for
Folks over 50, 2nd Ed.
by Linda Bowman
240 pages $12.95

A House Rabbit Primer
by Lucile C. Moore
264 pages $14.95

How to Find Your Family Roots
and Write Your Family History
by William Latham and
Cindy Higgins
288 pages $14.95

How to Speak Shakespeare
by Cal Pritner and
Louis Colaianni
144 pages $16.95

How to Win Lotteries,
Sweepstakes, and Contests in
the 21st Century, 2nd Edition
by Steve "America's
Sweepstakes King" Ledoux
224 pages $14.95

James Dean Died Here
The Locations of America's Pop
Culture Landmarks
by Chris Epting
312 pages $16.95

The Keystone Kid
Tales of Early Hollywood
by Coy Watson, Jr.
312 pages $24.95

The Largest U.S. Cities Named
after a Food
by Brandt Maxwell
360 pages $16.95

Letter Writing Made Easy!
Featuring Sample Letters for
Hundreds of Common Occasions
by Margaret McCarthy
224 pages $12.95

Letter Writing Made Easy!
Volume 2
Featuring More Sample Letters for
Hundreds of Common Occasions
by Margaret McCarthy
224 pages $12.95

Life is Short. Eat Biscuits!
by Amy Jordan Smith
96 pages $9.95

Loving Through Bars
Children with Parents in Prison
by Cynthia Martone
208 pages $21.95

Marilyn Monroe Dyed Here
More Locations of America's
Pop Culture Landmarks
by Chris Epting
312 pages $16.95

Movie Star Homes
by Judy Artunian and
Mike Oldham
312 pages $16.95

Offbeat Museums
The Collections and Curators of
America's Most Unusual Museums
by Saul Rubin
240 pages $19.95

A Prayer for Burma
by Kenneth Wong
216 pages $14.95

Quack!
Tales of Medical Fraud from the
Museum of Questionable Medical
Devices
by Bob McCoy
240 pages $19.95

Redneck Haiku
by Mary K. Witte
112 pages $9.95

School Sense: How to Help
Your Child Succeed in
Elementary School
by Tiffani Chin, Ph.D.
408 pages $16.95

Silent Echoes
Discovering Early Hollywood
Through
the Films of Buster Keaton
by John Bengtson
240 pages $24.95

Tiki Road Trip
A Guide to Tiki Culture in
North America
by James Teitelbaum
288 pages $16.95

ORDER FORM 1-800-784-9553

	Quantity	Amount
American Hydrant ($24.95)		
The Book of Good Habits ($9.95)		
The Butt Hello . . . and Other Ways My Cats Drive Me Crazy ($9.95)		
Calculated Risk ($24.95)		
Can a Dead Man Strike Out? ($11.95)		
Discovering the History of Your House. . . ($14.95)		
The Dog Ate My Resumé ($11.95)		
Dogme Uncut ($16.95)		
Exotic Travel Destinations for Families ($16.95)		
Footsteps in the Fog: Alfred Hitchcock's San Francisco ($24.95)		
Free Stuff & Good Deals for Folks over 50, 2nd Ed. ($12.95)		
A House Rabbit Primer ($14.95)		
How to Find Your Family Roots . . . ($14.95)		
How to Speak Shakespeare ($16.95)		
How to Win Lotteries, Sweepstakes, and Contests . . . ($14.95)		
James Dean Died Here: America's Pop Culture Landmarks ($16.95)		
The Keystone Kid: Tales of Early Hollywood ($24.95)		
The Largest U.S. Cities Named after a Food ($16.95)		
Letter Writing Made Easy! ($12.95)		
Letter Writing Made Easy! Volume 2 ($12.95)		
Life is Short. Eat Biscuits! ($9.95)		
Loving Through Bars ($21.95)		
Marilyn Monroe Dyed Here ($16.95)		
Movie Star Homes ($16.95)		
Offbeat Museums ($19.95)		
A Prayer for Burma ($14.95)		
Quack! Tales of Medical Fraud ($19.95)		
Redneck Haiku ($9.95)		
School Sense ($16.95)		
Silent Echoes: Early Hollywood Through Buster Keaton ($24.95)		
Tiki Road Trip ($16.95)		

Subtotal	
CA residents add 8.25% sales tax	
Shipping and Handling (see left)	
TOTAL	

Shipping & Handling:	
1 book	$3.00
Each additional book is	$ .50

Name —————————————————————————

Address—————————————————————————

City ———————————————— State ——————— Zip ——————

❏ Visa ❏ MasterCard Card No.: —————————————————

Exp. Date ———————————— Signature —————————————

❏ Enclosed is my check or money order payable to:

Santa Monica Press LLC
P.O. Box 1076
Santa Monica, CA 90406

www.santamonicapress.com 1-800-784-9553